Co-Parenting

by Jann Blackstone, PsyD

for dummies®
A Wiley Brand

Co-Parenting For Dummies®

Published by: **John Wiley & Sons, Inc.,** 111 River Street, Hoboken, NJ 07030-5774, www.wiley.com

For general information on our other products and services, please contact our Customer Care Department within the U.S. at 877-762-2974, outside the U.S. at 317-572-3993, or fax 317-572-4002. For technical support, please visit https://hub.wiley.com/community/support/dummies.

Wiley publishes in a variety of print and electronic formats and by print-on-demand. Some material included with standard print versions of this book may not be included in e-books or in print-on-demand. If this book refers to media that is not included in the version you purchased, you may download this material at http://booksupport.wiley.com. For more information about Wiley products, visit www.wiley.com.

Library of Congress Control Number: 2026940081

ISBN 978-1-394-37534-9 (pbk); ISBN 978-1-394-37536-3 (ebk); ISBN 978-1-394-37535-6 (ebk)

SKY10155236_042726

Table of Contents

Introduction

As you begin this journey through *Co-Parenting For Dummies*, it helps to understand the philosophy that shaped this book. Families do not end when relationships do. They reorganize, expand, and continue to shape the lives of the people within them. *Co-Parenting For Dummies* was written from that understanding.

My approach to co-parenting developed gradually, not from theory alone but from lived experience. I have seen the impact of divorce and remarriage from multiple perspectives: as a professional supporting families for over 30 years, as a parent and bonus parent navigating change, and as part of an extended family system myself. Over time, I began to notice that children did not struggle most with divorce itself; they struggled when the adults around them lost sight of how their behavior shaped a child's emotional world. That realization led me to focus less on blame and more on conduct — how former partners speak to one another, how they show up at milestones, and how they create an environment where children are not asked to carry adult tension.

My calling in this work has always been rooted in staying in the present and in the daily choices that allow families to create the life they want now rather than remain defined by what came before. Co-parenting is not only about managing what was lost; it is about moving forward with intention, building something steadier, and showing children that growth is possible even after relationships change. Every decision parents make today becomes the emotional landscape those children grow up within tomorrow. I believe the greatest gift we can offer them is stability created by adults who are willing to resolve conflict thoughtfully and take radical responsibility for their own part, rather than waiting for a co-parent to change. When parents shift their focus from proving who is right to asking how they can respond differently, the entire family system begins to steady. Teaching people how to navigate conflict with accountability and clarity is, for me, a way of advocating for children whose lives are shaped by these choices.

I may present as the expert, but I do not rise to the occasion perfectly every time myself. I, too, find moments of frustration, disappointment, or anger and have to steady my responses in order to find my higher self. For years I led with emotion, feeling like a victim, like I was unseen. Over time, I learned that I contributed as much as I received, and out of that work grew what I call Good Ex-Etiquette, or to be clearer, "Good Behavior After Divorce or Separation." It is not about politeness for appearance's sake. It is about emotional leadership after a relationship ends. Good Ex-Etiquette asks parents to shift from romantic partners to partners in parenting, recognizing that while the romantic relationship may end, the responsibility to create a stable family system does not. It emphasizes respect in communication, clarity in boundaries, and a willingness to cooperate even when agreement is not possible. Most importantly, it centers the child's experience rather than the adults' unresolved history. The concept of Good Ex-etiquette was so well received over the years that a Q&A column was born. Now syndicated by Tribune Content, it appears in newspapers and websites all over the world. Everyone is looking for direction.

Throughout this book you will notice I use the word bonus, a term I personally coined after years of searching for language that felt more accurate and more hopeful than "step." Traditional labels were created for a different era and can carry unintended emotional weight, suggesting hierarchy or replacement rather than connection. I know my family struggled with dated labels. That's why we started to use the term, bonus. Today, many families grow and change without marriage, and children often form meaningful bonds with adults and siblings who do not fit neatly into older terminology. Bonus is not simply a title — it is a concept and now a community — people who unite in their desire to move beyond negative narratives and demonstrate firsthand to their children that estranged parents can grow, cooperate, and lead with maturity. It reflects addition rather than subtraction. A bonus parent, bonus sibling, or bonus extended family member is not a substitute for anyone else; they are an added layer of care that develops through consistency, shared experience, and commitment. In many ways, the word holds the same meaning it does elsewhere in life: a bonus is a reward for effort, something earned through showing up. Once a bonus, always a bonus. "It's a step in the right direction."

As you move through the pages, you will find practical guidance alongside real-life examples that reflect the complexity of modern families. I use stories — real-life examples — to drive these subjects home.

For example, it's easy to say, "Don't badmouth your co-parent," but many people don't fully understand what actually constitutes badmouthing, so the instruction falls flat. But if I tell you a story about a child's reaction to her mother saying, "I wish he would just move on," while standing in line at the supermarket, now you begin to understand what badmouthing does to a child — and hopefully choose not to do it. "Don't badmouth," is one of the ten rules of good ex etiquette, as described in Chapter 16 (rule number three, to be exact).

Many readers expect a list of rules at the start, but lasting change does not come from memorizing principles alone. It comes from understanding the context in which those principles matter. By the time you reach the last chapter, you will have seen these ideas at work across different situations and relationships. The Ten Rules then serve as a summary — a way to gather the themes of the book into clear, practical guidance you can return to whenever family life feels uncertain.

If there is one message I hope readers carry forward, it is this: co-parenting is not defined by the end of a relationship, but by the choices adults make afterward. Children thrive when the adults in their lives commit to stability, respect, and cooperation, even when circumstances are imperfect. Families can evolve without losing connection. With thoughtful intention, former partners, bonus family members, and extended loved ones can create an environment where children are free to grow without feeling divided.

This book is an invitation to approach co-parenting with clarity and steadiness — to move beyond survival and toward a way of relating that honors both the past and the future.

You don't have to read this book from beginning to end to get what you need. Like most *For Dummies* books, it's designed to be a resource you can return to whenever a question comes up or a situation feels challenging. Use the table of contents or the index to jump straight to the topic you're facing right now. If you decide to keep reading beyond that section, you'll find deeper insight and context, but the goal is simple: clear guidance you can access quickly, right when you need it.

If you have a question or you need co-parenting help, please feel free to visit me via the Bonus Families website, at `www.bonusfamilies.com`.

About This Book

Co-parenting doesn't come with a clear instruction manual, yet millions of parents are expected to figure it out while managing emotions, logistics, and the everyday needs of their children. *Co-Parenting For Dummies* is designed to give you practical guidance, a steady perspective, and realistic strategies for raising children across two homes without losing sight of respect, cooperation, and emotional stability.

Drawing on decades of experience working with separated parents, bonus families, and extended family systems, I combine practical strategies with real-life insight so that you can navigate the challenges that come with separation, divorce, and blended family dynamics. In this book, you explore how to communicate more effectively, create workable parenting plans, support your children through transitions, and approach milestones with confidence rather than confusion. Throughout the chapters, I introduce tools and perspectives that encourage collaboration without requiring perfection.

Because every family situation is different, this book doesn't offer rigid formulas. Instead, you'll find adaptable ideas you can shape to fit your circumstances, whether you're newly separated, years into co-parenting, or adjusting to new relationships and life stages. The goal isn't to eliminate challenges, but to help you move through them with clarity, respect, and empathy while keeping your children at the center of your decisions.

Foolish Assumptions

I assume, perhaps wrongly, that you . . .

- Care deeply about your children and want to create as much stability as possible, even when the adult relationship feels complicated
- Are open to looking at your own communication habits as well as the dynamics between households
- Want practical ideas you can use in real life, not rigid rules that ignore the emotional side of co-parenting
- Understand that cooperation doesn't mean you have to agree on everything, but you're willing to find respectful ways to move forward
- Believe that small, thoughtful changes can make a meaningful difference over time

Language Used in This Book

First, I use the term *bonus* to refer to children who biologically belong to your partner. It's a more positive way to refer to a stepchild. *Step* implies wicked, and it doesn't match the way many families feel about each other. *Step* also implies marriage, so it doesn't apply to those who don't marry when they bring children into the world. *Bonus* is positive, all-inclusive, and independent of marriage.

Second, I try to stay away from gender-exclusive pronouns. Most of the time, I use *they* instead of writing out *he or she*. Besides, rarely does a specific gender play a part in the examples I use.

Third, I use the words *divorce* and *breakup* interchangeably. *Divorce* implies marriage, yet all the principles listed in this book are based on having children, not being married.

Icons Used in This Book

Throughout this book, you'll see small icons designed to help you quickly recognize different types of guidance and examples. Think of them as gentle signposts that highlight moments worth slowing down for.

TIP

Here, you'll find straightforward ideas you can try right away. These suggestions are meant to make communication clearer, transitions smoother, and everyday co-parenting decisions feel more manageable.

REMEMBER

When you see this icon, pause for a moment. It signals an important perspective or principle that can help you focus on what matters most: your children's emotional well-being.

WARNING

This icon points out common pitfalls that can unintentionally increase tension between households. The goal isn't to criticize, but to help you recognize patterns that may create unnecessary stress for you or your children.

Occasionally, you'll see deeper explanations about family dynamics, child development, or communication patterns. These sections offer additional context if you're curious about the "why" behind certain strategies.

How This Book Is Organized

Co-parenting doesn't unfold in a straight line. It evolves as children grow, relationships shift, and new experiences reshape the family landscape. Throughout this book, you'll explore practical strategies for communicating more effectively, managing transitions between homes, supporting your children emotionally, and navigating major milestones with steadiness and respect.

Each part focuses on a different stage of the co-parenting journey, from laying a strong foundation to handling everyday realities and preparing for life's biggest celebrations. Along the way, you'll find real-world examples, practical tools, and reminders that meaningful change often happens through small, consistent choices rather than dramatic overhauls.

Part 1: Building the Foundation

Co-parenting begins long before schedules are finalized or holidays are negotiated. It starts with understanding what co-parenting truly means and recognizing how your mindset influences the way you communicate and collaborate. In this part, you explore the foundations of cooperation, including setting realistic expectations, defining shared goals, and developing communication habits that support your children rather than deepen conflict. By the end of Part 1, you'll have a clearer sense of how to approach co-parenting as a shared responsibility rather than an ongoing struggle.

Part 2: Making Co-Parenting Work Day to Day

Once the groundwork is in place, it's time to focus on the practical realities of living between two homes. This part explores the day-to-day logistics that often create the most stress, including navigating the back-and-forth lifestyle, introducing dating into the family system, and establishing parenting plans that reflect real-life needs rather than ideal scenarios. You'll also look at financial topics such as child support and spousal support, learning how to separate practical agreements from emotional reactions so decisions remain focused on stability.

Part 3: Finding Balance

Co-parenting isn't just about agreements on paper; it's about how those agreements show up in everyday life. In this section, you learn how to build a supportive co-parenting team, create emotionally safe environments in both homes, and help your children adjust to the realities of living in two households. You'll also find guidance for managing your own stress so that your responses remain thoughtful rather than reactive, allowing you to model resilience and emotional steadiness for your children.

Part 4: Managing Special Occasions and Child-Centered Milestones

Birthdays, graduations, and coming-of-age celebrations can bring both joy and tension for co-parents. This part offers practical ways to approach these events with clarity and cooperation so children feel supported rather than caught between households. You'll explore how thoughtful planning, respectful communication, and child-centered decision-making can turn potentially stressful occasions into meaningful opportunities for connection.

Part 5: The Part of Tens

Sometimes, you need quick reminders you can return to when things feel overwhelming. This section gathers concise, practical lists designed to keep you grounded, including essential ex etiquette guidelines and examples of everyday phrases that can either escalate conflict or encourage cooperation. Think of this part as a handy reference you can revisit whenever you need clarity and a reset.

Beyond the Book

This book also comes with a free online Cheat Sheet, which highlights key co-parenting responses to help stop arguments before they happen. You'll also learn how to manage the legalese that might be part of your co-parenting arrangement. You'll learn some helpful co-parenting responses to nip arguments in the bud, and you'll find the C.A.R.E. Co-Parenting Problem-Solving Agreement. Finally, we've provided a short "I" statement exercise that is helpful whenever you find yourself in a difficult situation where emotions can get in the way of good communication. Visit `www.dummies.com/go/coparentingfd`.

1 Building the Foundation

IN THIS PART . . .

Understand what it means to be a co-parent

Shift from conflict to collaboration

Get your mind in the right place to work together

Learn what good communication is and how to interact with someone you can't get along with

IN THIS CHAPTER

» Putting your children first

» Examining why co-parenting is so important

» Introducing co-parenting with C.A.R.E.

» Moving forward

Chapter 1

Understanding What Co-Parenting Means

Let me begin with an analogy designed to explain what co-parenting your children after a parental breakup truly means.

Imagine that you and your partner have been together for eight years. You have three children, aged 7, 5, and 4. You recently started a new job that requires your family to relocate. The stresses of starting a new job, moving, and having three young children have put a huge strain on your relationship, and you and your partner are considering breaking up. As a diversion from your troubles, you decide to take one last family vacation — a train trip over the mountains to the Grand Canyon.

At the time of this story, you're at one end of the train, and your partner is at the other. Your three children are sitting in the middle car, playing video games on their tablets. As the train rounds a turn, loose rocks fall onto the tracks, and the train derails. Alarms begin to sound. Your partner's end of the train pitches to one side, and it's difficult to get to one another. You can hear both your children calling for you. As more rocks begin to fall, the train pitches even more, and the kids tumble toward your partner's end of the train. The kids struggle to keep their footing, but they must be careful. Too much shaking might dislodge the train from the tracks and cause it to tumble down the hill.

I'll stop the story here for a second. Amid all this confusion, someone hands you a new script saying that you and your partner are no longer together. Your relationship ended a year and a half ago. Do you say, "Cool! Since we're no longer together, this train wreck is your problem!" Or, with your partner's help, do you figure out a way to save your kids? That, precisely, is the definition of co-parenting.

To further explain, whenever you see the prefix *co* in front of a word, it implies "together," "jointly," or possibly "in common." It indicates a partnership or collective action — something shared equally between individuals. Co-parenting isn't just a word. It's also a call to action, an urgent directive for estranged parents to put their own issues aside in the name of their children.

In this chapter, I introduce the concept behind true co-parenting and examine why it's so important for parents to create a calm and loving environment for their kids after a breakup. I begin by establishing the premise of co-parenting, which is, "Put your children first," and why that should always be the primary motivation when making decisions with your co-parent. I also examine how your breakup has affected your children and how co-parenting with C.A.R.E. minimizes their confusion.

Putting the Children First

If you asked me for a co-parenting mantra, a positive phrase or affirming statement that you can say to yourself for motivation or encouragement, I'd have to say, "Put the children first." This is the criterion on which to make all co-parenting decisions. If you find yourself looking for answers and aren't sure where to turn, using your children's well-being as your measure when faced with a major decision makes any choice easier.

REMEMBER

Forget about the principle of the thing when disagreeing with your co-parent and make your love for your children the principal thing.

Sure, it's a play on words, and something I tell co-parents all the time, but no truer words can be spoken. What's best for your children should be your guiding light, even if at times you must feel uncomfortable, admit you're wrong, swallow your pride, move, do without, or go slower in a new relationship than you want to. Once you have children, it's your job to put them before anything else.

Your children didn't ask for this breakup. If you've decided to turn your children's lives upside down, you should legitimately consider those children first. Putting your children first is a call to your higher self and should be all the motivation you need to adjust your co-parenting approach from combative to collaborative.

Examining Why Co-Parenting Is So Important

For those who had a nasty breakup, the thought of working with someone who has so infuriated them in the past may seem impossible. How ridiculous to believe that parents who couldn't get along when they were together could get along after their breakup.

But it's not so ridiculous. Since the mid-1980s, when joint custody was introduced, custody laws have required estranged parents to share their children's time after they break up. And considering the number of marriages that end in divorce, not to mention parents who have never married but no longer live together, that means a huge percentage of children now live in two homes: Mom's house and Dad's house. The anxiety this creates — anticipating a move every few days, living with different family members, different rules, sleeping in a different bed, even eating different foods — can be overwhelming, not only for the children, but for the parents who anticipate their children leaving again. It adds an undertone of desperation to everyone's life.

Not knowing exactly what to do, many parents just retreat to their corners, living separate lives and expecting their children to do the same. Even though countless studies have proven that children fare better when their parents take a cooperative approach to parenting them after a breakup, many don't take this knowledge to heart. They believe a breakup makes them autonomous, able to make decisions for their children on their own.

The reality is something completely different. Joint custody parenting plans force a child to live in two homes. The very nature of joint custody asks children to check their allegiance each time they leave one parent's home and go to the other's. It's natural for people to compare, so when children go back and forth between homes, they inwardly consider which bedroom they like best or which parent makes the best pizza. Children often compartmentalize their approach to cope with the back-and-forth. In my own bonus son's case, I found that the snacks he preferred at his mother's home weren't the snacks he preferred at mine. I was amused to hear that he ate fruit cocktail at his mother's home, while bean burritos were his preference at my house. When I bought fruit cocktail to eat at my house, he looked at me like I was crazy. "I don't eat fruit cocktail here." He'd compartmentalized his food choices. Fruit cocktail at Mom's. Bean burritos at Dad's.

But there's something even more important to consider. When parents are raising children under the same roof, cooperation while parenting is implied. If a child speaks disrespectfully, it's common for the other parent, or even another adult in the home, to step in and say, "Don't talk to your mother (father, Aunt Mary, and so on) like that!" That united front helps children learn boundaries and respect.

However, once parents separate, the incentive to support one another can quickly disappear. So, when a child is disrespectful post-divorce, it's easy for a parent to say something like, "I understand, honey. I used to hate it when he talked to me like that, too. Just ignore him." That kind of response sends the message that it's acceptable to disrespect the other parent. But, of course, it's not.

REMEMBER

Whether you're raising your child under the same roof or in separate households, the standard for respectful behavior should remain the same. Your child needs to see both parents supporting each other's roles, not undermining them.

Co-Parenting with C.A.R.E.

This is where co-parenting with C.A.R.E. comes in. C.A.R.E. is an acronym for communication, acceptance, respect, and empathy. It's a useful co-parenting tool to remind estranged parents and extended family how to approach their co-parenting challenges.

Communication

When asked, most co-parents say that their lack of communication is the first thing they'd like to improve. So, for that reason, the *C* in C.A.R.E. stands for communication. This includes not only speaking but also listening to your co-parent to ensure they feel understood. In co-parenting, how you choose to see a situation can either fuel conflict or foster cooperation. Shifting your perspective doesn't mean excusing bad behavior; it means choosing to lead with understanding rather than judgment. That small shift can open the door for better communication, fewer misunderstandings, and ultimately a more stable and peaceful environment for your children.

Although I touch on improving your communication throughout this book, I cover it extensively in Chapter 4.

Acceptance

The *A* in C.A.R.E. stands for acceptance. Acceptance is the cornerstone of building a strong co-parenting alliance. People have different histories and preferences, and that guides their actions. That's why acceptance is so important. It means acknowledging your co-parent as they are — flaws, strengths, and history rather than holding on to expectations of how you wish they would behave.

Acceptance doesn't excuse harmful behavior, but it does allow you to come from a place of reality rather than frustration. When you accept your co-parent, you reduce the emotional resistance that reinforces conflict and creates space for cooperation. It opens the door to focusing on shared goals, like the well-being of your child, instead of disagreeing purely to make a point. Ultimately, acceptance transforms tension into collaboration and turns co-parenting from a battleground to a functional partnership.

Respect

R is for respect. Treating your co-parent with respect means approaching them as your equal and recognizing that your co-parent's perspective holds just as much weight as your own. It's the willingness to pause, listen, and consider their feelings, needs, and ideas, even when they differ from your own. This doesn't mean you have to agree or give in, but it does mean valuing their role and experiences as legitimate. When both parents operate from this mindset, it shifts the relationship from a battle of wills to a partnership, showing children that differing viewpoints can coexist with understanding, cooperation, and dignity.

Empathy

E is for empathy. Displaying empathy means putting yourself in the other's shoes to feel what they're feeling or understand their point of view. If you assume your co-parent is acting out of malice or trying to make your life harder, you're most likely to respond defensively or even aggressively. But if you pause and consider the possibility that they're struggling, too, or simply doing the best they can with the tools they have, it changes the entire dynamic. Using empathy when communicating fuels respect by offering them the same consideration you'd like in each situation.

Key principles of co-parenting with C.A.R.E. Co-parenting with C.A.R.E. allows parents to problem-solve together on every level. You'll see how to incorporate the C.A.R.E. strategy throughout this book.

» **Child-centered focus:** Placing your children's emotional and physical well-being above all else is at the heart of conscious co-parenting. Every decision, conversation, and interaction should be guided by the question: "Is this what's best for my child?"

» **Mindful communication:** Using calm, respectful, and clear language reduces the risk of conflict and keeps conversations constructive. Stay focused on parenting, not the past.

» **Cooperation and unity:** Parents present a united front, even if they're no longer together. When children see both parents working as a team, they feel stable and secure.

» **Managed emotions:** Acknowledge your emotions, but don't let them lead your interactions. Conscious co-parenting requires you to respond, not react.

» **Shared vision:** Agree on a long-term vision for your child's future. When both parents are looking forward rather than staying stuck in the past, it becomes easier to collaborate and make joint decisions.

Raising healthy kids with C.A.R.E.

To successfully raise children after a breakup, you need to Communicate with your child's other parent regularly — sometimes weekly, sometimes daily. Accept that reality early and make the necessary emotional adjustments. Respect your children enough to no longer put them in the painful position of watching their parents continue to argue long after the relationship has ended. Finally, put yourself in their shoes by feeling Empathy. Being party to parental conflict not only creates confusion for children but also leaves a child feeling helpless, torn, and unsure of where they belong. Your children deserve peace, and it's up to you to model how mature adults handle difficult interactions. Offer your children direction, not more confusion.

The following story highlights how parents' poor communication and ongoing conflicts can affect children in unsuspected ways. In this case, the parents believed they were co-parenting effectively, but their arguments, lack of clarity, and putting their child in the middle fueled her anxiety, causing her to withdraw from friends and family.

> Madeline and Peter had been divorced for four years. They thought they were co-parenting just fine, but occasionally locked horns when trying to make decisions for 10-year-old Emma. Their biggest arguments were always about money. Unable to make ends meet, Madeline decided to return to court to seek increased child support, but it ended up being an amount that Peter couldn't afford. Peter

continued to pay the original amount, and the back child support kept piling up. When Peter bought a new truck, he was confident Madeline would be upset. Believing honesty to be the best policy, the next time Emma came over, Peter explained the entire loan procedure, including how Grandpa helped with the down payment. Then he told Emma that when her mother asked about the new truck, she could just explain what he told her.

Emma had listened to her dad's explanation, but she didn't understand a word of it. She had no idea what a down payment was or why Grandpa was now involved. Thinking that she would get into trouble if she didn't pass on the information exactly as she'd been told, she clammed up and didn't say a thing to her mother except that she didn't want to go back to her father's home.

Anticipating her mom's reaction when she found out about the truck, Emma started having trouble sleeping and had no appetite. Madeline was concerned but forgot about the changes she noticed in Emma when she saw Peter's new truck. She lost her temper right in front of Emma, calling Peter all sorts of terrible things and ending with "deadbeat dad." Not understanding what that was, Emma became more withdrawn. Neither parent understood what was wrong. Both blamed the other for the change in their child.

I first heard of this family's problem when I was asked to mediate their child support disagreement. Because Peter wasn't paying the full amount, Madeline thought it was fitting to reduce his time with his daughter. After all, Emma had said many times that she didn't want to return to her dad's home, so reducing Peter's time with Emma seemed like a logical request. I was called upon to determine if a change in the parenting plan was appropriate.

As Madeline, Peter, and I went through the mediation process, it was easy for me, an outsider, to understand what was going on, but it wasn't so easy for them to understand that their inability to communicate was contributing to the problem. It wasn't that Emma didn't want to see her father. She just hated being put in the middle of her angry parents, and she figured that if she refused to return to her dad's, she wouldn't have to take sides. Using her 10-year-old reasoning, if she stayed put, she wouldn't have to choose. This was a huge revelation for these parents because they firmly believed they were doing everything right. But their daughter's behavior drove home the fact that it wasn't the parenting plan that needed to change; it was their approach to co-parenting. They needed to start from scratch, adopt a more cooperative spirit, and improve their communication. They, like so many parents after a breakup, had to accept once and for all that it wasn't Madeline versus Peter, but Madeline *and* Peter *for* Emma. That realization — understanding that they were no longer partners in life, but continue to be partners in raising their child — made all the difference. They finally saw why working together was so important for the well-being of their child.

Your Work Isn't Done . . .

Your children love you, and they deserve an active, loving relationship with both of you — at the same time. You don't have to live together, but you must cooperate with each other if you want healthy, secure children. The thing that's often overlooked is that parents are teaching their children how to have a relationship with someone both before *and* after a breakup.

REMEMBER

Your work isn't done when you choose to break up. That's when your work starts. Until now, all your kids have seen is chaos. You must change that. It's why parents working together after a breakup is not only important, but imperative. Your children's well-being depends on it.

Adverse Childhood Experiences (ACEs)

For years medical and mental health professionals have known that difficulties in early life negatively influence outcomes later in life. This was finally documented in 1995–1997 in the landmark study that Dr. Vincent Felitti and Dr. Robert Anda conducted titled *The Adverse Childhood Experience Study.* The study measured the responses of 17,000 Kaiser Permanente members about their childhood experiences with various traumas, including domestic violence, drug addiction, mental health struggles, and neglect.

A 10-question questionnaire was used, and a number score was assigned to the intensity of the trauma that someone endured.

TIP

You can find that questionnaire at `www.bonusfamilies.com/ACE questionanaire`, and at `www.dummies.com/go/coparentingfd`.

REMEMBER

Parental separation is counted as one of the primary adverse childhood experiences (ACEs) that contribute to the potential risk for health and social problems later in life.

Light at the end of the tunnel

Even though research suggests that children with divorced parents often show higher rates of anxiety and depression compared to those from intact families, it's important to note that this doesn't imply that every child from a divorced family will experience these challenges. Over time, a significant number of children can navigate these difficulties successfully, especially when their parents collaborate well while co-parenting.

The impact of divorce on children is mainly shaped by the *level of parental conflict*, the strength of the child's support system, and the child's own ability to cope. In favorable conditions, many children not only cope with the changes but also thrive.

How well children cope with a parental breakup and the aftermath is clearly based on how well the parents cooperate with one another as they raise their children. But there's something in it for the parents, too: lower stress levels, reduced anger and frustration, less tension, and the promise of a positive future.

Truthfully, it's nothing special to fight with your ex. Most feel that way and buy into typical vindictive, combative behavior for years after their breakup. What's special is overcoming your animosity to work together in the name of your children. Becoming a supportive co-parent is something to be proud of, and that takes true dedication and integrity. Now you have a positive legacy to pass on to your children.

It's time to get to work.

IN THIS CHAPTER

» Sensing that change is needed

» Modeling positive behavior for your children

» Having a positive mindset

» Being open to course corrections

Chapter 2

Setting the Stage for Collaborative Co-Parenting

Co-parenting in the true sense of the word is more than just raising your kids together after a breakup. It's changing your directive from fighting with the enemy to collaborating with an ally, all in real time. There's no rehearsal. Co-parents learn on the job and must be able to immediately correct courses when they see a problem.

This chapter focuses on the internal work co-parents must do to shift from conflict to collaboration. It begins with a simple but essential desire to make a change. From there, it explores the mindset needed to stay on course and make sound decisions in the best interest of your children. I talk about why letting go of the past is critical to improving communication and building trust, and I look at how to recognize what's not working so you can make the necessary adjustments. Successful co-parenting doesn't happen by accident. It happens by intention, awareness, and a willingness to grow.

Shifting from Combative to Collaborative

Most co-parents, particularly those just beginning their co-parenting journey, find the shift from combative to collaborative to be extremely challenging. After a breakup, few feel compelled to cooperate. And, at the time, it feels so foreign when collaboration is suggested that it takes a while to shift gears. I see it all the time in my clients. They're so used to saying no to one another because of their unpredictable past that they can't even consider that there might be a "yes" in there somewhere. So, when they're asked to trade a weekend or even just an afternoon, rather than consider a compromise or a favor and say, "Sure," it's an automatic, "No!" They secretly have no desire to cooperate, and that sets the stage for ongoing tit-for-tat disagreements. "You said 'no' when I asked, so I'm saying 'no' to you!"

Remember that it's about the kids

Co-parents start to collaborate when they realize that it's not about them but about their children. And while it's not possible to control your co-parent's behavior, you can lead by example. When your child sees you working through disagreements with maturity and care, they know they're safe, and their transition from house to house will be easier for them to navigate.

Lose the labels

One simple change that can make a big difference after a breakup is how you refer to your former partner. Instead of calling them your "ex," begin calling them your "co-parent." It's a small shift in language, but a powerful one. "Ex" keeps the focus on the past and what was lost. "Co-parent," on the other hand, is forward-focused and centers on what still matters: your shared responsibility in raising your child. This change in terminology sets a more respectful tone, reframes your relationship, and sends a clear message to your child that both parents are still present and important. By using "co-parent" instead of "ex," you give each other an upgrade.

Laying the Groundwork

Begin by considering four key components that will lay the groundwork for better co-parent interaction:

- Recognize the need for a change.
- Be the change you wish to see.

» Check your mindset.

» Be open to a course correction when you sense a problem.

Countless co-parents know the way they interact isn't effective, but they don't know what to do about it. As a result, they make no changes because they don't know what changes to make. To complicate the issue, most couples still break up exactly the way they did in high school. It doesn't matter that they're older now. They decide to part, they dig in their heels, they say terrible things about one another, their friends take sides, and they throw hate stares at each other standing by their lockers. Social media has become the lockers now, and people throw hateful words instead of hateful stares, but the rationale is still the same. The big difference? Most didn't have children in high school, and that completely changes the playing field. Now, parents must set an example.

Often, co-parents hope the courts will solve their disagreements. If they can't agree, they figure going back to court is sure to solve the problem. That's doubtful. Most of the problems co-parents face center on their inability to get along and solve problems together. A judge can't order you to stop being angry or to change your attitude. Those things come from within, and a desire to put your children before anything else.

Recognizing the Need for a Change

So, the first component to laying the groundwork for collaborative co-parenting is parents recognizing that something must change. Either they're just in the beginning stages of co-parenting, or what they've been doing isn't working. That's when they decide to commit to approaching each other differently than they have in the past.

The following is a firsthand accounting of an incident that happened during a mediation session a few years ago. It was so inspiring that it has always stuck with me, and I pass it on because it clearly depicts when the light bulb goes on, and parents recognize *together* that they need to change.

> A little background: These were "older" first-time parents, in their mid-30s. Both were extremely educated, met each other at a party, and got pregnant with twin girls. The parents came to me when their girls were 8 months old. The mother and father walked into my office for mediation. The mother carried a laundry list of everything the father was doing wrong. Both sat quietly until, without warning, she blurted out, "I want sole custody!" Her voice was emphatic, barely below yelling. "My daughters are going to get UTIs if he's not more careful! He needs supervised visits!"

At the time, their parenting plan included two-day visits and one overnight each week with the father. They had agreed to this when the twins were born. Now the mother wanted to restrict his time entirely. In joint custody, supervised visits are one of the most extreme limitations, just short of no contact.

The father looked stunned. "Supervised visits?" he said quietly. "These are my babies, too."

The mother continued. "He doesn't even put the girls in their car seats properly! I take pictures when I pick them up." She scrolled through photos on her phone and stopped at one showing her daughter in a safety seat. "Look at this. I can fit my entire fist under the straps!"

She explained she used her fist as a gauge to check how tight the straps were. I looked at her hands, then his. He stood about six feet three inches, and she was maybe five feet five inches.

"Look at the difference in your sizes," I said gently. "I think he's doing exactly what you asked, but his fist is much larger than yours."

The father nodded. "I thought it was tight enough. But why didn't you just tell me? You waited a month and brought pictures to the mediator?"

The mother sighed. "I try to co-parent. I really do."

"Really?" I asked. "Because nothing you've said has anything to do with co-parenting."

She looked stunned. "What? I'm telling you everything that's wrong. I'm being honest."

"That may be true," I said, "but you're telling the wrong person. I don't change diapers or buckle car seats. Dad does."

She grew more agitated. "I think he should make a doctor's appointment and have the doctor show him how to clean a little girl."

"Why don't you show him?" I asked.

"What?" she said, taken aback. "It's not my place! We were never really together. I barely know him!"

"Well," I said, "it sounds like it's time to get acquainted."

I looked from one to the other.

"Mom, meet Dad. Dad, meet Mom. Your co-parent for life."

The room went quiet.

"You think breaking up means you just walk away," I continued. "But you don't have that luxury now. You have twins. Your children need both of you. Regardless of how you feel about each other, they depend on you both. You're not in this alone. You actually have built-in help."

They both looked at me with blank stares.

"Two people who share a child can bond, if not in love, then in purpose. You don't have to be partners in romance, but you are partners in parenting. Someday, you may each have partners who love your children, too."

Then I added, "So, the next time Dad picks up the girls, set aside 30 minutes and show him how to properly clean a little girl."

The mother sat very still. "Oh my," she finally said. "I've been approaching this all wrong. I guess I need to change my attitude."

She turned toward the father.

"I am sincerely sorry."

The father looked at her for a moment.

"Thank you," he said softly, tears welling in his eyes.

I really didn't expect a turnaround that quickly. In fact, I'd never seen it happen so fast. No change was made to the parenting plan, but to the parents' attitude. The parents realized they had to work together for the children they both loved, and they started the process right there in my office.

You can, too. I'll tell you how.

Leaving the past in the past

When a romantic relationship ends, it's natural to carry scars from the past. Words were said, trust may have been broken, and feelings were hurt. But when you're co-parenting, holding on to that history only weighs you down and, more importantly, it weighs down your child.

Your role has changed. You're no longer romantic partners, but you'll always be partners in parenting. That means it's time to leave behind the old battles and begin building a new kind of relationship — one centered not on what went wrong between you, but on what's right for your child.

WARNING

The truth is, if yesterday's pain colors every exchange with your co-parent, the two of you will stay stuck in the very dynamics that ended the relationship. Your child will feel that tension, and they'll begin to associate "family" with conflict. Children need to see their parents working as a team, even if that team exists in two separate households.

TIP

So, how do you move forward? How do you make that change? You do so by repeatedly reminding yourself that the past isn't where you live anymore. You don't need to re-argue old points or win battles that no longer matter. You need to show up in the present as the parent your child needs today.

Allowing your co-parent to improve

If you say you want a better co-parenting relationship, you must leave room for growth. Don't expect perfection, but *do* acknowledge progress. You might be surprised at how much can shift when you stop looking for what's wrong and start noticing what's improved.

> "Jasmine and I recently agreed we could get along well enough to exchange our daughter at each other's homes instead of meeting at a Starbucks halfway between our hour-long commute. Our two-year-old would get fussy when we stopped, so it seemed like a better plan.
>
> A month ago, Jasmine brought our daughter to my home for the first exchange. I walked outside to greet them and saw Jasmine holding our daughter while rifling through the garbage can. I was furious. It's filthy, and she was leaning over the can with my daughter in her arms. I can't get past it. Every time I have to talk to Jasmine, that's all I picture. I want to scream. In Jasmine's defense, the incident was discussed during their weekly co-parenting session. She had been looking for a favorite mug and was convinced her co-parent, Ayan, had thrown it away. Rather than ask him, she checked the garbage. She apologized and promised it would never happen again, but Ayan would not let it go. He saw it as an invasion of privacy and was furious.
>
> "This is exactly how she always acted," he insisted. Each week, he brought it up, and the tension prevented them from forming the new co-parenting bond they needed.
>
> "I want to exchange at Starbucks," he said. "I don't want her coming to my house."
>
> Eventually, Jasmine gave up. "I tried. He will never change. I'll never apologize again. Let's just go back to Starbucks."
>
> If you read between the lines, the real issue wasn't mugs or garbage. It was the past. Both Jasmine and Ayan held on to their old image of each other and ignored the progress they had made.
>
> Originally, they had chosen to exchange their child at home so their toddler wouldn't have to stop midway during the drive. It was a thoughtful decision made for their child's comfort. Now they wanted to undo it because of their own discomfort.

> Successful co-parenting requires an open mind and a willingness to focus on present behavior. Mistakes will happen. The key is to acknowledge them, commit not to repeat them, and move forward.
>
> "Oh, but you don't understand what they did!" some parents say.

It doesn't matter. What happened between you in the past cannot be changed. Your children don't care who was right or wrong. They love both of you and need you to work together for them now.

REMEMBER

There's a disclaimer to "It doesn't matter." The one thing that affects how much interaction between estranged co-parents is acceptable is safety. Your safety and your child's safety. Safety is also the gauge by which Family Court and Child Protective Services (CPS) determine how often parents see their children.

- If the family background has domestic violence or any type of abuse that will influence the children's safety, a parent's time with their children will be affected.
- If a parent has an active addiction or untreated mental illness, whereby they're unpredictable and a child is unsafe, that could affect the time a parent might spend with their children.

A NOTE OF ENCOURAGEMENT

Try not to lose faith if you find old frustrations bubbling up. That's normal. But when they do, pause and ask yourself one question: "Will bringing this up help my child, or does it only justify my own hurt?" If the answer is the latter, let it go. Your child deserves your peace more than your past.

When you make the choice to leave history behind, you open the door to a healthier future. You're not erasing what happened, but you're refusing to let it dictate how you move forward. And in doing so, you give your child the priceless gift of watching the two adults they love the most rise above old wounds to create something new: a stable, cooperative, and respectful parenting relationship.

That's not just leaving the past in the past. It's modeling the very resilience you want your child to carry into their own future relationships. At the end of the day, it's not about who was "right" in the past. It's about being the best co-parent you can be now. And that begins by turning the page and writing a new chapter — one that focuses not on what broke you apart, but on what will hold your child together.

REMEMBER

But keep in mind that there can't just be accusations of these things. Judges can't just make arbitrary decisions. There must be a documentation of the history to help the agencies make their decisions. However, sometimes incidents aren't reported, and no paper trail to document previous problems. This complicates the ability to make an accurate finding. Still, for the majority of co-parents, the safety of children with the other parent isn't the issue. Just trying to coordinate the back-and-forth life and get along without losing their cool in front of the kids after a breakup is the primary hurdle.

Fighting in front of the kids: Why it matters more than you think

How many times have you made small compromises to keep the peace with someone with whom you don't entirely see eye to eye? Maybe you forgave a close friend after a big argument because your relationship mattered more than being right. Or perhaps you tolerated that co-worker who once ate your lunch or smiled through a conversation with your demanding boss. Everyone has people they choose not to walk away from — or simply can't walk away from — so they adjust, let things go, and move forward.

Your co-parent falls squarely into that category. No one's saying you need to become best friends, go shopping together, or take up golf. But you do need to be courteous and civil — especially in front of your children. Whether it's a school concert, a parent-teacher conference, or the sidelines of a Little League game, your presence together affects your child far more than you may realize.

I can't tell you how many children of estranged co-parents have shared heartbreaking stories about what it feels like when both parents attend the same event, but can't seem to coexist. Your children are frightened and embarrassed at the same time. They're frightened because when parents are out of control, their children don't feel safe and wonder, "Who will take care of me when things get tough?" They feel embarrassed that others will see how out of control their parents are and think less of them. It's tough to be proud of your parents when they're acting foolish in public.

Often, parents tell me, "I don't know why my child is so upset. We barely spoke to one another." But avoidance speaks volumes, and your children hear it loud and clear.

One father told me, "Sometimes I don't even go to the game if I know her mom's going to be there," as if his absence solves the problem. But here's the hard truth: When you avoid or disrespect your child's other parent while your child is present, it's not just uncomfortable for the child. It's emotionally damaging as well. Yes, those are strong words, but they're true. You're emotionally abusing your child when you openly disrespect their other parent. It's a scar they'll take with them for life.

Children take their emotional cues from their parents. When they see the two people they love most ignore each other, or worse, exchange cold glances and cutting remarks, it changes how they feel and how they learn to behave.

Here's why: Children learn more by watching than by listening. That means they're not just hearing your words; they're studying your tone, your posture, your interactions. It's called observational learning, and it's hardwired into the brain through something called *mirror neurons*. These neurons help children mimic what they see: everything from facial expressions to emotional responses.

So, when you show disrespect to their other parent, you're teaching your child how to behave in their future relationships. It's unfortunate, but if children are constantly exposed to conflict, they'll view stressful interaction as normal and seek it out in their own relationships when they get older — not because they like it, but because it feels familiar. That's quite a legacy to leave behind.

Staying focused on what your children need

Your children don't need perfect parents. They don't need you to agree on everything. What they do need is the reassurance that, even when you disagree, you'll do so respectfully — and never at the expense of their sense of safety and stability.

So, the next time you're tempted to roll your eyes or walk the other way at a school event, consider what message that sends to your child. You don't have to sit next to each other at the school assembly but consider the same vicinity so your child can look in one direction and see both of their parents cheering them on. You're not just reacting to your co-parent; you're modeling how to treat someone important in their life. And that's a lesson your children are guaranteed to carry forward.

Being the Change You Want to See

The second component to laying the groundwork for collaborative co-parenting is one of the most powerful truths in co-parenting, but also one of the hardest to put into practice: "Be the change you wish to see." And yet, it's often the very thing that makes the biggest difference.

I can't count the number of times I've heard a co-parent say, "I'll start being reasonable when they do," or "Why should I take the high road when they never do?" It's a common and understandable response when emotions are raw. You may feel hurt, angry, or misunderstood, and the idea of being the one to "go first" can feel unfair.

But here's the truth: Waiting for the other person to change before you do keeps everyone stuck — including your children.

Stepping up with respect and kindness

Being the change in your co-parenting relationship isn't about giving in. It's about stepping into the parent and person you want to be — not in reaction to your co-parent's behavior, but in alignment with your own values. When you lead with integrity, kindness, and consistency, you set a tone that has the power to shift the entire dynamic.

Here's how co-parents, Gigi and Don, handled it when conflict arose as they were exchanging their children:

> My co-parent, Gigi, and I were constantly at odds. Nothing I said was right, and she questioned everything I did, from helping with homework to teaching our son how to bake. If I tried to defend myself, it always spun out of control, especially during exchanges when the kids were present. I'd feel anxious beforehand, and they could tell. My daughter became clingy and finally said, "I'm so sorry Mommy is so mean to you." That's when I knew something had to change.
>
> But I also knew telling Gigi the kids were picking up on the tension would sound like a personal attack and only make things worse.
>
> When I saw what our dynamic was doing to them, I decided I didn't want to live that way anymore. It didn't matter who was right or wrong. I just wanted our children to feel safe.
>
> So, instead of defending myself, when Gigi met me with another accusation, I responded with kindness and curiosity. I said, "This feels important to you, and I want to understand why, but let's talk about it when the kids aren't around. I'll do my best to listen."
>
> That stopped her in her tracks. All she said was, "Okay." For the first time, the exchange was civil.

When only one co-parent is invested

So many believe that it's impossible to co-parent if only one parent is invested. Co-parenting is indeed easier if both have the desire to work together. No one "wins" in a co-parenting power struggle, but children lose when conflict becomes the focus. You don't need to wait for an apology or for your co-parent to suddenly change their attitude. You can begin right now by modeling the behavior you hope your children will one day carry into their own adult relationships. Someone must go first. Be the change you want to see.

Here's a perfect example:

> I once worked with a woman named Carla who was constantly at odds with her co-parent. Every exchange turned into an argument. If he was late, she snapped. If he questioned something, she pushed back harder. She felt she was simply defending herself.
>
> One day, she decided to try something different. She told herself, *"No matter what he says, I'm going to stay calm and keep it about the kids."*
>
> At the next pickup, he arrived late and immediately started explaining why. Normally, she would have interrupted and corrected him. Instead, she simply said, "Okay. Next time, just text me so I know."
>
> He paused. Looked at her. And said, "Yeah. . . I can do that."
>
> That was it.
>
> The tension didn't disappear overnight, but it shifted. He became less defensive. Their conversations became shorter, calmer, and more focused. And over time, the conflict that had defined their relationship began to fade.
>
> She didn't change him. She changed her response. And that changed everything.

REMEMBER

Someone must go first. Let it be you — not because you're giving in, but because you're rising above. Your children will notice. And whether your co-parent says so or not, they probably will too.

Checking Your Mindset

After you make the decision that a change is necessary and you put that change in place, the third component to laying the groundwork for collaborative co-parenting is to "check your mindset." You'll see throughout this book that every suggestion for improvement begins with "check your thinking." The proper mindset sets the stage for proper behavior.

Thoughts become action

It's human nature to act in accordance with your thoughts. If you're angry, resentful, or holding a grudge, that's what you'll be thinking about when you enter a conversation, and you'll act accordingly. You won't be able to successfully put aside your own interests to find a compromise when necessary.

I often use analogies to better illustrate concepts. In this case, the analogy, or story, was offered by one of my clients during a co-parenting session. It easily demonstrates how your thoughts will control your actions — and reactions.

> Paula was very angry with her co-parent, Brian, but as a working parent, she rarely had time to herself except when she blow-dried her long hair in the morning. It took a while, and the noise of the dryer drowned out the sounds of the house. As she explained, it was the only time she could think uninterrupted.
>
> That's when the conversations with Brian began in her mind. She replayed what he had done to her in the past, and with every stroke of the brush, she grew angrier until her heart was pounding.
>
> Inevitably, around that time, Brian would call to confirm pickup after school, and Paula would bite his head off the moment she heard his voice. It became a morning ritual.
>
> It didn't become clear to Paula until we talked about triggers and rituals in a co-parenting class. Blow-drying her hair had become an anger ritual. While filling the time, her mind returned to the past, each thought piling onto the next until she exploded when Brian called.
>
> Every time she picked up the dryer and brush, the ritual began. Paula was the only one who could stop that thought process, but it would take practice to replace those negative thoughts with ones that allowed her to communicate calmly with Brian.

I cover triggers and rituals and how to control them in Chapter 4. But, for now, take this point to heart: Your thoughts about your co-parent, your situation, or even what you think about yourself have a direct impact on the way you behave, and those behaviors shape your child's experience.

Looking for the shift

Like Paula in the previous section, if your thoughts are filled with resentment — "He never listens," "She's trying to make my life miserable," — you'll naturally approach every interaction with defensiveness. That may show up as curt emails, tense drop-offs, or arguments over even the smallest details. Your child may not understand the exact thought in your head that prompts the angry responses, but they feel the result in the atmosphere around them.

On the other hand, when you shift your thoughts toward the bigger picture "My child deserves peace," "We both love our child," "This disagreement doesn't define us" — your actions begin to change. You pause before reacting. You choose calmer words. You respond instead of retaliating. You shift your focus from the past to the present, and your child feels that shift in their sense of security and their ability to trust that both parents are looking out for them.

It's a simple truth: Your thoughts become your actions, and your actions become your child's environment. If you feed your mind with bitterness, you'll feed your home with tension. If you feed your mind with patience and perspective, you'll create an environment where your child can thrive.

This doesn't mean ignoring hurt feelings or pretending co-parenting is always easy. It means recognizing the power of your mindset. When you choose to reframe your thoughts — focusing less on past wrongs and more on present responsibilities — you create a ripple effect. You're not just managing conflict better; you're modeling for your child how to handle challenges with dignity and grace.

TIP

So, the next time you catch yourself thinking, "This will never work," or "That miserable so and so," stop and ask: "What do I want my child to see right now: anger, or resilience?" That simple shift in thought can change your next action, and that action may change the entire tone of your co-parenting relationship.

In the end, co-parenting isn't just about logistics and schedules. It's about the thoughts you carry into each interaction. Because in this journey, what you think today often becomes what your child feels tomorrow.

Being Open to Changing Course

Sometimes you realize the path you're on isn't bringing you the cooperation, respect, or peace you hoped for. That's when it's time to "course correct," which is the fourth component for laying the groundwork for collaborative co-parenting. The need to correct your direction doesn't mean failure. It means recognizing that relationships — including a relationship with a co-parent — are living, breathing things that occasionally drift off track and need redirection to achieve the relationship you want.

TIP

Here's a quick list to prompt collaborative co-parenting behavior if you and your co-parent sense that you've fallen out of sync:

- » **Pause before you react.** Take a moment to reflect before responding. Take a breath or count to five. Just give yourself some time to get your bearings. Reacting emotionally can escalate the problem, while a calm response opens the door to resolution.
- » **Identify the real issue.** Often, the conflict isn't about the immediate problem. It's about an unmet need, past hurt, or miscommunication.
- » **Separate emotion from strategy.** Your feelings are valid, but your interaction should be based on what works, not what wounds.
- » **Talk with, not about, your co-parent.** Although venting with friends may calm you down at the time, it's important to discuss problems directly with your co-parent.
- » **Collaborate on solutions.** Instead of pointing fingers, ask, "How can we fix this together?" Or "I'd like to explore a solution we can both accept."
- » **Acknowledge your part.** Even if it's just 5 percent, own it. Accountability builds credibility and invites cooperation.
- » **Always bring it back to your child.** Ask, "What outcome here is best for our child?" That question alone can redirect the entire conversation.
- » **Agree to revisit the issue.** Not everything can be solved in one conversation. Set a time to check in and adjust as needed.
- » **Remember that it's not too late to pivot.** That's what being open to a course correction is all about. One misstep doesn't define the whole co-parenting relationship. What matters most is what you do next.

IN THIS CHAPTER

» Setting co-parenting goals

» Designing your personal plan for co-parenting your children

» Understanding when to return to court

Chapter 3

Establishing Co-Parenting Goals and Designing a Collaborative Plan

Co-parenting after a separation or divorce isn't about winning or losing. It's not about keeping score or proving who's "right." It's about creating a safe, nurturing, and predictable environment for your children — one where both parents contribute, support, and guide their growth.

The first part of this chapter is prep work. It's about getting your mind in the right place to work together and coming to an agreement about what you must do to approach co-parenting collaboratively. The chapter goes on to help you identify your core values or the shared hopes you have for your child's well-being, growth, and happiness. From there, the focus is on maintaining stability and predictability by creating routines and schedules your child can rely on. Equally as important is learning to support healthy relationships with both parents, ensuring your child feels free to love each parent without guilt or pressure. Finally, you'll see how to design your personal co-parenting plan that reflects your child's needs and your family's unique circumstances, providing a clear roadmap for working together successfully.

Identifying Core Co-Parenting Goals

Identifying your core co-parenting goals is the foundation of a collaborative co-parenting relationship. Before you can design schedules, make decisions, or resolve conflicts, you need clarity on what truly matters to your child's well-being. These goals serve as your guide, helping you navigate the challenges without losing sight of what's most important.

The key here is to identify what's vital to your lives as co-parents — together. Core goals aren't about controlling the other parent. They're about creating stability, consistency, and predictability for your child, while fostering respect and cooperation between you as parents. By clearly defining your priorities, you lay the groundwork for a co-parenting relationship that's purposeful, intentional, and, above all else, centered on your child's needs.

Remember, even though co-parents may be estranged at the beginning of their co-parenting journey, they still must put aside their differences and come to an agreement about what they want for their children. It always begins with mindset.

TIP

Both of you must ask yourselves:

- » What kind of parent do I want to be?
- » What kind of relationship do I want with my co-parent?
- » What do I want to model for my children?
- » What kind of environment do I want my child to experience in both homes?

Reflecting upon these questions will help shape every decision you must make moving forward. The following sections provide steps to help you identify your key co-parenting goals.

Step 1: Prioritize the child's emotional, psychological, and physical well-being

The first and most crucial step in establishing your co-parenting goals is to agree to put your child's overall well-being at the forefront of every decision. This is more than meeting their basic needs of housing, food, and water. It involves creating a total environment at both homes where your child feels safe, valued, and emotionally supported by both parents.

Protect your children from adult conflicts

A surefire way to damage a child's self-worth is to expose them to adult conflict. Children naturally internalize what they hear, particularly when it's loud, harsh, or aimed at someone they love. So, when a parent says, "Your father is so lazy!" the child just doesn't hear criticism of Dad. They hear it as criticism of themselves as well. "I'm half Dad. Does Mom think I'm lazy, too?"

"Oh, our child never hears us fight."

Of course they do. So many parents are confident they've shielded their children from their arguing, but those kids lived with you prior to the breakup. They knew what was going on, and even though study after study reminds parents what ongoing conflict does to their children, in most cases, it continues. Your kids may no longer be standing in the same room with both of you, but they're party to your exchanges, they feel the tension at their Little League games, and they're distracted by it at their school assemblies. Your children personalize your disgust for their other parent, and it changes who they are.

When you sense even the slightest negative interaction with your co-parent coming on, stop and take a breath. Being right isn't as important as the example you're setting for your children. I'll examine this at greater length in Chapter 13.

Avoid badmouthing

A child's identity is tied to both parents. Speaking negatively about the other parent when your child is within earshot puts the child in the painful position of deciding to whom they're most loyal.

> "I could tell my parents were arguing on the phone even though Dad closed his bedroom door. I heard him yell, "You bitch!" and it scared me. Mom's house is not that far, so I ran back to her house to make sure she was okay."

Support your children's emotional well-being by refusing to let your personal frustrations spill into their world. If you want to help your child build a strong, healthy self-image, start by protecting how they hear you talk about their mother or father.

Maintain consistent routines

As difficult as it may be to coordinate efforts with your co-parent, particularly if you're somewhat estranged, consistent routines at both homes for meals, school, homework, and bedtimes ensure your child will know what to expect on a daily basis. Consistence helps a child feel safe and secure. Disorganization will undermine all your good intentions.

For example, do you have a bedtime routine your child likes? Share it with your co-parent. They may not want to copy it exactly, but knowledge of each other's routines reinforces consistency and cooperation in both homes. Mutual involvement in your child's extracurricular school activities further fosters their emotional development in a positive way. Things like allowing the same friends to go to both houses to play and sharing the transportation to games and practices add uniformity to life as your children move from house to house.

When parents intentionally prioritize their children, they create a foundation of trust and security that allows the children to thrive. Look for ways to support each other in supporting your children. When you undermine your co-parent for any reason, you're doing a disservice to your children.

Ensure your child feels heard, validated, and loved by both parents

One of the most meaningful things parents can offer their children is the assurance that their voice and feelings matter. This starts with truly listening to their words and being sensitive to how they feel. If you don't agree with what your child is saying, don't dismiss them with, "That's not true" or "You're being too sensitive." That response diminishes their feelings, and they won't feel respected or compelled to further confide in you.

Help create an atmosphere where your child feels comfortable confiding in and seeking out both of you in times of trouble. When your child expresses sadness or worries, do your best to resist the urge to fix things in the hopes of protecting them from pain. Instead, offer phrases of validation like, "That makes sense," or even, "I understand why you might feel that way." That kind of response doesn't imply that you agree but recognizes your child's right to feel the way they feel. As a result, they feel heard.

Finally, children must be allowed to love both parents and feel loved by both parents. When children are assured of this, they no longer carry the burden of divided loyalties or guilt. Instead, they experience the security of knowing that their parents' love for them is stronger than any conflict between adults.

Step 2: Fostering healthy communication between co-parents

Healthy communication is the backbone of effective co-parenting. When parents commit to speaking with one another calmly, respectfully, and directly, they reduce misunderstandings and prevent unnecessary conflict. This means keeping conversations child-focused, avoiding blame, and choosing words that inform rather than inflame. Tools such as shared calendars, parenting apps, or written agreements can keep communication clear and consistent. Above all, approach each interaction as you would a professional business partnership, focused on problem-solving and cooperation. The ultimate "business" you're managing together is the well-being of your child.

Make it your business

The key here is to model your approach to problem-solving with your co-parent the same way you'd approach a business associate. If you were meeting with your boss to ask for a raise, you wouldn't walk in yelling, screaming, or threatening that if they didn't give you what you wanted, you'd make their life miserable. Granted, your co-parent isn't your boss, but it goes without saying that in that circumstance, you wouldn't storm out because you have to return to work the next day. Instead, you'd arrive prepared with your reasons of why you deserve a raise, you'd present them in an orderly fashion, and you'd remain professional.

Problem-solving with your co-parent isn't that different. Yes, emotions run higher, but the principle is the same. You can't storm out of the relationship. You'll be back the next day, week, or month because your ex is your child's other parent. They'll always have a say in decisions concerning your children. Approaching discussions with the mindset of professionalism keeps the focus where it belongs: on your child.

MAKE IT YOUR BUSINESS CHECKLIST

The following can help when problem-solving with your co-parent:

- **Agree on the method of communication:** While many courts encourage or require text-based communication, it's important to recognize its limits. Texting is useful for quick updates, but more complex or emotionally sensitive topics are often better handled through an email, scheduled phone call, video conversation, or, when appropriate, in person. Honor the method chosen.
- **Look for neutral territory:** A park, a coffee shop, or a restaurant works well, not one of your homes. That's your domain and not neutral territory. Being in public often keeps tempers in check. Make sure your meeting is away from the kids and always be on time.

» **Avoid alcohol or substances:** Even one drink can shift your attitude and make compromise harder. The introduction of alcohol and other mind-altering substances has a funny way of reversing agreements.

» **Come prepared:** Bring real solutions, not just demands. Ask for your co-parent's ideas and truly consider them.

» **Stick to one topic:** Don't pile on problems. Your co-parent will feel overwhelmed and shut down. If today is about prom attire, leave child support or problems with visitation for another meeting.

» **Keep your child front and center:** Place a photo of your child on the table or use your phone screen saver. When tempers flare, look at it. That's why you're there.

» **Write it down:** Once you've agreed, put it in writing, sign it, and keep a copy for both of you. It's not silly. It creates accountability and prevents backtracking later. When you approach problem-solving with structure, preparation, and respect, you not only resolve issues more quickly. You show your child what cooperation looks like. That's putting your child first.

MAKE IT YOUR BUSINESS EXERCISE

For this exercise, review the following list, and place a check indicating which of these business relationship skills you already use with your co-parent. Then place an X on the skill you haven't mastered. The purpose of this exercise isn't to blame others for a skill they haven't mastered but to understand how to make changes in your approach if you have yet to master them yourself.

__ **My co-parent and I have common goals for our child(ren).** If this were a working business relationship, you'd strive to be a team player with common goals.

__ **My co-parent and I have a plan in place for how we'll solve problems together — and we follow it to a tee.** If this were a working business relationship, there would be an agenda to follow during the meeting.

__ **When it's time to discuss something, I put myself in my co-parent's shoes and come prepared with a possible solution that isn't one-sided.** Always have a possible solution in mind. Then you have a place from which to negotiate.

__ **If we don't agree, I'm open to compromise when searching for solutions.** If this were a working business relationship, the result would be a solution. It wouldn't be fighting until one of you admits the other is right or bullying the other into agreement.

_ **I calmly listen to my co-parent's opinion.** If this were a working business relationship, you'd respect your co-worker enough to listen without arguing or being insulting. If you didn't agree with a co-worker's point of view, what would be your response? Probably, "You know, I don't" and then you'd calmly explain how you feel. Treat your co-parent with the same respect as a co-worker.

_ **I don't interrupt or cut my co-parent off in conversations.** If this were a working relationship, you would approach your co-worker with respect and allow them to explain their position.

_ **I'm able to discuss details or concerns with my co-parent without becoming insulting or emotional.** If this were a working business relationship, you'd both keep your emotions under wraps.

_ **I don't bring up the past to make my point or prove my co-parent wrong.** That approach doesn't even come into play in a working business relationship. Business relationships concentrate on going forward, not backward.

_ **I don't badmouth or talk disparagingly about my co-parent to friends, relatives, or in front of our children.** Gossip and badmouthing aren't tolerated in the workplace.

If there are Xs by any of these behaviors, you have some work to do.

Agree to respond respectfully and promptly to messages about the child

In the early stages of co-parenting, it's not unusual for parents to avoid one another, especially if the relationship ended badly. Passive-aggressive behavior, like ignoring texts, delaying callbacks, or refusing to respond altogether, is often a way to stay emotionally disconnected. But avoidant communication doesn't make things easier. It makes them worse. These patterns only build frustration, create distrust, and set the stage for bigger conflicts down the road.

That's when parents start to threaten each other with court. Many parents say they never want to end up back in court, but when communication breaks down, that's often exactly where they land. If you want to stay out of court and make co-parenting work, you must find a way to engage respectfully and consistently.

You need a new strategy, and it should be more than agreeing to see a mediator before you return to court. Your new strategy should head off going to a mediator. This new approach is for the time between "the problem" and employing a mediator. It's for when you're living with "the problem" and don't know how to address it.

Agree to share information about health, school, and extracurricular activities

Agree to compare notes. Keep each other informed. Do your best to avoid the *best parent trap.*

The *best parent trap* is an attitude I often see when one parent arrogantly believes they're the "better parent"— more capable, more tuned in, and more essential to the child's life. It often sounds like, "You didn't know Steven likes to bake? We bake together all the time." On the surface, it may seem like a harmless observation, but why it's being said isn't harmless. The implication is, "I'm closer to Steven. I know him better. I'm the best parent." The best parent trap also shows up when one parent doesn't pass on essential information about the child. Information is power. So, information is hoarded as if it's a covert spy operation.

The problem with this mentality is that it turns co-parenting into a competition and completely cuts off communication. And, while one parent may feel validated in the moment, when their child senses that their parents are trying to one-up each other or that one parent thinks the other is less important, it creates emotional confusion, questions of loyalty, and unnecessary pressure on the child. Children should never feel as if they must pick sides, compare love, or protect one parent's ego at the expense of the other.

REMEMBER

The best parent isn't the one who knows the most and keeps information to themselves. It's the parent who reaches out, shares information in the name of the child, and supports the collaborative effort.

Pause or reschedule conversations when emotions run high

In most instances, taking a break when emotions run high is excellent advice. It allows flustered parents to cool down, gather their thoughts, and come back to the discussion with a more organized mindset. However, taking a break can be a two-edged sword. On one hand, if emotions are running high, stopping to take a breath is a great idea, but it can also add gas to the fire if you don't tell your co-parent what to expect. Therefore, reply with a time to expect a response. "I need to take a step back and gather my thoughts. Give me a couple of hours to think about this, and I'll let you know my answer by 7 p.m."

Now, your co-parent knows you received the text or other form of communication, you aren't ignoring them, and they can stop pacing the floor or blowing up your phone for lack of communication. To continue to build trust, make sure you reply by the time you said you would.

Step 3: Maintaining stability and predictability

It helps children feel safe and secure when they know exactly what to expect. Sudden changes without explanations confuse your children and make them feel disorganized and anxious. This is then exemplified in a multitude of behaviors — crabbiness, moodiness, acting out, a change in their eating or sleeping patterns, and, for younger children, wetting the bed when they've been dry for months or years. Ironically, rather than considering that the child's schedule is inconsistent and confusing, unknowingly, parents will discipline the children for their poor behavior, which only complicates an already complicated issue.

Keep parenting schedules consistent

Be clear about which days your children will transition between homes, where the exchange will occur, at what time, and who will be responsible for transportation. Children should never be surprised by an unfamiliar driver. They need to know in advance exactly who will be picking them up and taking them to their next destination.

Parenting plans can be confusing, particularly for younger children who don't yet understand the days of the week. These children often ask, "Where will I sleep tonight?" — a question that reveals their deep need for predictability. When parents switch days without explaining why, children can feel unsettled and unsure of where they belong. Keeping schedules consistent and communication clear not only eliminates confusion but also provides the stability children need to thrive.

Help your child feel organized by purchasing the same calendar for both homes, and fill them out together using different colors to designate the time they'll spend at each home. This will also help young children who don't have a clear understanding of the parenting plan to learn the days of the week.

Set clear boundaries around new relationships or major life changes

An essential part of setting co-parenting goals is to agree about how you'll approach dating and the introduction of new partners.

If you think about it, most of the advice you find about dating after a breakup starts with when you meet someone new and become serious. Then the advice covers when and how to introduce the children, but that's starting the discussion in the middle.

It's more than likely that both co-parents will date a few people prior to finding a new partner who best complements them and their children's lifestyle. That's why now, before anyone new enters your life, you should establish clear guidelines for how to conduct yourselves while dating. Remember, this will be your children's first glimpse of their parents as single people. They've already witnessed conflict and the pain of separation. The way you and your co-parent approach the transition to dating will leave a lasting impression, shaping how your children approach their own relationships as they grow older and start to date themselves.

So, agree on your dating boundaries. While I'll go into this in more detail in Chapter 6, it's important to start thinking about what's appropriate and what's not when it comes to dating after separation. Consider discussing and agreeing on expectations such as these:

- We'll only date when the children are with the other parent.
- We won't talk about our dating lives or introduce casual partners in front of the children.
- We agree that no one will meet the children unless both parents are aware and the relationship is serious.
- Once a relationship becomes serious, we'll inform one another out of respect and transparency.
- We'll agree on how and when to introduce a new partner to the children to help ensure it's a positive, well-timed experience.

Respect each other's time and household rules

Not only must you come to an agreement about how you'll date in front of the children, but also how you'll present dating to one another.

> "I just started dating a woman I really liked, and she stopped by for a glass of wine last Sunday afternoon. One thing led to another, and we ended up in bed. At the most inopportune moment, my ex walked into the house searching for our daughter's stuffed animal. Evidently, she couldn't take her nap without her "Baby Dog," and she'd left it in her room at my house. My ex had a key for emergencies and thought I was out for the day because my car was in the garage. My girlfriend lost it. I never saw her again."

Situations like this highlight why respecting each other's time and household rules is so important when co-parenting. Even when dating, it's essential to consider that your home remains a shared space with your child, and unexpected visits from a co-parent can happen. Setting clear boundaries around timing, privacy, and expectations can prevent these awkward or upsetting incidents. It's also a reminder that transitions, like introducing someone new, require planning, patience, and transparency, not only with your co-parent, but also with a potential partner so that all feel respected. Of course, slipups happen, but don't consider them to be backsliding. Use slipups as a learning tool and make the necessary adjustments for the next time.

Step 4: Encouraging positive relationships with both parents

Children should never feel they must choose sides. They need the freedom to love both parents without guilt, pressure, or fear of disappointing either one. Supporting your child's relationship with the other parent doesn't mean you've given in or that you necessarily agree with your co-parent. It simply demonstrates that you love your child enough to put their needs ahead of your own.

Children thrive when they enjoy consistent, meaningful contact with both parents in an environment that feels emotionally safe. So, if your child says they miss their other parent while they're with you, don't take it personally. Instead, comfort them by encouraging a quick phone call, sending a cheerful text, or finding another small way to ease their feelings. Remember, this isn't about your hurt feelings or guarding your time. It's about raising secure, emotionally healthy children who feel free to love both of their parents without fear of letting either one down.

Designing Your Co-Parenting Plan

Up to this point, I've focused on preparing your mindset, laying the groundwork for cooperation, respect, and child-centered thinking. That foundation is critical because, without it, even the most carefully written parenting plan can unravel.

Now it's time to move from theory to practice. I'll explore the day-to-day logistics of co-parenting and the specific agreements you and your co-parent must establish to keep things running smoothly. These details, how schedules are honored, how information is exchanged, and how decisions are made, are what transform co-parenting from an abstract ideal into a workable, productive partnership that truly benefits your children.

Setting up co-parenting logistics

Co-parenting logistics simply means having a clear structure in place so both co-parents know what to expect and how they'll work together. Establishing guidelines for communication, decision-making, and financial responsibilities reduces confusion and keeps the focus on raising your child in a stable environment. Whether it's deciding how and when you'll share information, outlining how major choices about education or health will be made, or clarifying financial commitments, these logistical agreements are the backbone of productive co-parenting.

Schedules

Agree to abide by the parenting plan schedules that are in place. And if there are changes, agree upon how far in advance a change must be requested. Seven days? Two weeks? Spur of the moment, okay?

Regarding vacations, most parenting plans allow both parents to take vacations with their children. Each vacation usually requires a 30-day notification; however, it's important to note that this is a notification, not a request. There's a difference. Minor changes, like switching a weekend, are requests, and those kinds of requests must be agreed upon between the parents.

So, how far in advance do you agree to ask each other for a change? And, if something comes up at the last minute, do you agree to be flexible?

Decision-making protocols

Parents must decide what decisions should be made jointly and what may be made autonomously. Healthcare, religion, education, and extracurricular activities are usually made jointly. You don't necessarily need to run autonomous decisions by your co-parent first. These are things like, "Bedtime is usually 9 p.m., but it's a weekend, so you can stay up until 10 p.m." That's when the child returns to the other parent's home and balks at bedtime. "Mom lets us stay up until 10 p.m." They aren't lying. Mom did make that judgment call, but it was a one-time judgment call, not a regular occurrence. Have an answer ready.

Public Appearances and Expectations

Additional considerations that you must discuss and agree upon with your co-parent:

- Will you attend school functions or extracurricular activities together? For example, what about the winter assembly in which Mary Louise plays the flute?
  - How will we manage it?
  - Will we both attend or alternate activities?
  - If we attend at the same time, where will we sit?

If co-parents are estranged, sitting together may cause undue stress on both the parents and the children. If that's the case, consider sitting in the same vicinity so your child doesn't have to search for either of you, just not next to each other if you feel uncomfortable or a disagreement is looming.

Determining financial responsibility

Child support is usually calculated using a computer program that analyzes the time the child spends with each parent in relationship to both parents' salaries. Each state uses a different computer program. Check with your attorney or the Superior Court Child Support Office in your state for help with filing for child support. You can also agree on an amount among yourselves. If you do agree, write it down, both sign and date it, and if you like, you can file your agreement with the court in the form of a court order.

Consider these questions when discussing extracurricular activities, medical and dental bills, and unforeseen extras: Will the cost for medical and dental bills be split between the parents, or will they be assigned to one or the other? What about extracurricular activities? How will unforeseen extras be handled — things like cheerleading outfits or soccer cleats?

Anticipating conflict

Co-parents will disagree at some point. Even those who have learned to get along over the years face conflict at times. That's why it's important to anticipate problems and have a plan in place for how you'll constructively disagree and then find a way to agree.

Without a plan for co-parenting conflict resolution, co-parents approach disagreements just as they did when they were together. Some clam up; some scream until they're blue in the face and then retire to their corners; and some get insulting. Most see poor results. Therefore, a new approach to conflict resolution is necessary. Have an idea of how you'll approach a problem before it surfaces.

- What will we do when we disagree?
- How will we address disagreements?

Some co-parents do better with a model to follow, a sort of step-by-step guide that helps them solve problems and brings them to compromise.

I often use a four-step model to help keep co-parents on track. The following example demonstrates how two co-parents addressed a problem. Of special interest is how the mother, Elyse, initiated using the four-step model. So many parents have no idea how to start. As you read through the scenario, you'll see Elyse was direct. She just asked, "What about using the model we learned in co-parenting class?" Her co-parent, Robert, immediately agreed.

When Elyse and Robert first separated, they promised each other they'd "Keep things steady for Shane." But three months later, Shane was complaining about stomachaches every Wednesday — the day he switched houses and went straight to basketball practice from the exchange.

One Wednesday, Elyse helped Shane buckle his seatbelt slowly, clutching his basketball as he got into Dad's car.

"I'm always late," Shane murmured while staring at his feet. "Coach said if I'm late again, I won't start this weekend."

Robert immediately became defensive. "We're not *always* late," he said, sharper than intended. Elyse did her best to stay calm, "You're getting him there after warm-ups. That's late, Robert."

Shane shrank a little in his seat. Two parents, two homes, and he was caught in the middle.

That night, Elyse texted Robert. Instead of blaming him, she tried something new. "This isn't working for Shane. Can we try the problem-solving model we learned in co-parenting class?"

Robert's first instinct was to fire back, but he paused. He texted back, "Yes. Can we talk when he's asleep?"

They agreed on a quick video call once the house quieted down.

Using Elyse and Robert's conflict, I'll walk you through the four steps for peaceful resolution.

TIP

You can find the Four-Step Problem-Solving Model Using I Messages document at www.dummies.com/go/coparentingfd. You can also find this on the Bonus Families website at www.bonusfamilies.com/4StepModel.

1. Identify the problem

Elyse almost began by reminding Robert that he was always late, but she caught herself. Step one is "identify the problem," *not the person.*

She began, "Shane is arriving late for basketball on Wednesdays, and it's making him anxious. He thinks he's going to lose his starting spot."

"From my side," Robert noted. "Leaving work, picking him up, and getting across town in time is tight. But yes, the problem is Shane's anxiety and the repeated lateness."

They weren't pointing fingers. They were naming the issue. That's the first sign that they're becoming a co-parenting team.

2. Come to the table with a solution

This is an important aspect of problem-solving together. Suggest a solution to the proposed problem. If you don't, you come to the table with something you see as a problem and expect your co-parent to come up with a solution. They may not even know there *is* a problem, and that will cause resentment.

"My idea," she said, "is that I drive Shane straight to practice on Wednesdays. You pick him up after. That way, he's never late."

Robert came prepared, too, and offered his ideas. Two parents. Two ideas. Two attempts at fixing the same problem. That's teamwork, not perfection.

3. Negotiate

This step is where many co-parents slip into old patterns. You might hear things like, "It always has to be your way!" Or "You're so controlling!"

When a co-parent hears either of those statements, they immediately want to defend themselves. Then the co-parents are arguing about what the other said or did, and discussing not the problem that needs to be solved. In this case, Shane was late, and it embarrassed him. Using the model, Elyse and Robert stayed focused on Shane.

They talked through real drive times, realistic work flexibility, and alternate exchange points closer to the gym. Then tension rose.

"You don't understand what my job expects," Robert said.

"And you don't understand how this affects Shane's whole evening," Elyse replied.

Both were silent after that. They didn't want this discussion to end up like all the others — in a shouting match. They took time to reflect on where to go from there. Then Robert said, "Let's stop. This isn't about our schedules. It's about Shane not feeling sick every Wednesday."

They were putting the model into practice and realized that their conversation was getting off track. That reset the discussion to what Shane needs. The ability to reset without blame or fault is the heartbeat of effective co-parenting.

4. Compromise

After talking it through, they landed on a plan. Elyse would have to drive a little more than she wanted, but she was willing to compromise to relieve Shane's stress. Robert agreed to check with his supervisor to see if he could leave a little earlier on Wednesdays.

They also agreed to tell Shane together: "Mom and Dad noticed you were worried about being late to basketball. We made a new plan: Mom will take you; Dad will pick you up and make sure your gear is ready. You don't have to worry anymore. We've got it handled."

That reassurance is as important as the schedule change.

REMEMBER

Children relax when the adults show them, "The team is on it."

Two weeks later, Shane jogged to Robert's truck after practice, cheeks flushed and smiling. "Coach let me run point tonight!" he said. "And I wasn't late at all."

Later, as Elyse dropped him off, Shane paused before going inside and thanked his mom for "fixing Wednesdays." He said the same thing to his dad once he got into the house.

So many times, parents tell me their children don't know about the conflict between them. Of course, they know. They live with both parents. Two homes. One team.

And that's the four-step problem-solving model in action. It looks so simple that many are skeptical of how effective it can be, but if you apply it step by step, it works, and you stay on track.

Checking in and evaluating the plan

Another great way to stay on track is to schedule periodic check-ins and reviews to evaluate what's working and what needs tweaking. Depending on your parenting plan, decide how often you need a check-in. If your children live with each of you for a week at a time, once a week, when they return to the other house might be a viable choice. However, if your children follow a 2-2-5-5 plan or even a 2-2-3-3 plan (see Chapter 8 for explanations of these parenting plans), you may need to check regularly to ascertain how their transitions are going. The key here is to decide between the two of you when a check-in is necessary and stick to the schedule.

Tracking progress and celebrating wins

Tracking your progress helps you measure your growth even when it seems slower than you like. And I'm a huge fan of celebrating your successes. It reinforces hope, motivates you, and reinforces cooperation. When you and your co-parent acknowledge even small victories (a smooth transition day, a respectful conversation, or consistency in the schedule), you build momentum and trust. These moments are proof that working together can produce tangible results for your children. Now you're co-parents!

When You Can't Agree: Knowing When to Return to Family Court

Returning to family court doesn't solve everything. Judges can enforce schedules, issue orders, and draw lines in the sand, but they can't fix faulty communication patterns, power struggles, and old emotional wounds that keep bringing back the past. That part is up to you.

So, if you and your co-parent are at a standstill, ask yourself, "What's the plan instead?" Are you willing to return to mediation? Communicate through a co-parenting app? Sit down with a neutral third party who can help you design a long-term strategy, not just a temporary ceasefire? If you want a different outcome, you need a different approach.

Going back to court may feel like a proactive method for change, but often it's just a detour back to the same dead end. Your child deserves a co-parenting team that can communicate effectively to manage differences without constantly asking a judge to step in and do the parenting for you.

REMEMBER

The real work happens outside the courtroom. That's where respect is built, and it's where your child learns that even hard disagreements can be managed with maturity, patience, and C.A.R.E. It's your behavior that generates trust.

C.A.R.E. BEFORE COURTROOM CHECKLIST

C — Communication

- Have I clearly stated my concerns in calm, respectful language?
- Did I avoid blame, criticism, or personal attacks?
- Am I listening to understand, not just to argue my point?

A — Acceptance

- Am I expecting my co-parent to do things my way instead of allowing room for differences?
- Can I accept that there's more than one "right way" to parent?
- Is the disagreement about preference, or is it truly about my child's health and safety?

R — Respect

- Am I respecting my co-parent's importance in our child's life, our child's time with their other parent, and my co-parent's boundaries?
- Have I considered their schedule and obligations as equal to my own?
- Would I want to be spoken to or treated the way I'm managing this situation?
- Am I asking my co-parent to do something I wouldn't do?

E — Empathy

- Can I identify what my co-parent might be feeling now?
- Would I accept the solution I'm proposing as fair?
- How might my child be affected if I let this conflict continue?

So, before you return to court believing it's your last resort, consider the C.A.R.E. Before Courtroom Checklist below.

Use this tool whenever you feel tempted to "lawyer up" or threaten court. It will help you slow down, reflect, and choose a child-focused path forward.

TIP

You can find a more extensive checklist at www.bonusfamilies.com/CareBeforeCourtroomChecklist and the Dummies website at www.dummies.com/go/coparentingfd.

Reflect and tweak your approach

After going through the C.A.R.E. Before Courtroom Checklist, ask yourself whether the issues you're facing belong in court. If the court can help, then it's time to call an attorney or file yourself if you feel confident.

But, if it's a co-parenting issue, ask yourself what the next step you can take is to resolve this disagreement peacefully. Options include mediation, co-parenting help from a professional, or even just a cooling-off period.

REMEMBER

Every time you solve a disagreement without going to court, you teach your child that adults can solve problems with maturity, compassion, and respect.

IN THIS CHAPTER

» Improving communication with your co-parent

» Breaking the negative emotion chain reaction

» Stopping misunderstandings that lead to miscommunication

» Employing practical communication tools to overcome conflict

Chapter 4 Communicating Effectively

Have you heard the term *communication breakdown*? Up to this point, *communication breakdown* has become a buzz phrase for an inability to problem-solve together. Someone will observe, "Oh, they don't get along. It's a communication breakdown." And everyone automatically knows what that means. The two people are at an impasse with no chance of improvement.

In this chapter, I'm going to finally break down what good communication is and how to successfully interact with someone you can't get along with. I didn't say *like* because that's not necessary for problem-solving in the best interest of your children. But, surprisingly enough, you may find it to be a by-product of your improved communication because you may grow to understand their motivation and be able to discern what they're really saying rather than merely reacting to hateful words. Of course, the examples and exercises offered in this chapter will center on improving communication with your co-parent, but you'll see that the suggestions also apply to conflict with just about anyone. You can use the same tools for a disagreement with your co-parent that you use during a disagreement with your boss or your children. The goal is not to "win," but to learn to comfortably negotiate and come to a compromise. It's to walk away with both parties feeling heard and respected. The disagreements may not stop completely, but you'll have the tools at your fingertips and know what to do when conversations spin out of control.

Improving Your Communication Is Key

I'm starting this chapter with an example of a typical point of conflict that came about due to poor communication. As with all examples in this book, I've changed the names.

A typical communication breakdown

During a co-parenting class with two divorced parents, I witnessed the following conversation. It's a perfect example of how a breakdown in communication affects your ability to take an honest look at problems and find a solution together.

> A little background: These parents have been divorced for four years. They have a 9-year-old daughter, Makela, who lives with each of them for a week at a time.
>
> "Makela is embarrassed to go to school when she's with her father," her mother said. "He doesn't know how to do her hair, and now she refuses to stay on school nights. I told him why, and he thinks I'm putting her up to it."
>
> Dad laughed it off. "You're putting ideas in her head. You don't want me to have time with her. You're making a big deal out of nothing."
>
> "That's not true. She said she's embarrassed."
>
> This wasn't just about hair. It was a culture gap. Makela's mom is Black. Her dad is white. Mom wears braids: Dad shaves his head. When they were together, those unique differences brought them closer. Now, they divided them, and Makela was caught in the middle.
>
> Dad didn't believe something like hair could matter this much. To him, it felt like manipulation. But hair and grooming were part of Makela's daily life with her mom. Dad wasn't part of those conversations, so he missed their importance. Trust broke down, and communication followed.
>
> I explained to Dad that if he wanted Makela to feel comfortable staying with him on school nights, he needed to learn how to help with her hair. She might not have told him it was a problem, but she would tell her mother, and the conflict would continue.
>
> "That's exactly what happened," Mom said. "And he thinks it's me."

It wasn't. This had nothing to do with love or preference. It was about Makela growing up, becoming aware of how she looked, and trying to fit in at school while moving between two homes.

The solution was simple: Dad could learn via YouTube tutorials, or Mom could show him how to do Makela's hair. But neither option was obvious to these two co-parents because they rarely communicated and never asked each other for help. They thought avoiding each other would reduce conflict. Instead, it left Makela to manage the gap between them.

"She's my baby," Dad said. "I didn't think this would matter yet. We fish; we do projects. I didn't think she cared about hair."

"She's in fourth grade, Louis."

Dad paused, then asked the question every parent asks: "Where did the time go?"

A resolution built on collaboration

REMEMBER

Here's something divorced parents must remember. Their child's life doesn't stop when they walk out their door and go to their other parent's home. Their child's life continues. They have one life but dual citizenship. They're active members of both parents' families — and in Makela's case, both cultures.

When parents don't live together, they must work even harder at coordinating efforts. For their children to flourish, they must acknowledge each parent's strengths and openly reinforce those strengths to their children. Teach your children to respect both parents, and they'll get the best of both of you. It's difficult, especially when you are at odds, but you must do it.

After much discussion, Makela's mother set aside time to teach her co-parent how to help with Makela's hair. It was a new approach, and Dad was skeptical. Mom brought the products she used at home and showed him what to do.

Later, they laughed as they told me how it went. They were often at odds, but this time they shared the story with ease. More importantly, they recognized they were modeling cooperation for their daughter in real time and made a point to keep it positive.

Makela wouldn't need their help for long, but for now, they were working together to support her.

The takeaway was apparent from a comment Makela's dad made in a discussion about how this situation might have been handled more successfully. "I should have believed Julia when she told me about Makela's concerns in the first place and asked her for suggestions. I'm so used to thinking that she is trying to get the better of me that I didn't see that she really was trying to tell me our daughter was unhappy.

WARNING

This approach isn't for everyone. If you and your co-parent are still highly reactive, working together in front of your child can backfire. Don't take something like this on unless you are confident you can stay respectful and focused in front of your children.

Numerous studies have observed that children as young as infants can sense the tension from parental fighting. Further, fighting can affect their emotional, psychological, and even their brain development. Learning disabilities and anxiety are no joke, and combative co-parents are in denial if they don't think it will happen to their children.

You're not collaborating with your co-parent because you're a pushover, forgiving someone who has wronged you. You're doing this for your children. Children notice tone, timing, and emotional regulation, not just words. Your goal now is to form a new relationship with your child's other parent because you both want the best for your children. It's an unselfish act with unselfish motivation.

At the end of each co-parenting session, if parents locked horns during the week, I ask them how they could have handled that situation more successfully.

REMEMBER

It's not only the big things that undermine everyday co-parenting and confuse your children. It's the smaller things like doing their hair or potty training, or coordinating after-school sports, practices, games, homework, bedtimes, and discipline. Coordinating efforts for those things builds trust — not as exes, but as co-parents — and helps you both help your children feel safe and secure.

Breaking the Negative Reaction Chain

As much as co-parents tell themselves that they don't care about their other parent, they do, and the words they exchange matter. If they didn't, I wouldn't have seen thousands of clients over the years complaining, "Did you hear what he just said?" or "She's lying!" And my favorite of recent, "And, now they're just creating this false narrative!" If estranged parents truly didn't care about each other's point of view, they could easily end the fighting by not engaging. That doesn't happen. Most want to keep the kettle boiling because that's the way they're used to interacting, and it's difficult to break the negative thought/negative behavior chain reaction.

While co-parenting, a "negative chain reaction" happens when a small disagreement escalates into a series of emotional responses and defensive behaviors.

Something as minor as a schedule change, a missed text, or a difference of opinion can spiral into tension and arguments.

This chain usually follows a predictable pattern. A trigger sparks a defensive reaction, the co-parent responds in kind, and soon both parents feel unheard, frustrated, and disconnected. Even minor disagreements spiral into full-blown conflict when you follow the same old emotional patterns.

Breaking the chain means choosing to lead with communication, acceptance, respect, and empathy — the C.A.R.E. model in action. I've talked about C.A.R.E. in previous chapters. When parents learn to truly communicate rather than merely react, to accept that they can't change the past, to show respect even in disagreement, and to empathize with both their children and each other, they create a new legacy — one built on cooperation rather than conflict, collaboration rather than confusion.

REMEMBER

Every conversation you have with your co-parent sets the stage for the next conversation. If it was a positive experience, you look forward to the next encounter. If it wasn't positive, you dread it. Since most must share their children's time after a breakup, making it an ongoing positive experience best serves your children.

Breaking the chain means choosing to lead with Communication, Acceptance, Respect, and Empathy — the C.A.R.E. model in action. When parents learn to truly communicate rather than merely react, to accept the past cannot be changed, to show respect even in disagreement, and empathize with both their children and each other, they create a new legacy — one built on cooperation rather than conflict, collaboration rather than confusion.

Step 1: Pause before reacting

The first step to breaking the negative chain reaction is to pause. Taking a deep breath, counting to five, or stepping away for a moment allows your brain to shift from an emotional reaction to an intentional response. Even a brief pause interrupts automatic escalation and gives you control over your next move.

TIP

The next time you feel triggered, silently say the words: "Pause and respond with C.A.R.E."

Step 2: Recognize that trigger awareness is essential

Identify exactly what set you off: a word, a tone, or a past memory resurfacing? Ask yourself whether you're reacting to the present situation or the past. Recognizing the trigger helps you respond thoughtfully rather than reflexively.

Keep a journal of recurring situations, phrases, and words that trigger you. Note what happened, how you felt, and how you typically reacted. Awareness is the first step toward change.

Step 3: Reframe your thoughts

Once you recognize the trigger, shift your mindset from blame to problem-solving. Replace statements like, "They're trying to control me," with, "How can we solve this for our child?"

Here's an example of a shifting mindset in progress: "You're impossible to deal with!"

Try saying, "I see we have different approaches. Let's figure out what works for (child's name)."

Reframing stops escalation and moves the conversation toward collaboration.

Step 4: Respond; don't react

Your response matters more than your initial emotion. First, use neutral, calm language and focus on "I" statements and child-centered communication. Then ask for your co-parent's opinion. Each of these techniques warrants its own discussion.

Using "I" statements

You're probably wondering what I mean by "I" statements.

When you're upset, there's a reason. It's usually because someone has said or done something that has rubbed you the wrong way. In that state of mind, it's natural to blame the other person for upsetting you, but when you do, it sparks a defensive reaction, and the conversation stops. Instead, they'll argue that they're not responsible, or they'll say they never do what you're accusing them of.

So, if you say, "You're always late!" your co-parent's natural response will be, "I am not!" Your natural response is then, "Uh, yes, you are, and it really pisses me off!" All of it is said with a further insulting accusation. The conversation then spirals out of control, and no one has addressed the real problem: Your co-parent wants you to be on time.

That's when it's helpful to use "I" statements to convey how you're feeling. There's a model you can follow, and it will feel awkward at first because rarely do stressed people talk like this, but it works if you stick to the program. After a while, using the "I" statement formula will become second nature.

This is how it works: Begin your sentence with "I feel," but be careful of the words that further explain the emotion. These are words like *you, like, that,* and *as if.* When using these words, you're expressing a thought or opinion, and most likely you're blaming the other person for how you feel. The goal is to express your feelings without blame. This invites a conversation and enables you to get to the root of the matter.

So, "You're always late!" becomes, "I feel anxious when my time isn't respected."

Now, if you add any of the four words previously mentioned as qualifiers, look how the feeling of the sentence changes.

"I feel anxious when *you* don't respect my time." Or, "I feel *like you* don't care if I have to wait for you at an exchange."

See the difference? You can further refine the "I" statement approach by offering the effect the questionable behavior has on you and then stating what behavior you'd like to see.

So, "I feel anxious when my time isn't respected" continues using the "I" statement model like this:

> **I feel/felt** anxious
>
> **when** my time isn't considered
>
> **because** I must be at work on time, or I'll lose my job.
>
> **And what I'd like is:** Please be on time.

"I feel anxious when my time is not considered because I'll lose my job if I am late. Please be on time."

That is a straightforward, unemotional request to be on time, said without blame. A co-parent can argue and respond negatively when they feel blamed, but not about a sincere request. "Please be on time."

TIP

If you would like to practice using I messages prior to a discussion with your co-parent, a worksheet guiding you through the steps is available at `www.dummies.com/go/coparentingfd`. This exercise is also available on the Bonus Families site at `www.bonusfamilies.com/Imessages`.

Asking your co-parent's opinion

Now that you've practiced "I" statements, you can take things one step further. Some background:

> Your current parenting plan includes an hour commute each way, and you're concerned that this is too long for your 18-month-old to sit in the car. You believe your co-parent will balk at a suggestion to change the parenting plan because they've mentioned how guilty they feel about moving after the breakup and being so far away from your son. Your co-parent is afraid it will affect their time with their child, so they're resistant to any new suggestions.
>
> Try this:
>
> "I feel concerned about the schedule. I think commute traffic may make (name of child) be in the car too long. He's so crabby when I get home. What do you think? Do you see the same thing when you get home? Can we put our heads together and work out a new plan for our child?"

Responding thoughtfully signals to your co-parent that collaboration is possible and prevents the conflict from spiraling. Asking, "What do you think?" and "Do you see the same thing?" asks your co-parent's opinion.

Asking their opinion does four things to improve your communication:

- **It communicates respect:** You're saying that their thoughts matter, and you're listening. That simple message can diffuse defensiveness and create an opening for cooperation. It demonstrates that you value your co-parent's role in your child's life, even if you disagree.
- **It invites collaboration:** When you ask for their opinion, you move the conversation from conflict to collaboration. Instead of pushing against each other, you begin working alongside one another, which models teamwork for your child.
- **It builds trust:** Trust is something that's sorely lacking in most co-parenting relationships. Even the smallest gesture to rebuild trust is useful. Every time you ask your co-parent what they think and genuinely listen, trust improves. Trust reduces tension and makes future discussions run more smoothly.
- **It encourages reciprocity:** When someone feels heard, they're more likely to respond similarly. By creating a pattern of asking and listening, you reinforce that communication is a two-way street — and you model that for your child.

You get all that from simply asking their opinion! Try it.

Step 5: Apply the C.A.R.E. model

When you feel the emotional chain reaction starting, actively practice C.A.R.E.:

> **Communication:** Speak clearly, focus on facts, and keep your child at the center of the conversation.
>
> **Acceptance:** Accept what you can't control and focus on your own behavior.
>
> **Respect:** Maintain civility and avoid sarcasm or blame.
>
> **Empathy:** Acknowledge your co-parent's perspective and feelings.

Step 6: Debrief afterward

After the situation has passed, reflect calmly. Consider what triggered your reaction, what strategies worked, and how you could handle similar situations differently in the future. Tracking your patterns helps you build stronger, calmer co-parenting habits over time.

REMEMBER

Breaking the negative reaction chain isn't about never getting upset. It's about choosing how to act when you do. A positive response protects your child's emotional safety and builds co-parenting skills over time.

Tricks of the Trade for Improving Communication.

The impact of texting on co-parenting communication

Before I start to officially work with clients, we meet just to get acquainted. I ask about their goals for co-parenting and what they feel they need to improve. Everyone — and I mean everyone — says, "We need to improve our communication. We can't talk to each other. All we do is argue."

Say that in court, and the order will become "communicate only in writing." This is done to verify the instigator of the disagreements. "Texting okay" is often added to the stipulation. But texting isn't a communication tool. It's a notification tool.

Technology has transformed how everyone communicates, and nowhere has technology had more of an impact than with separated parents. Texting has become the go-to method for exchanging information. On the surface, it seems efficient. Parents can send a quick note between meetings or while waiting in the school parking lot. However, the convenience of texting can also become the path of least resistance and blur the line between communication and confrontation.

You don't want to interface with your co-parent, but you need to pass on information? Text them. Or don't. That's an easy way to let your co-parent know, "You don't control me." Or, better yet, "You no longer control me."

The problem with text messages as a communication tool is that they lack tone, context, and visual cues. What was meant as a neutral statement can be read as sharp or dismissive. A parent might text, "Can you pick up Jamie at 5 instead?" The other parent might interpret that as, "You never help with pickup." When people are already carrying emotional residue from their past, even an innocent message can trigger a defensive response. When co-parents feel defensive, they're less likely to return a text, and communication breaks down. It's difficult to get back that positive texting momentum.

Another common problem is the tendency to overuse texting for emotional exchanges. Ah, those text wars. You know, those long, insulting back-and-forth texts that go on for days. Rarely is a problem solved like that, but co-parents engage in them repeatedly.

TIP

Texts are best reserved for the logistics of who, what, where, and when. They're not the place to rehash arguments, justify decisions, or analyze motives. The written word freezes a moment in time. Once sent, a message can't be softened unless you use emojis. Disagreeable co-parents rarely use winks and hugs.

TIP

Think **BONUS** when texting your co-parent: **B**rief **O**nly **N**ecessary **U**seful **S**tatements. No embellishment or overstating the case that could possibly be misunderstood or prompt a negative response. Keep it direct and to the point.

Editorializing

One parent I worked with, Laura, described how a single misinterpreted text spiraled into weeks of tension.

> She'd sent her co-parent, Ethan, a message saying, "Please don't be late again today." She meant it as a simple reminder, but Ethan read it as criticism and shot back a defensive reply. By the end of the day, both had said things they regretted. When they finally discussed it in person, they realized the argument could have been avoided with a short call or a calmer tone.
>
> The truth is, Laura was *editorializing,* and that's a sure-fire way to create a communication breakdown. When someone editorializes, they express their opinion about something in the guise of a request or by just stating facts. "I was just being honest!" No, you were editorializing. Angry or resentful co-parents do that all the time, not understanding how it undermines their communication.
>
> When you editorialize, you may start out with a compliment or by merely making an observation, but then there's that comment at the end that secures the last lick.

As a result, your co-parent will feel as if you're blaming them for how you're feeling and immediately get defensive. This is when co-parents tell me that their communication is terrible. "We just can't seem to get along." But they've been blaming and faulting each other for years, editorializing when they make an observation, asking or volunteering for help, or comparing notes about their children.

To stop editorializing, just state your case or observation without qualifying it negatively. Look for words like *but, like, as if,* or words that reference time, like *finally, again, now,* or *no longer*. Just state the positive, and don't qualify it with a negative follow-up word or qualifying sentence.

Laura said, "Please don't be late *again*." Adding the word *again* to the end of her request refers to a time frame, so it sounds like blaming. Jaime's response will be, "Again? What do you mean, again? I'm never late!" Even if Jaime's late all the time, he'll deny it when accused of it by Laura's editorializing comment. All Laura had to say was, "Please be on time, Jaime." Possibly adding, "I have to be at work by 9 a.m." End of story. The answer would then be, "Okay," or possibly, "I'll do my best." Neither response is defensive nor will provoke additional arguments.

An exercise designed to help you identify editorial qualifiers before you communicate can be found at www.dummies.com/go/coparentingfd. This will not only be helpful during conversations, but also when composing texts and emails.

Co-parenting works best when both parents communicate as if their child might one day read every message. That simple filter encourages respect and discourages impulsive or inflammatory comments.

Active listening

In-person communication brings back the tone, facial expressions, and timing that texting lacks, but it introduces a new challenge: listening to understand rather than listening to respond. Many co-parents approach conversations as if they're in a courtroom, waiting to make their case, rather than hearing the other person's perspective.

Active listening requires intention. It means slowing down enough to focus on what's being said instead of preparing a rebuttal. This kind of listening validates the speaker, even if the listener disagrees. Validation doesn't mean agreement; it means acknowledging that the other person's feelings or experiences are real to them.

Consider a situation between Dina and Marcus, who were struggling to align bedtime routines between their homes. When Marcus said, "The kids stay up too late at your house, and it throws everything off," Dina immediately wanted to defend herself. Instead, she paused and reflected back what was said, "I think what you're saying is the kids are tired when they come back to you, and that makes your mornings difficult." That small shift diffused tension and allowed Marcus to feel heard. Once that happened, he was able to listen to Dina's perspective without reacting. He could then respond, "Exactly." They had a meeting of the minds rather than a fight.

Words make a difference

Here's something else to consider. A common phrase used as an example for active listening or to prompt additional conversation on a subject is "Can you help me understand . . ." The end of the request might be "your point of view," or "why you feel that way," or "why you said that."

"Can you help me understand?" implies ability ("are you able to" or "is it a possibility"), not willingness, which can sound slightly condescending or challenging when tensions are high. So, basically, what you're asking your co-parent is "Is it possible for you to help me understand . . ." An angry co-parent will come back with, "I don't have to explain anything to you." Now you're thinking, "I'm trying to be nice, and that's what I get?"

Instead of *can* or *could*, try using words or phrases like these:

- "I'm curious why . . ."
- "I'd like to understand this better."
- "I'm trying to understand your point of view."
- "I want to make sure I understand exactly what you're saying."
- "I may be missing something. Tell me more about that."
- "I'd appreciate hearing how you're thinking about this."
- "Let's talk through what led to that decision."
- "Let's examine how we can make this work."
- "What was behind that choice?"
- "What were you hoping would happen?"

Any of those phrases prompts a more positive reply because you aren't asking if it's a possibility to understand. You're laying the groundwork for understanding.

Active listening builds trust because it communicates respect. It also models emotional maturity for children who are always observing how their parents handle differences. When kids see adults listen calmly and respond thoughtfully, they internalize that approach in their own relationships.

REMEMBER

Effective communication in co-parenting isn't about winning a debate; it's about preserving a cooperative relationship that benefits the child.

Understanding your triggers

A trigger is something that sets off a strong reaction, often tied to past experiences. It can be a tone, a word, a situation, or even a pattern you've seen before. When you're triggered, you're not just responding to what's happening in the moment. Your mind and body react as if there's a threat. That's why the response can feel immediate and intense. You may feel anxious, angry, or overwhelmed, or find yourself reacting more strongly than the situation calls for.

To identify your triggers, pay attention to patterns. Notice when your reaction feels bigger than the moment. Ask yourself what just happened, what it reminded you of, and what you were thinking or feeling right before you responded. Over time, those patterns become easier to recognize.

Triggers and rituals

Triggers don't just happen in the moment. They often build through rituals. A ritual is something you do repeatedly that gives your mind space to repeat the same thoughts. You may be getting ready in the morning, blow-drying your hair or shaving, and thinking about your co-parent. With each stroke of the razor, you revisit past frustrations. By the time you're finished, you're no longer just getting ready for the day; you are already upset.

Triggers don't just happen in the moment. They often build through rituals. Nothing new has happened, but your reaction is real. The ritual has activated the trigger.

Over time, these patterns become automatic. The thought leads to the feeling, and the feeling leads to a reaction, often before any communication has even taken place.

Breaking the pattern

You don't need to eliminate the trigger, but you do need to interrupt the ritual that feeds it.

Start by noticing when and where it happens. Is it during your morning routine? Driving in the car? Right before an exchange? Once you identify the pattern, make a small change. Shift your focus. Turn on music, a podcast, or something that redirects your attention. Changing the order of your routine also helps. Set an intention before you begin: "I'm not going there this morning." If the thought comes up, acknowledge it and let it pass instead of following it.

A different response

By the time you speak to your co-parent, your tone has already been set by what you've been thinking.

When you interrupt the ritual, you change the starting point of the conversation. You're no longer reacting to a story you've replayed. You're responding to what's actually happening.

You don't have to agree. You don't have to like what's happening.

But you do have to respond in a way that keeps your child out of the middle and moves things forward.

Curiosity as a communication tool

Curiosity is one of the most overlooked tools in effective co-parenting. It shifts the focus from blame to understanding. Instead of assuming the worst, curiosity asks, "What might be going on for the other parent right now?" or "What information might I be missing?"

When curiosity replaces accusation, defensiveness begins to dissolve. A parent who says, "Help me understand why you think this is best for our child," invites conversation instead of confrontation. It also signals that the goal is problem-solving, not power.

> For example, when Renee noticed her son coming home withdrawn after weekends with his father, she was tempted to accuse: "What are you doing to make him so upset?" Instead, she approached the situation with curiosity: "I've noticed Josh seems quieter after visits. Have you seen that too?" That question opened a productive discussion that led to discovering Josh was struggling with a new extracurricular schedule, not with either parent.

REMEMBER

Curiosity takes emotional restraint, especially when there's history or hurt. But it's the foundation of empathy. When parents are genuinely curious, they create space for solutions instead of conflict. It's not about prying or controlling. It's about seeking understanding so both households can better support their children.

Curiosity builds bridges where assumptions once stood. It transforms tense exchanges into opportunities for learning, and it reinforces a shared truth: Both parents love their child and are doing their best under difficult circumstances.

Even small shifts in language can improve understanding. Check out Table 4-1 for common negative words and phrases. Do you use any of them? Does your co-parent?

TABLE 4-1 Common Negative Phrases and Positive Alternatives

Negative/ Triggering Phrase	Positive Neutral Alternative	Why It Works
"You always . . ."	"It seems like this happens often . . ."	Removes exaggeration (*always*) and invites discussion instead of accusation.
"You never . . ."	"I've noticed it hasn't happened recently . . ."	Focuses on observation, not blame.
"You're a liar."	"That doesn't match what I understood. Let's compare notes."	Keeps the focus on facts rather than character.
"You don't care about our child."	"I'm worried that our child's needs might not be met. Let me explain what I see, and then I'd like to hear your opinion."	Expresses concern instead of judgment.
"You're impossible to talk to."	"This conversation feels hard right now. Maybe we can revisit it when things calm down."	Acknowledges tension but leaves room for repair.
"That's ridiculous."	"I see it differently. Let me explain my perspective and see if you agree."	Reframes disagreement as dialogue.
"You're wrong."	"I have a different view."	Keeps tone factual and collaborative.
"Calm down."	"Let's take a minute before we continue."	Avoids invalidating emotion (which "calm down" often does).
"You're just trying to control everything."	"I feel like decisions are happening quickly. Let's slow down and make them together."	Moves from accusation to joint problem-solving.
"That's not true."	"That's not how I remember it. Let's compare notes."	Focuses on how the behavior affects you rather than labeling the person.
"You're so selfish!"	"I'm feeling left out of the decision-making."	Encourages clarification rather than confrontation.
"You make me so angry."	"I'm feeling frustrated when this happens."	Takes ownership of emotion ("I" statement) instead of placing blame.
"You should . . ." or "You know what you need to do . . ."	"What if we tried . . ." or "Have you considered . . ."	Invites cooperation instead of giving orders.
"You're just being dramatic."	"I can see this is really important to you."	Validates emotion, even if you don't share it.
"I'm done talking about this."	"I think we've hit a wall right now. Let's pause and return to it later."	Words matter, especially between people who share the lifelong task of raising a child together.

Tact and timing

Even the most thoughtful message or conversation can fall flat if it's delivered at the wrong time or without sensitivity to the other parent's emotional state. In co-parenting, tact and timing can be as important as the words themselves.

Tact is the skill of saying what needs to be said without causing unnecessary harm. *Timing* is knowing when to say it. Together, they help parents communicate effectively even when the topic is difficult.

> Imagine Owen texting co-parent Rachel about a change in summer vacation plans. Frustrated, he fires off his message while she's at work: "You've switched weeks again. You can't keep doing this." Rachel, blindsided in the middle of a meeting, reads it as an attack. A situation that could have been solved with cooperation becomes a standoff.
>
> Had Owen waited until later in the evening and opened with a neutral tone — "I just saw the change in the vacation schedule. Can we look at this together?" — Rachel would have been more receptive. The issue wasn't what he said, but how and when he said it.

Timing also involves self-awareness. If one parent is angry, exhausted, or hurt, it's rarely productive to discuss sensitive matters in that moment. Pausing to regroup isn't avoidance. It's emotional intelligence. Saying, "This feels tense right now. Let's pick it up after dinner," allows space for emotions to cool so logic can take the lead.

REMEMBER

Children benefit when parents model this kind of restraint. They learn that strong emotions don't have to dictate behavior and that calm communication leads to better outcomes.

Tone

Tone often speaks louder than words. A single sentence can convey cooperation or contempt depending on delivery. The phrase "We need to talk" can sound like an invitation or a warning. In text, tone can vanish entirely, which is why it's so easy to misread messages.

When co-parents communicate, the goal is to maintain a tone that reflects mutual respect even when there's disagreement. Neutrality is powerful. It signals emotional control and a focus on the child's needs rather than the past relationship.

One father, Ben, once admitted, "It wasn't what I said; it was how I said it. My ex stopped listening halfway through." He learned to check his tone by rereading his messages before sending them and asking himself, "Would I say this to a co-worker?" That simple filter helped him reframe defensive or sarcastic remarks into practical, respectful communication.

Tone also carries through body language — crossed arms, raised eyebrows, sighs — all of which can undo the most carefully chosen words. In person, adopting an open stance and calm facial expression signals willingness to collaborate. In writing, that same openness is reflected through word choice: "Let's try to . . ." or "Let's explore the possibility of . . ." instead of "You should . . ."

Parents don't have to sound cheerful when discussing hard topics, but they need to stay composed. A calm tone fosters cooperation, while an accusatory one fuels defensiveness. The difference often determines whether a problem gets solved or simply recycled.

Empathy in action

Empathy is more than understanding another's point of view; it's the ability to hold space for that view even when it differs from one's own. Co-parenting requires empathy because it's built on shared responsibility amid differing experiences.

When Maya realized her ex-husband Trevor was struggling financially, she quietly adjusted their child's extracurricular budget so he wouldn't have to contribute as much. She didn't announce it or demand gratitude. She simply recognized that supporting their child meant being flexible about what each could contribute at the time. Trevor, in turn, made sure to take their daughter to every game and be fully present. He volunteered to man the Snack Shack and be an assistant coach. Their cooperation was not about perfection. It was about empathy. They both took a look at what they could do to support their daughter in ways where they could both show up.

Empathy helps parents remember that they're partners in parenting, even if they're no longer partners in life. It softens interactions, diffuses tension, and invites understanding. When one parent extends empathy, it often encourages the other to reciprocate.

Respectful communication as the foundation

Co-parenting communication is rarely perfect, but it doesn't have to be. What matters is consistency, intention, and mutual respect. Every text, email, or conversation is an opportunity to demonstrate maturity and prioritize the child's well-being.

When parents commit to speaking with respect, they create a climate of safety — not just for themselves, but for their children. Kids sense when communication is calm and collaborative, and it allows them to relax, knowing both parents are working together.

TIP

The guiding question in any exchange should be simple: Will what I'm about to say help or harm our ability to parent together? If it helps, proceed with confidence. If it harms, pause and reconsider.

The methods may vary. Some parents prefer structured communication apps, and others rely on in-person discussions, but the principles remain the same: clarity, compassion, and respect.

Co-parenting after separation is one of the hardest things adults can do, but when communication is thoughtful, honest, and kind, it transforms conflict into cooperation. In time, parents often discover that the skills they build out of necessity — communication, acceptance, respect, and empathy — become strengths that benefit every part of their lives.

Making Co-Parenting Work Day to Day

IN THIS PART . . .

Handle child transitions with composure

Learn the ins and outs of dating other people after a breakup

Get a handle on custody terminology and set parenting plans

Understand spousal and child support

IN THIS CHAPTER

» Coming to terms with your new life

» Defining the areas on which you must agree

» Handling school, extracurriculars, and religious training

Chapter 5 Accepting the Back-and-Forth Lifestyle

Seven-year-old Lily used to cry every Sunday night during exchanges. Her parents, Rachael and Mike, were newly divorced and still raw from the breakup. Rachael would buckle Lily into the back seat, lean in for one last hug, and whisper, "Call me if you are scared." Mike, trying to keep things light and upbeat, would cheerfully say, "We're going to have fun this week!"

Both meant well. But to Lily, it felt like she was abandoning one parent to please the other. Her tears weren't about the car ride. They were about guilt, confusion, and divided loyalty.

When I met with Rachael and Mike, I asked them to treat exchanges like passing the baton in a relay race. One runner doesn't drop the baton to hug it; they hand it off with confidence. The next runner picks it up and keeps moving. Rachael and Mike began greeting each other calmly, focusing on Lily instead of their feeling. They even created a simple ritual. A quick wave at the end of the driveway meant, "We've got her covered."

Within a week or so, the tears stopped. Lily stopped bracing herself for the exchange because Rachael and Mike had learned to accept the new rhythm to their life and to cooperate instead of competing.

REMEMBER

When parents handle transitions with composure, children learn that love doesn't stop at the curb; it travels with them from one home to the other.

For many separated or divorced parents, one of the hardest adjustments is accepting that they'll no longer live with their children full-time. The rhythm of daily life changes. Mornings once spent making breakfast or packing lunches become quiet, and weekends that were once filled with soccer games and birthday parties might now be spent alone. It can feel unnatural, even unfair.

But acceptance, the **A** in the **C.A.R.E.** model previously discussed, is the cornerstone of healthy co-parenting. The back-and-forth lifestyle, though challenging, can also become a steady rhythm that provides children with love, stability, and the comfort of knowing that both parents are still present and involved.

Accepting Your New Life

One of the greatest challenges of co-parenting after separation is learning to accept what you can't change. You can't change the past and what has happened, but you can choose to face today with an open mind. Acceptance isn't giving in; it's acknowledging reality. Acceptance, paired with cooperation, is when parents stop seeing each other as opponents and start working as partners. The transition from house to house becomes less about control and more about connection and creates a bridge that helps children move freely and confidently between homes.

This chapter is about the day-to-day operations of the back-and-forth life. It can help you define the areas where agreement is crucial and establish the rules of engagement that make shared co-parenting work in real life. I'll look at the practical and everyday necessities of how to maintain consistency between homes, honor each parent's personal autonomy, ensure open sharing of information, and align on school, extracurricular activities, religion, and worship.

REMEMBER

The goal is for this new lifestyle to become less about loss and more about the love for your child, balance, and teamwork. Although you may not have chosen this arrangement, your children now depend on you to make it work. The reality is that your children love both of you. They need both of you.

When parents hold on to the anger or refuse to cooperate, their children are caught in the middle, forced to adapt to adult conflict rather than adult cooperation. Instead of focusing on the loss of daily contact, focus on how to make the time you do have meaningful and predictable. Children thrive when transitions between homes are calm and consistent. They feel emotionally secure when both parents show that cooperation is possible, even when living apart.

Cooperation, on the other hand, is about giving your children the best version of both parents. It requires improved communication, patience, and the willingness to see your co-parent as a partner in raising your child, not an opponent. When you accept that each parent brings different strengths to the table, you open the door to balance. Acceptance and cooperation don't erase the pain of separation, but they do prevent that pain from running the household — and your life.

REMEMBER

Think of it this way: Children learn what they live. When they watch their parents manage transitions with respect, flexibility, and teamwork, they learn resilience. They learn that even when life changes, there can still be mutual love for their children. That's the true foundation of good co-parenting and the first step in mastering the back-and-forth lifestyle.

Defining the Areas on Which You Must Agree: The Non-Negotiables

Once you accept that your child will be living in two homes, the next step is identifying the areas where both parents must be in agreement. These areas aren't about control or convenience; they're about creating consistency for your child. When expectations are clear and predictable, children feel safer and less anxious. When they're not, the back-and-forth lifestyle becomes a tug of war.

In successful co-parenting, agreement is the glue that holds everything together. You don't have to agree on everything, but alignment is non-negotiable in some key areas.

REMEMBER

You don't have to be best friends, but you do have to be partners in raising your children after a divorce or separation. Every choice, from school decisions to holiday plans, should be filtered through one question: "Is this good for our child?"

What follows are the non-negotiables, things you must agree upon to keep your daily life running smoothly. When you agree on these foundational areas, everything else becomes easier to navigate, and this new back-and-forth life will be much easier to accept — for you, your co-parent, and your children.

1. Have clear expectations

Having clear expectations means setting realistic, agreed-upon goals right from the start. This eliminates misunderstandings, reduces conflict, and provides a stable environment for your children. Whether it's about exchanges, communication boundaries, or holidays, mutual understanding gives both parents a roadmap to what to expect. When expectations are transparent and consistent, both homes run more smoothly.

2. Maintain consistency between homes

Children need to know what to expect — from bedtime routines, homework rules, discipline styles, and even how the family eats dinner. You don't have to mirror your co-parent exactly, but the basics should feel predictable and familiar. When parents agree on core expectations, children relax and focus on being kids rather than referees and messengers for their parents.

I often tell parents, "If your child needs an instruction manual to go from house to house, you're not being consistent enough." Predictability equals peace.

3. Have respect for the other parent's role

Co-parents may not agree on everything, but when they disrespect their child's other parent, they chip away at half of their child's foundation. If you roll your eyes, sigh loudly, or make subtle digs, your child learns that love is conditional and divided. When you model respect, they learn that love can exist even among differences.

4. Transparency, not control: Keep the flow of information open

Keeping secrets and expecting your child to keep them is about the worst mistake co-parents can make. The following is *not* a good policy:

> "What goes on here stays here."

Of course, you want autonomy now that you're single, but co-parents must grasp that where they live isn't just their house; it's also where their children call home — both houses. Therefore, when your child volunteers information about what went on at Mom's or Dad's, they're not telling on their parent; they're sharing information about *their* life. They're not violating some secret pact. They're saying, "Guess what happened, Mom or Dad?" Your response can encourage them to be open and honest or teach them to hold in their feelings.

Even though you may not want your co-parent to know your business, remember that your child already knows what goes on at both homes. If you restrict what they can say, you're telling them not to share half their life. You're asking them to be two different people. Plus, you're setting up both yourself and your co-parent for failure.

Let's look at how secrets, or lack of transparency from house to house, can affect everyone's lives:

> Michael is six years old. His parents share his time equally. He was excited to tell his father some news.
>
> "Dad! Mom is buying a home at the beach! We're going to live there for the summer!"
>
> But as soon as the words left his mouth, he burst into tears.
>
> He remembered. His mother had told him not to say anything. "What happens here, stays here."
>
> Mom and Dad don't share information. They fear that anything revealed will lead to conflict or even court, so they keep their lives separate.
>
> But that's between them.
>
> Their child is paying the price.
>
> A child should never know more than either parent. It creates pressure no child should carry. Asking a child to keep secrets puts them in an impossible position. Abusers say, "Don't tell."
>
> There are quite a few different reactions that Dad can have in response to learning the information about the summer home. He could be angry at Mom for not telling him anything. He could be angry that she's buying another home and wasn't forthcoming about her expenses. He could be angry because she didn't go through the proper channels to request vacation time, and he wanted to take Michael somewhere in the summer. Bottom line: All the possibilities start with, "He could be angry . . ." And who will feel the brunt of that anger? Michael, because Dad was taken by surprise.

If the parents had shared information, Dad's reaction would be something to the effect of this:

"Well, yes, Michael. Mom told me about her plans to stay at the beach for the summer last week. She wanted to surprise you. We've worked out a special schedule."

Instead of "Your mother is buying a home? That liar! She's always telling me she has no money!"

And now Michael is creaking in his boots because Dad is angry, and Michael is the one who passed on the information. You can bet Michael will think twice about passing on information in the future. By not allowing Michael to openly talk about his life at both homes, these parents are teaching their child to make a judgment call to withhold information or lie to keep the peace. That lesson will follow him into adulthood.

REMEMBER

You *want* your child to talk to both parents about absolutely everything that goes on everywhere. No secrets for your child's sake. When information isn't shared, mistrust grows. Information isn't a power tool; it's a bridge to cooperation.

5. Keep the schedule predictable

Children count on seeing each parent. Once you agree upon a schedule, you should honor it. Frequent changes or last-minute cancellations create instability for children and frustration for parents. Life happens. There will be emergencies, illnesses, and unexpected work conflicts, but constant rearranging isn't fair to anyone.

TIP

Decide what constitutes being sick. Is it a cold, a fever, or strep throat? Then, decide when your child is sick if they'll continue to go back and forth or stay put until they're well. Finally, what constitutes "well?" Their fever broken? Has it been 48 hours since they've taken antibiotics? Once you decide, respect your agreement.

6. Maintain autonomy in each home

Accepting the back-and-forth lifestyle also means accepting that each household will have its own rhythm. One parent might enforce a strict bedtime, whereas the other might be more flexible. Both can still raise well-adjusted kids.

Resist the urge to micromanage your co-parent's home. You're not in charge there. Children benefit from learning that there's more than one "right" way to do things and that both parents are capable, loving adults.

7. Keep unified standards for health and safety

While flexibility is fine, some things aren't negotiable. Examples are car seats, helmets, medications, allergies, medical care, and basic hygiene. Children shouldn't have to remember which house is "safe" and which parent enforces the rules. Safety isn't a preference. It's a promise you make to your child.

8. Encourage the love of both parents

When push comes to shove in family court, primary custody is typically offered to the parent who's more likely to encourage a relationship with the other parent.

WARNING

If it's determined that you'll withhold a child or possibly undermine your co-parent, don't be surprised that you're granted less time with your child than you expected.

You're not competing for your child's love. You made the child together, and it's your responsibility to raise them together. That means you encourage them to call the other parent, to bring up fun memories, to speak freely without guilt.

Handling School and Extracurriculars

Managing your kids' schedule outside of your home can be especially trying. You must coordinate your children's schedule, your schedule, and your co-parent's schedule. This is where so many co-parents drop the ball. Communication is strained, and coordinating efforts seems impossible.

TIP

At the beginning of each school year, write an email to your child's teacher explaining the following:

- Your child has two homes, and you need two homework packets, two copies of the class newsletter, two of everything.
- Offer your child's parenting plan so the teacher knows where the child resides, just in case: "Edgar spends time with his mother on Mondays and Tuesdays. He stays at my home on Wednesdays and Thursdays. We alternate the weekends, Friday after school to Monday to school."

In addition, do the following:

- Make sure all contact information is up to date so the school can reach both of you.
- Make sure that both parents have access to the student portal online so both can stay up to date about school activities, like picture day or back-to-school night.
- If you know something you think your co-parent may not know, share it!

The same applies to extracurricular activities like sports, dance classes, music lessons, and art classes. These are opportunities to broaden your children's horizons, not for one parent to take credit or try to control the schedule. Work together to ensure transportation, fees, and participation are handled fairly. If you can both attend, all the better. Your child wants both of you there.

Check out this example:

> "My ex enrolls our kids in soccer each year but never checks with me, and it interferes with my time with them. I don't want to spend all my time with my kids driving them back and forth to practices and games."

First, of course, co-parents must coordinate efforts when enrolling their children in extracurriculars, but here's something that parents who feel their children's extracurriculars cut into their time should consider: It's not your time; it's your children's.

REMEMBER

If you and your co-parent were a couple, your time would be spent driving your children to practices. Your weekends would be filled with games and recitals. That shouldn't change because you're no longer a couple. You're still parents, and your responsibility is to support your children.

Supporting Religious Training and Worship

Faith can be deeply personal, and the differences in religious beliefs often become flashpoints in co-parenting. The key is respect, which is the *R* in C.A.R.E. If religion was part of your child's life before separation, maintaining that continuity provides comfort and familiarity.

If you have different beliefs, discuss them privately, not through your child. The message to your child should be simple: "Both of us want you to grow in faith and values." Encourage your child to participate freely and without guilt in the traditions of both households.

REMEMBER

Ultimately, the spiritual lessons your child learns about kindness, compassion, and forgiveness are strengthened when both parents model respect for each other's beliefs.

When parents honor these rules of engagement, they create a roadmap for success. The back-and-forth lifestyle becomes less about what was lost and more about what's possible, a cooperative rhythm that helps children feel secure, loved, and understood, no matter which home they're in.

Putting It All Together

When co-parents commit to cooperation and consistency, their children stop feeling like visitors in either home. They learn that, although their parents live apart, the love and stability surrounding them remain the same. You may not be able to control the back-and-forth itself, but you can control the tone, respect, and reliability in which it's handled.

REMEMBER

Children don't measure how many days they stay with each parent. They won't remember if they spent an extra day one week five years ago. But they'll remember how safe, seen, and supported they felt in both homes. When transitions are calm, information is shared, and both homes uphold the same values, children thrive.

If you have different beliefs, discuss them privately, not through your child. The message to your child should be simple: "Both of us want you to grow in faith and values." Encourage your child to participate freely and without guilt in the traditions of both households.

Ultimately, the spiritual lessons your child learns about kindness, compassion, and forgiveness are strengthened when both parents model respect for each other's beliefs.

When parents honor these rules of engagement, they create a roadmap for success. The back-and-forth lifestyle becomes less about what was lost and more about what's possible: a cooperative rhythm that helps children feel secure, loved, and understood, no matter which home they're in.

Putting It All Together

When co-parents commit to cooperation and consistency, their children stop feeling like visitors in either home. They learn that, although their parents live apart, the love and stability surrounding them remain the same. You may not be able to control the back-and-forth itself, but you can control the tone, respect, and reliability in which it's handled.

Children don't measure how many days they stay with each parent. They won't remember if they spent an extra day one week five years ago, but they'll remember how safe, seen, and supported they felt in both homes. When transitions are calm, information is shared, and both homes uphold the same values, children thrive.

IN THIS CHAPTER

» Rediscovering yourself and mindful dating

» Collaborating on your dating life with your co-parent

» Realizing how your children perceive your dating

» Troubleshooting when things aren't perfect

Chapter 6 Dating After a Breakup

When a relationship ends, many parents believe dating again is off-limits for the foreseeable future. The grief, the exhaustion, and the logistics of raising children between two homes can make romance feel like a luxury — or a betrayal. Yet, at some point, the desire to connect returns. You notice laughter again, or a spark of curiosity when someone asks about your weekend. That moment of interest is human, healthy, and necessary, but for co-parents, it's also complicated.

In this chapter, I discuss the ins and outs of dating after a breakup. The main concern, as you will see as you peruse the next few pages, is how you and your co-parent collaboratively approach dating someone else after your breakup and how you help your children adjust comfortably. It starts with getting clear about what you want in your next relationship and then mindfully putting one foot in front of the other. I then go on to discuss how following the C.A.R.E. model while dating keeps you focused. I hope to answer all the questions you might have when deciding to move on to your next chapter.

Rediscovering Yourself Before Rediscovering Love

Before you think about dating, you must explore who you are now. Every relationship, every breakup, affects who you are. Before, you measured happiness by what you and your co-parent needed. Now, it's time to rediscover what *you* want for the future.

Practicing mindful dating

Mindful dating is an approach to relationships that emphasizes awareness, presence, and intentionality, both with yourself and with others. Instead of rushing into dating or being driven by anxiety, expectations, or external pressures, mindful dating invites you to slow down, pay attention to your experiences, and make choices that align with your values.

Mindful dating begins with self-awareness. This is for everyone, not just one gender or the other. It's less about looking for "the one" because there may be a few "ones" in your life. It's more about making sure you're ready to be in a relationship again and how this new relationship can shape your children's attitude about partnership, sex, and resolving conflict.

So, before you start dating again or as you evaluate your new relationship, take time to reflect on the kind of partner who truly fits into your life now. Not just who you were before your last relationship or becoming a parent, but who you've become through this journey.

You may want to create a Mindful Dating List like the one shown in Table 6-1 to help you get your thoughts in order. It's a way to sit down with yourself and weigh exactly the kind of partner you want to complement your life and the lives of your children.

Draw a line down the center of a piece of paper. On the left side, list your desires; on the right side, list your reasons. See Table 6-1.

TABLE 6-1 Sample Mindful Dating List

Desires	Reasons
They have a steady job.	I want a partner who shares in the responsibility, not another dependent.
They have children or are comfortable around them.	Parenting changes priorities, and I need someone who understands my commitment to my children.
I want more children.	Although not a deal breaker, I want a partner who will at least discuss the possibility.
They respect my co-parenting boundaries.	I want a partner who values peace over drama.
They're emotionally available.	They're ready to move on. I don't want to fix someone; I want to move forward together.
They live a healthy lifestyle.	I want longevity and energy in the life I'm building.
They communicate calmly and directly.	I've lived through conflict. I want a partner who values problem-solving, not arguing.
They have a good sense of humor.	Laughing at the same jokes is important. It keeps us connected.

Falling into old patterns

So many times, parents re-create the same relationship again and again. This has to do with what they've seen and experienced in the past, starting from when they were very young. Similar relationships are re-created each time, not because they feel good, but because they seem familiar. You know that feeling. You've experienced it before. Perhaps you've even heard that people who have experienced domestic violence in one relationship often face it again in the next relationship. Unfortunately, studies verify this to be true. So, this time, think about it:

- What have I learned from my past relationship?
- What does emotional safety look like for my children and me?
- What qualities make me feel calm, respected, and seen?

When you take the time to answer these questions before you start to date, you reduce the chances of falling into old patterns. Instead of choosing between loneliness and fear, you choose between self-awareness and confidence. Don't be afraid to enlist the help of a professional to help you get your thoughts in order.

A therapist or life coach can be a wonderful guide to help you get clear on what you want and how to go about getting it.

When Laura's marriage ended, she promised herself she wouldn't repeat old patterns.

"I was always the fixer," she confided. "I was drawn to people who needed rescuing. I mistook chaos for chemistry."

She made a list like the one in Table 6-1 — not hobbies or height, but qualities she needed to build a healthy future. When she met Marcus, a father of two, she was clear: her son came first, and she wanted to take things slowly.

Marcus didn't just agree — he respected it. On nights she was home with Ethan, he would text, "I hope you're having a good mom-and-son night."

Laura recognized the difference: a healthy partner doesn't compete with your priorities — exactly what she had written on her list.

Collaborating Your Dating Life with Your Co-Parent

One of the biggest misconceptions about dating after a breakup is that it's a completely personal decision — what you do on your time is your business. While that's partly true, it's not entirely accurate when you're a parent. You and your co-parent may no longer live together, but you do share a child, and the choices you make ripple through that child's world. That is why mindful dating invites collaboration, not secrecy.

Dating collaboratively may sound absurd, especially if you and your co-parent struggle with getting along, but before you begin dating, it's important to talk with them about how you both want to approach this new chapter. The conversation isn't about permission; it's about preparation. It's about mutual respect and predictability. When both parents know what to expect, that predictability trickles down to their children, and they feel safer.

It will be helpful to have this talk as early in the process as possible. Agree on basic boundaries like these:

- When will the children be introduced to a new partner? (Not until a relationship is serious.)
- How will you explain your dating to your children?

» What language will you use to describe someone new (a "friend" until both parties agree that you're more than friends)?

Using C.A.R.E. as a guide for dating

I talk about C.A.R.E. throughout this book when it comes to co-parenting, but the concepts can apply to dating as well.

Communication

Children rarely announce their discomfort directly. They show it through behavior.

> Eight-year-old Evan became quiet each time his mom's boyfriend, Rick, visited. When asked what was wrong, Evan shrugged and said, "Nothing." But one night, when Rick corrected him for interrupting, Evan blurted out, "You're not my dad!"
>
> His mother's first instinct was to defend Rick, but Evan wasn't challenging authority. He was expressing fear about his place in the family.
>
> A mindful parent listens for what's beneath the words. Evan didn't need a lecture about manners. He needed reassurance that his relationship with his mother was secure.

When children express frustration about a new relationship, resist the urge to correct them or make it better. Instead, listen and validate what they're feeling. "I can see that made you uncomfortable. It's okay to tell me when something feels off. Let's figure it out together."

When communication is calm and direct, children learn that their emotions matter and that they don't need to act out to be heard.

When a child voices discomfort about your dating life, pause before responding and consider what they may be trying to tell you. Do you need to make adjustments, or are they looking for reassurance? Then:

Acknowledge their feelings: "That sounds hard."

Reassure them of your love, invite them to share more, and listen without judgment.

Acceptance

Acceptance is a reminder that there's no single "right" timeline for integrating someone into your life. Every family's story unfolds differently, and acceptance means recognizing that your timeline, your child's timeline, and your co-parent's timeline may not be the same.

> Jordan and Elise are a good example. Both divorced around the same time. Jordan's ex relocated to another city, while Elise shared custody of her two sons. At first, their situations seemed similar, but their emotional histories soon surfaced. Jordan's ten-year-old daughter was still hoping for her parents to reconcile, while Elise's sons were eager for their mother to "have fun again."
>
> Jordan wanted to move quickly. Elise wanted to take it slow. Their children were in very different places, and both parents had to accept what was not what they wished it to be.

When you accept the differences, you model tolerance. When you force sameness, you create stress.

Respect

Respect in co-parenting goes far beyond politeness. It's the acknowledgment that two households, two sets of traditions, and two emotional climates must coexist for your children's well-being.

> Maya and Diego divorced after 12 years. They were cordial, but cautious. When Maya began seeing Henry, she assumed Diego didn't need to know the details until Henry showed up at a school event and sat beside her. The next morning, Diego emailed, "A 'head's-up next time would have helped. The kids were confused."

Your first thought might be that Diego was jealous. But his reaction wasn't about jealousy; it was about respect. Respectful co-parenting means keeping each other informed enough to maintain stability for your child. Surprises might be fun in dating, but they're stressful in co-parenting.

REMEMBER

Respect also governs privacy. If your co-parent's door is closed, metaphorically or literally, don't enter uninvited. Don't scroll their social media for clues about their relationship or use your child as an informant. Children should never be messengers between homes. Mindful dating asks for restraint, not secrecy. Restraint is mature. Secrecy breeds confusion.

Empathy

Empathy is what turns defensiveness into connection. It's the ability to imagine the world through someone else's eyes — your children's, your co-parent's, and your new partner's.

> Becky, a divorced mom, moved out of the family home in March. By summer, she had met Max, a kind man who shared her love of hiking. One evening, her

9-year-old son, Oliver, burst into tears after she mentioned a weekend camping trip. "If you go camping with Max, you won't want to camp with Dad anymore!"

Becky's first instinct was to dismiss his fear. "Don't be silly. You know I love camping with both of you." But she caught herself. That response would only add to Oliver's confusion as he adjusted to the time between his dad and her new relationship. Instead, she stepped into his perspective. She imagined the campsite through his eyes: one parent missing, another person in their place.

Empathy allowed her to say, "You're right. It will be different. But a difference doesn't mean worse. We'll still have our own trips, and I'll make sure you go camping with Dad, too." Dad's importance wasn't erased. It was reinforced, and so was Max's importance — not by comparing the two, but by reinforcing both of their importance.

Dating on your own time

Most likely, you'll date quite a few people before you settle on someone who fits easily into your new lifestyle after a breakup. That's why dating *on your own time* is so important. So what does that mean?

REMEMBER

You date when the kids are with their other parent, grandparents, or extended family, or with trusted friends.

Doing so creates space and balance. It allows you to focus fully on your children when they're with you and to explore your adult life without forcing your kids to carry their weight of it. They don't have to worry about competing for your attention, and you don't have to worry about how they'll react to someone new before you're ready.

Being Aware of How Your Children Perceive Your Dating Life

Children usually look at their parents' dating in one of two ways:

- They either see the new person as a potential forever partner — someone who could change their lives again — or they've watched so many introductions come and go that they stop trusting anyone will stay.
- They expect a breakup.

Both reactions come from the same place: self-protection.

In the first case, a child's hope can make them vulnerable to disappointment. They may begin daydreaming about a wedding or a new bedroom at your partner's home before you've even decided if the relationship is right. When it ends, the child experiences another kind of breakup, losing not only their partner but the imagined future built around them.

There is also the possibility that they have grown close to your partner's children. They may have been introduced as "brothers" and "sisters," but after the breakup, what are they? Your children may wonder if they can still see them, and you may question whether it's healthy to support that relationship.

This is something to consider when becoming a couple: If this doesn't work out, how will you explain the breakup to your children? It is especially important if the children remain in the same school district. They will continue to see each other and may still want to spend time together as friends.

Handle this with care. These children didn't ask for the breakup. Demonstrate kindness and empathy. Consider how they are experiencing the loss and respond accordingly.

In the second case, children who have been introduced to a series of short-term partners often stop investing emotionally. "Don't get attached," they tell themselves. "They won't be around long." Over time, they begin to lose trust in adult romantic relationships.

That is why it is so important to wait until a relationship has real potential before introducing your children. Dating casually is perfectly fine, even healthy, but your children don't need to meet everyone you date. Introductions are significant moments. Protect them.

Many parents learn this the hard way:

> Take Nate, a father of two boys who attended a co-parenting workshop I was teaching in California.
>
> After his divorce, he began dating right away. "I just wanted to feel normal again," he admitted. "I wanted to move forward."
>
> In the first year, his sons, ages 7 and 10, met three women he dated. Each seemed promising until it wasn't. After the third breakup, his oldest son said, "Dad, maybe don't make us meet anyone else for a while."

Nate realized his son wasn't being critical. He was tired and confused. He had already lived through the end of one family and didn't have the emotional capacity for more goodbyes.

Nate took a break from dating for over a year. When he eventually met someone new, he moved slowly, giving his children time to heal and rebuild trust.

"It's not about hiding my life," he said later. "It's about giving them back their sense of security. I wasn't thinking about them. I was thinking about myself."

That's mindful dating in action: awareness, restraint, and compassion for everyone involved.

Communicating with Your Co-Parent about Dating

It's easy to say, "It's none of your business," but when you share children, certain things *are* shared business. You don't need your co-parent's approval, but you do owe them awareness. That's not a courtesy; it's respect. When they know what's happening, they can support your children through the transition instead of being blindsided by it.

These conversations flow best when you approach them straightforwardly and with honesty. Choose a neutral tone. Stick to the facts, not feelings. For example:

"I wanted to let you know that I've started seeing someone. It's early, but I'll keep you informed before there's any introduction to the kids."

That's it. Simple. Respectful. Predictable.

REMEMBER

When your co-parent does the same, avoid sarcasm, jealousy, or competition. Even if it stings to imagine your ex with someone new, model maturity. Take a breath before reacting. Your children are watching how you manage this stage. Every calm response builds their character and their sense of security. Every hostile response teaches them that love equals unresolved conflict.

When your co-parent refuses to collaborate

Not every co-parenting relationship is collaborative. As a matter of fact, if you're reading this book, yours probably isn't. Some co-parents refuse to discuss dating at all, or they use it as a power play, questioning your choices, interrogating the children, or withholding information about their own relationships. You can't force collaboration, but you can set an example. Don't get into a tit-for-tat war based on "If they're going to do ______, well, I'm just going to do that, too." Your children will be able to relate to that behavior perfectly because it's childish.

If your co-parent won't engage, here's how to move forward:

- **Set your standard anyway.** Decide your own introduction timeline and stick to it.
- **Inform, don't ask.** Think B.O.N.U.S., which stands for brief, only necessary, useful statements. "I'm seeing someone. I haven't planned any child introductions, but you should know just in case the subject comes up." Later, another text: "Our relationship has grown into something. It's time to introduce the kids. I'll let you know before the kids meet them so we can stay on the same page."
- **Shield the kids from adult conflict.** If your co-parent questions the kids, prompt them to say, "Please talk to Mom (Dad) about that." Then back up your child by repeating the same thing to your co-parent. "Please talk to me if you need clarification about anything. Please don't ask the kids. It puts them on the spot, and they may not have all the information."

When your co-parent starts dating

No matter how prepared you think you are, hearing that your ex is seeing someone new can sting. It's one thing for you to move on; it's another to picture your ex with someone else or your children with another adult in their life.

You may feel jealousy, fear, or even protectiveness. That's normal. The key is to manage those feelings privately, not through your children. They should never feel they have to choose between supporting you and liking your co-parent's new partner. Don't teach your children to compare. No one will win.

REMEMBER

Remind yourself that your ex's dating life isn't a reflection of your self-worth. What matters is how you both handle it. Children flourish when their parents show mutual respect, even when emotions run high.

What most parents report when their co-parent starts to date isn't so much that they're jealous. More accurately, they struggle with someone else performing the same tasks they do for their kids, like tucking them into bed or cooking their favorite meal.

"Those rituals are my job," one dad told me. "And I don't want anyone else doing them for my little guy."

When Jeffery heard that his co-parent, Renee, had begun dating, he didn't hide his discomfort, but he managed his response with intention.

In a private phone call, Renee shared that the relationship was serious and that she felt it was time for Jeffery to meet her partner. Out of respect, she suggested a quick coffee meeting. She also let Jeffery know she was planning a birthday party for their oldest child and would be inviting them both.

Jeffery forced himself to go.

"I told myself it was for my son, and honestly, it wasn't terrible. We laughed and talked about the upcoming World Series while my son ran between us. It was obvious he was excited we were both there, and I was glad I could do that for him. I realized it was my pride that was making things hard."

TIP

Parents often feel they must attend special events together to support their children. If you're not ready, don't do it. Parents who are uncomfortable being in the same vicinity won't provide the stability their presence is meant to offer.

Deciding When to Introduce the Children

When and how to introduce your children to someone new is one of the most sensitive transitions a co-parent will navigate. The right time depends less on months passed and more on emotional readiness — yours and your children's.

A good rule of thumb is to wait until you've seen someone long enough to envision a future together. That doesn't mean you need to know whether marriage is in the picture, but it should mean you've had enough time to see how they handle real life, the hard conversations, the stress, the scheduling conflicts.

When you know this person could be part of your long-term story, that's the time to introduce them. Do it slowly, and in stages. Start with a short, casual meeting. Maybe an ice cream outing, a walk in the park, or pizza and an arcade. Keep it light. Avoid labeling the relationship too early. "This is my friend, Jordan," is often all you need at first.

TIP

When both of you agree that the relationship is serious, it's time to share more with your co-parent. This is where collaboration comes back into play.

When parents handle introductions with mutual respect, they reduce their children's anxiety about their original breakup, getting used to going back and forth between their parents' homes, and meeting someone new. Kids pick up on tension faster than adults realize. If you and your co-parent can communicate calmly and predictably, your children will see dating as a manageable change rather than another emotional earthquake.

Avoiding social media pitfalls

Children shouldn't learn about your dating life from Instagram or Facebook. Neither should your other parent. Even if you keep your relationship private, remember that kids see shared screens, hear notifications, and notice tagged photos. The order of operations matters:

1. Tell your co-parent first (briefly and respectfully).
2. Tell your children next (using age-appropriate language).
3. Post later, if at all, and only once your children are comfortable and your relationship is truly stable.

TIP

If your new partner wants to post first, be clear: "I choose not to be public about my personal life until my kids have adjusted." Healthy partners understand; they won't equate patience with secrecy.

Presenting sexual boundaries without hypocrisy

Few topics are as delicate as how parents present intimacy to their children.

> When 13-year-old Naomi's dad moved in with his girlfriend, she confided in her mother, "He tells me not to rush into sex, but he moved in with her after six months."
>
> That's how it appeared to Naomi. In reality, her father had been seeing Lisa for over a year. Naomi simply didn't know. And truthfully, her father hadn't considered how it would look to his daughter. He didn't realize he was sending a mixed message.

If you tell your child that physical intimacy should follow emotional trust, but they see you skipping steps, they'll notice. Again, perfection isn't necessary, but consistency and predictability are.

Dana and Mark were married for nine years before separating. They shared custody of their two children and prided themselves on keeping things stable. But one Sunday evening, after returning from their dad's house, their oldest, 12-year-old Tyler, said, "Mom, there was a lady in Dad's bed when I went in to say good morning."

Dana froze. She and Mark had dated in college, and she assumed they shared similar standards around privacy and parenting. She wasn't judging his new relationship, but she couldn't ignore their son's discomfort. The next morning, she called Mark, determined to keep the focus on their child.

Addressing a difference in morals

Disagreements about values or dating practices can escalate quickly if parents fall into old patterns of blame and jealousy. But when managed with structure and respect, they can strengthen the co-parenting dynamic.

The following four-step model can help you navigate conversations like these with clarity and empathy, keeping the best interests of the children in the forefront. Here's how Dana and Mark managed it.

TIP

You can find the Four-Step Problem-Solving Model Using I Messages document at `www.dummies.com/go/coparentingfd`. You can also find this on the Bonus Families website at `www.bonusfamilies.com/4StepModel`.

Step 1: Identify the problem

Start by stating your concern clearly, without accusation or assumption.

Dana started with calm curiosity.

> "I'm not making any judgments about how you manage your personal life. I know you care about Marcia. I'm just concerned because Tyler was uncomfortable. He said he saw someone in your bed when he came to say good morning. Did you know he saw that?"

This simple open-ended question gives Mark space to respond without feeling attacked. It's not about catching him off guard or proving him wrong. It's about opening the door to understanding and collaboration.

> "No, I didn't realize," Mark admitted. "She left so early. I thought we were being discreet."

Step 2: Suggest a child-focused solution

> Dana continued with compassion. "Tyler was embarrassed. He doesn't want to say anything to you because he's afraid you'll be mad. He's saying he'd rather take a break from your house. He just needs reassurance. Maybe you could talk to him and let him know you understand how he feels — maybe even apologize for the confusion."

The focus isn't on punishment or criticism. It's on helping their son feel safe, heard, and comfortable in both homes.

Step 3: Negotiate

Mark responded thoughtfully.

> "I feel terrible about that. Do you think I should talk to him right away, or should I wait a bit?"

Asking for input from your co-parent signals mutual respect. It tells them you value their insight as a fellow parent. You're not just "the ex."

> Dana replied with this. "Maybe give him a day or two. I'll talk to him tonight and let you know how he's feeling."

Step 4: Compromise

Mark agreed about waiting, but not for Dana to run defense and tell him how his son feels about the situation.

> "Alright, I'll wait until tomorrow evening when I see him again, and then I'll talk to him. But I want to talk to him firsthand. I want him to know that he can talk to me, too. I don't want to tell you not to talk to our son. I appreciate your willingness to help, but I have to figure this out with him myself. I didn't handle this well, and I have to own this and fix it. I'll let you know how it goes."

Notice how both parents stayed on task. They didn't drift into personal grievances or moral judgments. The goal remained consistent: to meet their son's needs first.

C.A.R.E. in action

The brief exchange covered in the previous four steps demonstrates every element of the C.A.R.E. approach:

- **Communication:** Dana was honest and clear, focusing on Tyler's experience instead of blaming Mark for his choices.

» **Acceptance:** She acknowledged that Mark's relationship was part of his life and didn't shame him for it.

» **Respect:** She phrased her concern as a question, not a criticism.

» **Empathy:** She put herself in Mark's position and offered a path forward that protected both him and their child.

TIP

Before confronting your co-parent about something that upsets you, pause and ask yourself:

» Am I addressing this because it truly affects our child or because it hurts my feelings?

» Can I express my concern without blaming or judging?

» Is there a way to turn this conflict into a moment of collaboration?

When parents lead with empathy and structure, differences in morals stop being battles and start being opportunities to model emotional maturity for their children.

Respecting each other's space

REMEMBER

Although it's unwritten, the primary rule of dating while co-parenting is to *never* show up at your co-parent's home unannounced. That small courtesy communicates, "I respect your privacy, and I expect the same in return."

One father once told me about a time when his ex came into his home while he was on a date.

> "She thought I wasn't home because my car was in the garage, and she wanted to grab our son's backpack. But I was, and my girlfriend and I were, well, indisposed." My girlfriend had no idea how closely we co-parented and was mortified. After my co-parent left, my girlfriend got up, left, and now won't return my calls."

Collaborative co-parenting isn't just about avoiding conflicts; it's about anticipating how your actions affect others. When you respect boundaries that have been put in place — like never showing up at your co-parent's home unannounced — you create an atmosphere where everyone can relax and coexist peacefully.

If you still have keys to your co-parent's home, return them unless you've discussed otherwise and have rules around using them, such as during an emergency. Predictability will keep everyone — especially new partners — calm.

Answering your children's big questions

"Do you still love Mom (or Dad)?" is the question that catches just about every parent off guard. Add to that, "Will you ever get back together?" and you've got the big breakup question combo. Behind these questions isn't curiosity. It's fear. Children crave stability, and when they see their parents moving on, they're afraid that their old world, which felt familiar, will disappear for good. And they're afraid that you'll forget about their other parent, whom they're desperate for you to continue to love.

The classic answer is, "I'll always love your mom (dad), but we can't live together." It sounds reassuring, but it can confuse your children. Love, to a child, is forever, like you love them. So, if you "love" their other parent, shouldn't you be together?

A mindful response strikes a balance between truth and comfort:

> Your dad and I care about each other because we're your parents, and we both love you very much. We've learned we're happier living in two homes, but we will always work together to take care of you and keep you safe.

REMEMBER

The goal is to close the door gently, not slam it in their face or leave it open just enough for false hope. Children can handle change if you make it clear that their security doesn't depend on your relationship status.

Taking It Slow When Your Date Has Children

Dating someone who has children adds another layer of complexity to the dating dynamic. Not everyone moves at the same pace.

Every child processes change differently. Just because your kids are ready to meet someone new doesn't mean your date's children are. And vice versa. You may find yourself eager to create one big happy bonus family, but moving too quickly often backfires.

Take your cues from your children. Notice their energy, their comfort, their silence, and the times they withdraw. Instead of planning a big family outing right away, start with casual times together: lunch in the park, pizza at the arcade. Your date's children don't owe you affection. Your relationship will develop slowly through consistency over time.

Ben and Tasha had been dating for 8 months. Both had children. Ben's twins were ten, and Tasha's daughter was eight. Excited to bring everyone together, they planned a "family" dinner.

But they hadn't done the proper preparation, and everything fell apart quickly. Within minutes, Ben's twins were loud and teased Tasha's daughter about her "princess pajamas." Tasha jumped in and defended her daughter. Ben scolded his twins, and soon everyone was upset.

Afterward, Tasha reflected on the evening. "We thought we were ready, but we skipped steps. We tried to make them a family before they even liked each other. Truthfully, they barely knew each other. I don't know what we were thinking."

They were thinking, "We love each other. Of course, our kids will, too. They will meet and immediately melt into a loving family because that was *our* goal."

REMEMBER

That's at the heart of mindful dating: understanding that love between adults doesn't automatically translate to connection between children. Relationships take time. When adults slow down and are mindful of the feelings around them, everyone feels safer.

Setting Boundaries When Your New Partner Doesn't Respect Your Co-Parent

Respect is contagious, but so is resentment.

Take Leo and Darcy's situation: They divorced when their daughter, Chloe, was six. A few years later, Leo started dating Erin, a woman who adored his children but couldn't stand his ex. "Why do you still text her?" Erin complained whenever Leo and Darcy discussed Chloe's soccer schedule.

Erin's tone began to influence Chloe, who became anxious during exchanges. "Erin says Mom's too strict," she whispered one night.

Leo didn't realize his silence was agreement and meant that the things Erin was saying were okay. By not correcting Erin, he allowed her to shape the family narrative, and Chloe was caught in the middle.

When your partner criticizes your co-parent, it might feel validating at first, but allowing it to continue teaches your children that disrespect is acceptable. The healthier approach is to set a firm, but kind boundary:

"I appreciate that you're protective of me, but Darcy and I are partners in raising Chloe. We don't badmouth each other in front of her, nor do we allow anyone else to. That's important to both her and me."

Setting the boundary doesn't mean you're choosing your ex over your partner. It means you're choosing maturity over drama and protecting your child from unnecessary loyalty conflicts.

TIP

If your new partner expresses frustration about your co-parent, pause and do some soul searching:

1. Are they reacting to real behavior or insecurity about the past?
2. Have I shared too many private details that feed that insecurity?
3. What boundary can I clarify that supports both relationships?

These are important questions to consider when moving forward in a new relationship. Often, when you first meet someone, you share uncensored stories about your ex. You might describe how they hurt or betrayed you, or even admit that they were the love of your life, not expecting the new relationship to become serious.

But when it does, those early confessions don't disappear. New partners don't forget what you've shared.

REMEMBER

It's important to distinguish that loyalty to your co-parenting partnership doesn't diminish the romantic feelings you have for your new partner. If you've shared too much in the past, you may have to backtrack a little and clarify your position. Explain that there's no comparison. One is your partner in raising your child. One is your partner in life. Make the distinction evident.

Knowing What to Do When Things Go Wrong

Even the most well-intentioned plans can hit bumps. Perhaps your co-parent introduces a partner before you're ready. Or your child resists your new relationship. Maybe your new partner struggles with jealousy about your ongoing communication with your co-parent.

When that happens, return to the principles of C.A.R.E.

» **Communicate** honestly and early.

» **Accept** the feelings — your own and others' feelings are valid, even when they're inconvenient.

- **Respect** boundaries, both logistical and emotional.
- **Empathize** with everyone involved, especially the children.

TIP

If your new date or partner becomes jealous of your relationship with your co-parent, guide them away from referring to them as your ex and make sure they refer to them as your co-parent. To a new partner, "ex" is filled with romantic connotations. It means former lover, and that's sure to conjure up all sorts of questionable images in their head. Co-parent refers to the present relationship — a nonromantic collaborative partnership formed in the best interest of the children you both share. It's more like a joint business venture than a love lost.

If conflict persists, don't be afraid to seek professional guidance. A family therapist experienced in breaking up and starting over can offer neutral ground and tools for moving forward. Sometimes just having a structured space to talk and air differences can defuse tension before it escalates.

REMEMBER

Dating after a breakup isn't a one-time event. It's an ongoing adjustment. Give yourself permission to learn, stumble, recalibrate, and grow.

Dealing with breakups after introductions

Despite all your hard work, some relationships will end after your children have met your partner, maybe even moved in together, or even remarried. How you handle that goodbye matters just as much as how you handle the hello.

What children want to know is what this means for their lives. What will change, and what will stay the same?

- Tell the truth gently, "We care for each other, but we decided not to be partners anymore. It works best for us."
- Avoid blame. Children don't need the fine print; they just need the headline.
- Maintain continuity. Your routines will be the same. You'll still be in Ms. Nelson's class, and our Friday Night movie night will remain."
- Invite conversations about feelings. "It's okay to miss them. We'll put our heads together if you want to talk to them or spend time together. (This is especially true if your children have gotten close to their children.)
- Don't rush into something else. Give yourself and your children time to process the loss.

Consider this example:

> Sherilyn was very close to Markie when she was married to his father, Bruce. But when they broke up, Bruce told her not to contact Markie again. Both Sherilyn and Markie mourned the loss. Sherilyn felt she was abandoning a little boy who trusted and loved her. Markie couldn't understand why his bonus mom had disappeared.
>
> Because little was said about the breakup, Markie blamed himself. Unable to put his feelings into words, he lost his appetite and had trouble sleeping. His mother, unaware of how close he was to Sherilyn, didn't understand the change. Concerned, she took him to the doctor, but everything checked out.
>
> Bruce didn't seem concerned about how the breakup affected his son. He was done with Sherilyn, and the boundary was clear. He believed Markie was resilient and would "get over it." When asked about their son's behavior, he simply repeated, "He'll get over it."
>
> He might. But how parents help their children "get over it" matters.
>
> Bruce was operating from an old-school divorce mindset, believing the door should be closed after a breakup. He wasn't considering that his son might need help processing the loss. As much as Bruce disliked Sherilyn, his son may have needed continued, thoughtful contact to adjust.
>
> The key is this: Love your children more than you hate your ex.
>
> Even though Sherilyn wasn't Markie's mother, cutting off contact without explanation left him to make sense of the loss on his own. Like many children, he blamed himself: "It must be me or something I did. That's why she's not talking to me."
>
> Bruce and Sherilyn needed to decide whether continued contact would benefit Markie based on his needs, not Bruce's anger, and agree on what that would look like.
>
> There is no one-size-fits-all answer. Some children can gradually let go of a parent's former partner. Others form deep bonds that continue. Given Markie's strong reaction, involving a professional to guide the transition would have been wise.

Modeling love and respect

To end this chapter, I want to remind you that your children are always learning from you, especially when you think they aren't looking. The way you speak to your co-parent, the patience you show when plans change, the kindness you extend to your new partner: These moments become the blueprint for how your children love and resolve conflict in their own lives now and as they enter relationships when they're older.

Healthy dating after a breakup isn't just about finding love again. It's about modeling what love and a healthy relationship should look like. You'll make mistakes. You're human. But when you allow your children to see that adults can treat each other with kindness even after heartbreak, they'll realize that relationships can end and there can be new beginnings without destroying the people experiencing them.

Your dating life, if handled mindfully, can become one of the greatest emotional lessons your children will ever receive.

Use the worksheet in Table 6-2 to pause and reflect before taking on your next relationship.

REMEMBER

When in doubt, pause. Mindful decisions create lasting peace.

TABLE 6-2 **Mindful Dating Self-Check**

Questions	Reflection
Have I fully grieved the end of my prior relationship?	
Am I dating because I feel ready or because I feel lonely?	
Can I distinguish the difference?	
Have I discussed my approach to dating with my co-parent?	
How might this new connection affect my children emotionally?	
Am I proud of the example I'm setting for my children?	

IN THIS CHAPTER

» Understanding custody considerations

» Examining equal custody schedules and step plans

» Incorporating special factors and situations into plans

» Looking at separation anxiety

» Assessing which parenting plan is best for your child

Chapter 7 Establishing Parenting Plans

Your parenting plan is the schedule by which you and your co-parent will share your children's time after your breakup. Your parenting plan outlines when each of you will see your children after you no longer live together.

Most parents anticipate sharing their children's time equally, but each situation is different, and the allocation of time between parents really depends on what's best for the children. Plus, your children's needs will change over time, so staying flexible about your time together is important. The parenting plan that works for your children now may not be the right parenting plan for them in a few years. Stay open to making the necessary adjustments as time goes on.

In this chapter, you discover custody terminology and find out how the custody of your children is determined once you no longer live together. I also explain specific parenting plans and help you assess why one parenting plan may work better for your children than another. You also get an important look at separation anxiety, how it affects your children at various ages and stages of their lives, and how to address it at each stage.

Determining Who Gets Custody and Why

Nothing is written in stone regarding whether and how parents have custody of their child or children. An effective parenting plan is personalized to fit the needs of your family's lifestyle and takes many aspects of your lifestyle into consideration. You and your co-parent can ideally work together to evaluate the factors involved in your situation and develop a custody agreement that works for everyone. This section helps you with that task.

Custody terminology explained

Before you delve into the factors involved in your custody decisions and associated parenting plans, you need to get a grip on the related terminology. The following terms commonly describe custody for co-parenting:

- **Legal custody** describes the situation in which you have legal custody of your children that secures your legal right as a parent to make decisions and sign documents concerning your children's health and welfare.
- **Joint legal custody** means that both parents can legally make decisions for their children. Most custody agreements require parents with joint legal custody to meet and confer prior to a final decision being made.
- **Sole legal custody** also referred to as *primary custody*, means that only one parent has the right to make decisions. When a parent has sole custody, they don't have to consult the other parent before making decisions.
- **Physical custody** refers to the location where the children reside, but equal or joint physical custody doesn't necessarily guarantee parents equal time with their kids. Joint physical custody just means the kids live with both of you. The parenting plan you choose designates the days and times the children are with each of you.
- **Shared custody and equal custody** sound the same, but they're dissimilar in a special way. Shared custody means exactly what it sounds like: The parents share custody (including the decision-making, care, and feeding of their children). However, shared custody may not be equal custody in terms of the time spent with the children.

Comparing shared custody and equal custody

In this section, I compare two parenting plans. In one plan, the child lives mostly with one parent and sees the other parent every other weekend. In the other plan, the child alternates one week with one parent and one week with the other. Both parenting plans are regarded as shared custody, but only the alternating week plan represents equal custody.

Equal custody schedules work best in these scenarios:

- The parents live close enough to each other that the children can easily attend their school from both homes.
- The parents' work week supports the children's schedule, and exchanges are easy to maneuver.
- The parents can communicate with each other cordially and solve problems straightforwardly.
- Badmouthing and bickering are kept to a minimum.
- The children are emotionally equipped to switch homes on a regular basis.

The theory behind an equal custody parenting plan is that it allows your child to build a close relationship with both parents. However, in some situations, an equal parenting plan may be detrimental to your child's adjustment. For example:

- When only one parent cared for the children most of the time before the breakup. Most equal parenting plans require the child to spend days — or at times a week — away from each parent.

  REMEMBER

  If your child is very young — or if you were the primary caregiver before separation — equal custody may not be the best solution immediately after a breakup. A sudden shift that requires your child to be away from that primary caregiver for extended periods can be emotionally and psychologically difficult.

  In these cases, a step plan approach that allows the child to slowly adjust to living in two homes can be helpful (see "Considering a step plan" later in this chapter).
- When parents continue to fight and argue after their separation, regardless of whether the altercations take place in front of the children. Even if your children can't hear the arguments, they can feel the resulting tension. Countless studies show that ongoing conflict between parents can affect their children's psychological, emotional, and even physical development.

Looking at parental history

When deciding on custody arrangements, angry co-parents often try to paint each other in a poor light by using each other's past as a reference for why one parent should have more time with the children than the other. However, many factors you may think will make a difference when deciding custody really don't affect the decision. Here are two examples:

- **Infidelity:** While infidelity is technically still illegal in 16 states, these laws are rarely enforced, and the law is often considered outdated. States like Arizona, Florida, Kansas, Illinois, Massachusetts, Oklahoma, Idaho, Michigan, Wisconsin, Minnesota, Utah, New York, Mississippi, Georgia, South Carolina, and North Carolina still have adultery laws on the books. Still, even in these states, adultery is typically categorized as a misdemeanor, and prosecutions are rare. However, infidelity may become a factor if you can prove that it negatively affected a child's well-being. Infidelity leading to instability, neglect, or exposure to unsafe situations could, however, influence a court decision.
- **Past drug or alcohol abuse:** This may not be a factor when deciding custody in some courts if the parent has a history of drug or alcohol abuse but is now clean and sober, especially if they've been clean for years.

The courts believe that a child deserves time with both parents, and all decisions are made in the best interests of the child. First and foremost, this means they consider factors like the child's emotional and physical well-being, the stability of the home environment, and the parents' ability to meet the child's needs. Infidelity or past drug use don't automatically disqualify a parent from having custody of their children, especially if your relationship began with infidelity or your co-parent has proof that you took drugs together in the past.

Here are situations that do have a significant impact on custody decisions:

- **The existence of an abusive past:** This is especially relevant when the parents share a child. In many states, there is a rebuttable presumption that a parent found guilty of domestic violence against the other parent will not be awarded sole or joint custody. This presumption can only be overcome by a preponderance of the evidence, such as completion of a court-approved batterer's intervention program.
- **The existence of past child abuse:** There are different types of abuse to be considered here. Of course, sexual abuse would prevent custody or even visitation, but other types of abuse a court may consider detrimental to a child are past neglect and physical or emotional abuse.
- **A parent who's currently abusing drugs or alcohol:** In addition, a court will look for signs that indicate the children aren't safe in that parent's care.

But you can't just accuse your co-parent of wrongdoing. A judge makes the determination based on the evidence presented when the custody case comes before them. There must be proof — something like an active restraining order to prove domestic violence or the incompletion of batterer's classes, recent DUIs to prove substance abuse, or a substantiated CPS finding for caretaker absence or neglectful parenting choices. When you can demonstrate proof of wrongdoing, the court has a basis on which to consider whether joint custody of the children is appropriate.

Evaluating how well co-parents get along

Although most family courts support parents sharing their children's time after a breakup and hope they can co-parent their children fairly, sometimes the parents' relationship is extremely volatile, and they can't make decisions without the discussion erupting into an argument.

In cases like this, the courts must choose a primary parent. Making this choice is a difficult decision for a judge. Still, because the criteria for all decisions in family court are "in the child's best interests," and based on the belief that children deserve a loving relationship with both parents, the final decision is often made by determining which parent is most likely to foster a positive relationship with the child's other parent. If a judge believes you won't support your child's relationship with their other parent based on your own animosity toward that parent, a judge may make the decision to grant primary custody to your co-parent.

REMEMBER

Receiving primary custody of your child doesn't preclude the necessity for you to co-parent. No matter what the parenting plan is, parents must work together in the best interests of their children.

When mental health concerns exist

Health-related issues can play a role in custody decisions and parenting plans. Your health, or your co-parent's, may affect what arrangement is best for your child. Consider this example:

> "Although my children's mother is now under a doctor's care and takes medication, she was unpredictable in the past and was diagnosed with bipolar disorder two years ago. I don't believe she should have time with our children."

Many believe a co-parent's mental health diagnosis is all that is needed to gain custody. This is not true.

We know this mother was diagnosed two years ago and is currently under medical care and taking prescribed medication to regulate her mood. That reflects a proactive approach to managing her condition. Unless there are additional concerns, this sort of diagnosis alone would not be the final determiner to decide custody.

Examining Equal Custody Parenting Schedules

Professionals suggest that children will adjust best after a parental breakup if they have ongoing and constant contact with both of their parents. Several schedules associated with parenting plans offer the opportunity for this type of parental contact, but each has positive and negative aspects to consider. In this section, you find out about commonly used schedules that offer equal custody for parental plans.

The 2-2-3 schedule

If you choose the 2-2-3 schedule, as shown in Figure 7-1, during the first week, your child spends two days with one parent, two days with the other parent, and three days back with the first parent. In the next week, the parents will switch the number of days with custody. The figure shows a 3 p.m. exchange because that's a commonly used after-school exchange time. When you adopt a custody schedule, you can adjust the exchange times and location to fit your family's needs.

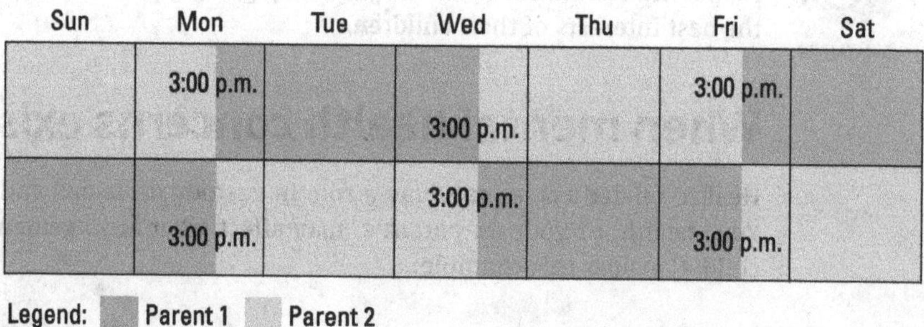

FIGURE 7-1: The 2-2-3 custody schedule.

Here are the positives:

» The child or children will have the encouraged "ongoing and constant contact" with both of their parents.

» The plan works well for infants and toddlers and younger children who don't yet understand the concept of time or the days of the week.

» Young children may have difficulty being away from a primary caregiver for multiple days at a time. This parenting plan allows them to see both parents every few days.

And here are the negatives:

» Lots of exchanges to plan for and execute.

» Switching different days throughout the week can make staying organized more difficult for both you and your school-aged children.

» Your children may not understand where they're supposed to stay on specific days. They may often ask for clarification.

» If parents don't communicate well, with constant back and forth, the following may happen:

  - An inability to communicate well can lead to frustration and ongoing conflict between parents.
  - Disorganization may lead school-aged children to have difficulty turning in homework on time.
  - Parents may forget to sign school papers, such as reading records.
  - The children's teachers won't be sure of which parent to contact on what day when they need to discuss something.

If you can't easily solve a problem when working with your co-parent, this parenting plan will be a challenge. The 2-2-3 schedule requires you to interact with your co-parent every few days to stay organized.

For any equal parenting plans that shift days during the week, buy a calendar and color-code the days on which the children will be with you, and add another color for when they'll be with their other parent. Make a calendar for each child's room at both homes, and for your co-parent, your children's teachers, and possibly their on-site after-school childcare provider, so you'll all be in sync in case of emergency.

The 3-4-4-3 schedule

If you choose the 3-4-4-3 schedule, depicted in Figure 7-2, your child will spend three days with one parent, four days with the other parent, and then four days with the first parent and three days with the other parent.

Sun	Mon	Tue	Wed	Thu	Fri	Sat
3:00 p.m.			3:00 p.m.			
3:00 p.m.				3:00 p.m.		

Legend: Parent 1 Parent 2

FIGURE 7-2: The 3-4-4-3 schedule.

Here are the positives:

- This plan may work well with your work schedule.
- The transition schedule is convenient when the goal is to keep an equally shared custody plan in place as your child moves to longer time periods with each parent.
- This plan works well for children around ages 6–9 or older who can easily be away from either parent for three or four days at a time.

Here are the negatives:

- Like the 2-2-3 schedule from the previous section, some of the days on which each parent has custody shift each week, which can make staying organized difficult. You must be able to comfortably plan and stay flexible with your co-parent, coaches, the school, and childcare.
- Keeping the kids organized can be a challenge when they switch homes in the middle of the week. Take special care with monitoring homework.

REMEMBER

This parenting plan requires ongoing parental interaction. If you don't get along well with your co-parent, forcing your children to go back and forth between homes every few days is doing them a disservice. The goal is loving, ongoing contact with both parents to help the child cope with living in two homes after their parents' breakup, not adding to their anxiety by forcing them to be in the middle of their battling parents.

The 2-2-5-5 schedule

The 2-2-5-5 schedule is shown in Figure 7-3. It's one of the most common shared-custody parenting plans.

Sun	Mon	Tue	Wed	Thu	Fri	Sat
	3:00 p.m.		3:00 p.m.		3:00 p.m.	
			3:00 p.m.			

Legend: Parent 1 Parent 2

FIGURE 7-3: The 2-2-5-5 schedule.

If you choose the 2-2-5-5 schedule, your children will spend Monday at 3 p.m. to Wednesday at 3 p.m. with one parent and Wednesday at 3 p.m. to Friday at 3 p.m. with the other parent. Each parent would also alternate weekends, from Friday at 3 p.m. to Monday at 3 p.m. When the parents' designated weekend attaches to their regularly scheduled days, the child is with that parent for five days in a row. Exchange times can be easily adjusted to coincide with after-school childcare or the parents' work schedules.

The positives:

- Great for adolescents aged 10–14 who can comfortably stay for five days with each parent.
- Your child is with you on the same day of the week each week and alternating weekends. As a result, scheduling is more predictable. Children know at which home they'll stay, and so do their teachers, friends, and coaches.

The negatives:

- You must be able to comfortably plan and stay flexible with your co-parent, coaches, the school, and childcare.
- Keeping the kids organized can be a challenge when they switch homes in the middle of the week. Take special care in monitoring homework.
- It's not recommended for high-conflict co-parenting. This parenting plan requires ongoing parental interaction. You must be able to solve problems easily, or your children won't fare well.
- When children enter high school, they may have so many extracurricular activities and responsibilities that switching homes in the middle of the week becomes bothersome. This is when families often opt to move to a parenting plan that alternates weeks: one week at each parent's home.

The 7-7 schedule

The 7-7 schedule is also known as alternating weeks. You probably don't need a figure for this one, but Figure 7-4 is included for the sake of being complete.

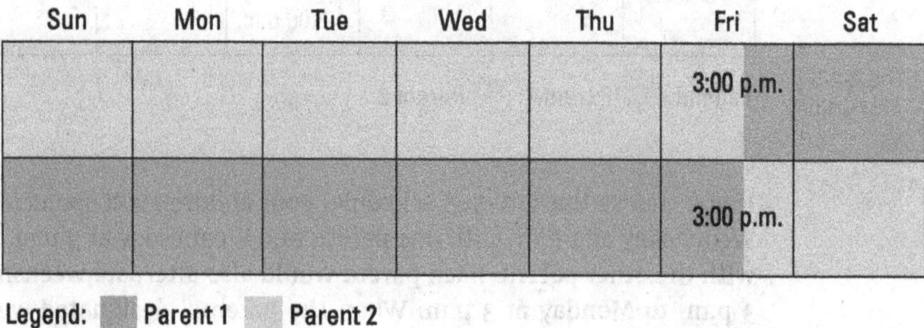

FIGURE 7-4: The 7-7 schedule.

This schedule is often referred to as "week on, week off," which translates into seven consecutive days with one parent, then seven consecutive days with the other one.

There are different ways to execute this parenting approach. When exchanges occur after school on Fridays, there's a little downtime before the school week starts. Children have time to relax at the other home after the exchange and possibly finish their homework and laundry before returning to school on Monday. However, some families prefer to exchange the kids on Sunday evenings or Mondays after school because it works best for the parents' work schedules.

However, when exchanges are on Sundays or Mondays, kids don't have much time to get organized before the school week starts or bone up for a test after the weekend. Switching on Monday after school may also require some additional coordination, such as an extra trip to the other home to exchange clothes or sports equipment when the children participate in extracurricular activities.

Parallel parenting

There's an irony associated with this 7-7 schedule. It's the schedule suggested most often when parents get along well, *and* when parents are at odds and can't work together. The approach is just different.

- **If co-parents get along well,** they can compare notes and stay on top of everything their children do. Their children can easily see their parents setting a good example as they problem-solve as co-parents.

* **If parents can't get along,** their children simply live with each of them for seven days, and their parents rarely interact with one another.

This approach to parenting after a breakup is referred to as *parallel parenting.* The parents lead separate lives as their children go back and forth between their homes. The parents don't coordinate efforts and make their own parenting decisions when the children are with them.

The greatest negative to parallel parenting is that the parents rarely talk, and their children know it. It's easy for estranged parents to ask a child to pass on information. "Tell your mother" or "Tell your father" becomes commonplace and puts the children right in the middle of their battling parents.

TIP

When children are told to pass on information, for fear of getting it wrong or causing arguments between their parents, they may feel as if they must rely on their own resources and fill in the blanks. They may choose to lie, alter the message, or withhold information, thinking it might keep the parents from fighting or even promote a reconciliation. If parents choose to parallel parent, they must make a concerted effort to establish a workable mode of communication between them and keep their children out of the middle.

The positives:

* This schedule is often chosen when children reach middle school, typically around sixth or seventh grade, when they can be away from a parent without feeling anxious. It also works well in high school, when teens need more flexibility and can drive themselves to activities.
* This schedule also works well for sharing the summer break. The 7-day stretch with each parent allows for taking vacations without interrupting the children's regularly scheduled time with their other parent.

The negatives:

* This isn't the best plan for young children who have trouble being away from either parent for more than a few days.
* If parents can't communicate well or at all, it's easy for children to manipulate them, tell them something that isn't true, or say that the other parent granted permission to do something when they really didn't. If parents don't check in with each other, their children have free rein to raise themselves.

THINKING OUTSIDE OF THE BOX

The courts can assign a parenting schedule, but the key is how you live it and how that parenting schedule truly affects your children. Think outside the box and do what works for your family. You don't have to maintain a conventional parenting schedule; you need a workable schedule so your child can form a bond with you and your co-parent.

Here's a great example that two of my clients worked out between themselves, which was difficult to put on paper in the form of an order; however, this is the schedule they used to raise their child after their breakup. Their son, William, was 6 when they began.

> Parent A worked Monday through Friday, 12 p.m. to 7 p.m. Parent B worked 6 a.m. to 3 p.m. It was difficult for parent A to pick up their child after school, and it was difficult for parent B to drop off the child at school in the morning. Neither of the parents worked on the weekends. And these parents lived two miles from one another.

Writing a court order that reflected exactly how they lived the parenting plan was next to impossible, so it was written that

> "The parents shall share their child's time equally by mutual agreement."

That language isn't enforceable by law because it gives no schedule for someone to enforce, but these parents worked well together and trusted each other. This is what the parents decided to do:

> From Monday after school to Friday after school, the child resided with parent A, and the child was with parent B from Friday after school to Monday after school. Here's the caveat to the order: Parent B picked the child up after school, fed him a snack, monitored his homework, fed him dinner, and returned the child to parent A for the night at 7:30 p.m.

So, parent A woke up with the child, fed them breakfast, and got them off to school. Since the child spent less time with parent B, the parents agreed to assign spring and fall break to parent B. And since parent A had no formal weekend time with the child, the parents assigned the second weekend of each month, Friday after school to Monday to school, to parent A. These compensations were noted in the order.

Taking Unique Factors into Account

When building a parenting plan, start with what the child's schedule was prior to the breakup — the status quo — and build from there. Prior to the breakup, did you have a workable routine in place for how you cared for your children? For example,

- You both agreed that one of you would stay home with your child and the other would work.
- You both worked part-time so you could care for the child at different times, or one parent worked days, and the other worked nights.

Regardless of the details of your previous lifestyle, you can start there to keep the disruption to your child's schedule to a minimum. Then look at other factors presented in this section to determine the best co-parenting plan for you and your children.

The distance each parent must travel

Many parents move after a breakup. They want to start a new life in a new neighborhood, establish new friends, and start over with a new partner. Moving even a short distance away can affect how often people see their children. Even living in the next town over adds time to exchanges and makes it difficult for your children to maintain friendships.

REMEMBER

You may think that moving won't affect navigating the parenting plan, but it will. It will also complicate how effectively your children adjust to this new back-and-forth life.

Although courts have individual opinions about the preferred distance a child should travel to school, the logistics associated with attending a school more than 30 minutes away from a child's home can be problematic. For example,

- Your child must wake up earlier than usual, interrupting their normal sleep patterns.
- Morning traffic can be unpredictable and cause your child to be late or marked absent.
- Living in a different neighborhood can make participating in after-school extracurricular activities more difficult.

So, if one parent lives farther than 30 minutes away from their child's school, the child will likely live predominantly with one parent when school is in session and visit the other for dinner visits, on the weekends, and during school breaks.

Your work schedules

A parent's work hours can also affect their child's parenting plan. For example, if one parent works nights and the other works days, maneuvering an equally shared parenting plan can be difficult. One parent is usually assigned to primary physical custody.

This means that the child lives primarily with one parent and visits the other, even though both parents maintain joint custody status. Circumstances are even more difficult when both parents work the night shift, and the children attend school during the day. In these cases, the time when the children can be with either parent is affected. Parents may need help from extended family or friends for transporting the children to school. And they may need before- or after-school childcare.

The age of your child or children

The age of the child plays a huge part in how long they're comfortable being away from each parent. The psychological community changes its recommendations all the time, but typically, professionals suggest that a child younger than 1 or 2 shouldn't be away from the primary caregiver longer than one or two consecutive overnights per week. Once the child reaches 3, then three nights a week might be appropriate. This is just a rule of thumb. It really depends on the individual child's ability to adjust.

The number of overnights isn't a concern for older children and teens. Therefore, a toddler would have a completely different parenting schedule than a teenager.

Accommodating a child who has special needs

When a child is said to have special needs, it means they have a condition or disability that requires individualized support to successfully learn or complete various tasks. Your child may have a chronic illness or a mental health challenge. Or your child may need a tutor or an Individual Education Program (IEP) offered at a specific school that's closer to one co-parent's home than the other's. All this can influence how you address the parenting plan.

Consider this situation from an email I received:

> My co-parent and I have a child with autism. He is regarded as high functioning, but he has extreme mood swings and emotional meltdowns. Even so, he is my son, and I want to spend as much time as possible with him. He currently spends most of the week with his mother, and I see him on the weekends. I'd like to have him

with me every few days. I think seeing me more often will be beneficial. His mother disagrees, and since we don't speak, I often petition the court to change the parenting plan, but they don't listen, and our parenting plan has been the same since we divorced six years ago. I'm not sure what to do.

When I receive messages like this one, I like to point out the red flags, and this email has quite a few:

» The first red flag that flashes the brightest is that these parents don't speak to each other. Raising a child diagnosed with special needs can be a challenge in the best of circumstances. These parents need each other's support and must compare notes to give their child the best life possible.

» The second red flag is something that's often overlooked when designing a parenting plan for an autistic child: how much they crave order and consistency. Children with this diagnosis struggle with change, so a parenting plan that requires them to go back and forth every two days isn't in their best interests. This father is generally looking for ways to spend additional time with his child, but requiring this much back and forth may not be the answer.

» The next flag involves the child's emotional health. It's not uncommon for autistic children to suffer from anxiety. They may have panic attacks, and as this father mentioned in his original query, his son occasionally has emotional meltdowns. Knowing this, a consistent routine that supplies a stable, predictable schedule would be more desirable than switching homes every few days. This may be the reason the court won't consider the parenting plan Dad suggests.

The correct approach to ensuring the best parenting plan at this stage is a multi-step approach:

1. **Listen to the professionals' advice regarding joint custody.**

   Don't try to do this on your own. Although everyone thinks they know what's best for their kids, when a child has special needs, there are all sorts of variables you may not see. Things like drug interactions or drug side effects are one example. Consult the professionals treating your child, and design a plan that incorporates coping strategies they've seen work for children with special needs.

2. **Reach out to local support groups for emotional support and suggestions.**

   Other parents may be out there going through exactly what you're facing. They can be a wonderful resource for help and support.

3. **Improve your communication with your co-parent.**

During my work as a co-parenting counselor, I often hear, "I don't see my kids enough." I always give the same advice: "Work on your relationship with your co-parent, and chances are you'll see your child as much as you want."

TIP

Of course, you can go to court and fight it out to achieve the custody situation you want, but the essence of good co-parenting is reaching out to your co-parent with good intentions based on the best interests of your child. When you get along with your co-parent, special requests are more likely to be honored, rather than ignored.

REMEMBER

Court-ordered parenting plans are put in place to prevent arguments between disgruntled parents. The order is a default. If you can't get along, then follow the court order. But if you can and you work well with your co-parent, it's easy to modify the order, either temporarily or forever. And you're not breaking the law if you follow your new agreement. The key is that *you must agree*. If you don't agree, you must follow the court order.

FLEXIBILITY IN COURT-ORDERED CUSTODY AGREEMENTS

A notification in most custody orders states something to the effect of, "The terms and conditions of this order may be changed as the needs of the children and parties evolve. Any changes should be made in writing, dated, and signed by the parties. If the parties desire a change to become a court order, it must be filed with the court in the form of a court document." This is language from a custody order in the state of California, but orders from each state incorporate similar language.

Bottom line: If you get along with your co-parent, and you want some extra time with your child, you need to pick up the phone and say, "I have the afternoon free, and I'd love to take our son for ice cream." Since you're now of like mind and both of you are looking for ways to cooperate, your co-parent shouldn't resent the request, thinking you're just trying to take away their time with their child, but welcome the request because they know the child will thrive by having a balanced relationship with both parents. Your co-parent's reply: "Great! Come get him."

Taking it one step further, your co-parent might add, "Will you bring him home afterward, or do you want him to spend the night with you tonight?" At this juncture, you may feel this kind of co-parenting relationship is a pipe dream. It's really not. If you both continue to put your child first, time can be adjusted on an ongoing basis. That's co-parenting at its best.

Adjusting Parenting Plans for Special Situations

Life is full of surprises, and what's true today may not be true in a year or so. A parent could lose their job or be promoted and transferred to another state. A child could develop an illness or need to recover from an accident. You may experience all sorts of unforeseen obstacles in life. Parents must learn to be flexible to accommodate the unforeseen challenges life may throw. The parenting plan you put in place for your children today may not fit your lifestyle in a year or two. A modification might be necessary. The modification doesn't have to last forever. It could be long-term, or it could be short-term, depending on how long it takes to address whatever your family is facing.

Modifications may be granted if you can prove a "change of circumstance." A change of circumstance could be:

- **Changes in the child's health or educational needs:** For example, the child could be diagnosed with something that requires them to live closer to a particular hospital. Or there's a better academic program for a child diagnosed with special needs at a school closer to one of the parents' homes.
- **Changes in the child's schedule:** For example, the child must attend special education tutoring at a particular facility or travel for extracurricular activities.
- **Changes in a parent's job or health:** This might be a job promotion and relocation, loss of employment, or a parent being diagnosed with a terminal illness.

A parenting plan may require a *temporary modification*, as I further explain in the sections that follow.

Making changes when physical health issues affect parenting

Suppose that you were just diagnosed with cancer, and you have months of chemotherapy ahead of you. Your doctor informs you that the medicine will make you weak and sick, and you may find caring for your children to be difficult. Or suppose you've struggled with alcohol in the past and decided to take responsibility by going into rehab. Both are reasons to change the parenting schedule and allow your co-parent to shoulder the weight; however, both examples may only require a temporary adjustment. As the ill parent, once you finish your cancer treatment or complete your rehabilitation program and are well enough to care for your child, you and your co-parent may return to your original parenting plan.

The court loves co-parents to support one another. Judges praise parents who step up to the plate when their co-parent is ill. However, some parents aren't forthcoming, and once their co-parent has recovered from whatever they faced, they refuse to return to the previous parenting plan.

Don't be that person. If you're the one who's well, keep in mind that the stress associated with your children being withheld will only slow down your co-parent's progress. Plus, it will greatly affect your children and could backfire. Your kids will be worried and will probably want to spend as much time as possible with their other parent, particularly if that parent has been ill.

It's not uncommon for children to reject the manipulative parent when they figure out that they were at the root of their inability to return to their parents' home.

Be sensitive to your children's concerns. Support your co-parent. Talk openly with your children about returning to the status quo.

Tailoring a plan to your specific lifestyle

Flexibility is an important component of making your children's parenting plan workable for all concerned.

> When my bonus daughter was 16, she asked her mother and father to consider another schedule. Until that time, her parents — me included — had shared her time as she went back and forth between our homes every other week.
>
> At 16, she could drive, she was a cheerleader with many social obligations, and the week-on/week-off schedule was just too much for her. She never knew where her good jeans were, which caused all sorts of chaos. After much discussion, it was decided that the parenting plan would be adjusted to two weeks with Mom and two weeks with Dad.
>
> This sounds like a long time for any child to be away from a parent, and in truth, it was. But by this time, we had been sharing custody of her and her brother for ten years, and we had an open-door policy. Because the parents lived less than a mile away from each other, the agreement was that the children had to sleep at the designated parent's home at night, but they could come and go between the homes during the day at their leisure.

The moral to this story is how important it is to stay flexible and make adjustments in the best interests of the child. It was gratifying to see what we'd put into action. My bonus daughter felt comfortable enough to talk to both her parents at the same time. Everyone put their heads together and came up with a new plan that worked for all. There was some negotiation and some compromise, but the final decision was the right one for our family.

Don't be afraid to tailor an unconventional parenting plan or adjust what's already in place if it makes your children's lives easier. They didn't ask for the breakup, but they must live with it. Therefore, make any adjustments with them in mind.

Considering the nesting approach

Nesting is an unconventional approach to sharing parenting time after a breakup. Easily described, it's when the kids stay put, and the parents move in and out.

> Consider Scott and Leanne and their son, Jacob, who uses a wheelchair. His home was fully adapted to meet his needs, with wide hallways, ramps, and accessible fixtures. When they divorced, they realized that moving him between two homes that were not equipped for his disability would be a hardship. Instead, they chose to "nest," with Jacob remaining in the family home while each parent took turns living there every two weeks.
>
> While nesting can work well in situations like this, it requires careful consideration. Parents must communicate effectively, stay aligned, and be willing to resolve issues quickly. It can also be expensive, as it often requires maintaining additional living arrangements.

Nesting can become complicated when a parent enters a new relationship. Most partners are not willing to move in and out of a home every two weeks or share space connected to a former partner. While some couples find ways to make it work, nesting is typically best suited for unique situations and may not be sustainable long term.

Considering a step plan

As noted in the section "Comparing shared custody and equal custody" earlier in the chapter, a step plan can be important for helping younger children adapt to spending time with both parents who no longer live together — especially if one parent was the primary caregiver before the breakup.

A typical step plan for a toddler may start with hourly visits, progressing to 4 hours in a day, then to all-day visits, then to two all-day visits in a row, and then to those two days becoming overnights. When you design and implement a step plan, you should establish an agreed-upon duration for each step, say 6 to 8 visits for each step. The duration can be more or less, depending on the specific needs of your child.

TIP

The key to developing a successful step plan is to put your child's interests and safety first. Most parents are eager to progress to overnight visits with their children and want to hurry the process, but don't be selfish. Your child's adjustment is important. A typical timeframe for working up to an overnight visit for an infant or toddler takes between three and four months. The process moves much faster for older children. Depending on the age of the child, a step plan may not be needed at all.

Here are other scenarios to consider when you think about step plans:

- If you and your co-parent lived together prior to separation and your child knows you both well, a step plan to work up to an overnight visit may not be necessary.
- If you lived together, but a primary caregiver existed prior to the breakup — for example, one parent stayed home all day with the child while the other saw the child after work for a few hours — then a step plan may be the best way for your child to get used to their new life. In those cases, you should take the age of the child and how long the parents have been apart into account when setting up the duration for each step of the plan.
- Suppose that your child is one year old when you separate. One parent stayed in the family home while the other moved out and is couch surfing with friends. Because the couch-surfing parent has no real place for the child to sleep, even though the child feels comfortable with both parents, having overnights at this time may not be in the child's best interests. After the parent who moved out establishes a more stable lifestyle, you can put overnights in place.

Adding Holidays and School Breaks Schedules

To ensure the holidays run smoothly, it's best to have a holiday schedule in place. It will help you stay organized and know what to expect. Sometimes parents think they don't need one and will work it out as the holidays approach, but even the most congenial co-parents will disagree at times when changes are made on the spur of the moment. Without a holiday schedule, planning can be overwhelming, and co-parents and their families may find it difficult to coordinate time and gift-giving with extended family. You can always adjust the schedule if you agree to make changes — and if you don't agree, you have a prepared holiday schedule in place for you to follow.

REMEMBER

Most holidays are alternated between the parents. For example, in even years, the children spend Christmas Day with one parent, odd years with the other. School breaks are treated in a similar fashion. Spring break with one parent in even years, odd years with the other. Or, rather than alternate, permanently assign spring break to one parent each year and fall break to the other.

Your holiday and school break schedule is another place where you must exercise flexibility. Whether you decide to alternate holidays or permanently assign them, as the years go by, things change, children grow older and move out, and people are added or leave the family. Be flexible as life changes.

TIP

You can use holidays to make up for a discrepancy in your parenting plan. For example, if a parent has Monday through Friday with their child because they attend school from their residence, the other parent could be assigned spring or fall break each year, or possibly the majority of the summer months to compensate.

The key, however, to making any parenting plan work is to stay open to negotiation when a change in the schedule is desired. It's best for your children if you can discuss changes easily — switch weekends, plan vacations, and cooperate in their best interests.

Forgotten holidays

This is where your effort to communicate effectively really pays off. Go through the calendar together and make sure you've included all the holidays that are important to both you and your children and add them to your holiday schedule. Do your best to coordinate your efforts. Holidays that you may not see as important may be very important to your children or to your co-parent.

Here are some days that are often left off the holiday schedule:

- **Halloween:** Most children will tell you that Halloween is one of their favorite nights, but parents continually omit this day from their parenting schedule, thinking it's no big deal. It is for your kids. Trick-or-treat is a favorite kid pastime, and uncertainty and last-minute arguments about where the kids will collect their candy and treats are certain to color your children's memories of a favorite day, not to mention remind them of how poorly their parents get along. Whether you alternate Halloween with your kids and co-parent, make sure you keep your animosity under wraps and allow your children to happily celebrate the day.
- **Children's birthdays and parents' birthdays:** Birthday milestones are often overlooked when designing a parenting plan, and this can cause big arguments. Remember to designate the day to one parent or the other and come to an agreement prior to the date for how your child's birthday will be celebrated. As

time moves on and co-parents become more cordial with one another, both might attend their children's milestone celebrations and include extended family from both sides. But that's not always the case, and forgetting to designate where your child will spend their birthday can cause serious disagreements between family members. Also, if celebrating your birthday with the kids is important to you, remember to add that day to the parenting plan as well.

Religious holidays

Religious holidays like Christmas, Hanukkah, and Easter are often designated in the parenting plan. Still, other religious holidays like Passover, Rosh Hashanah, Yom Kippur, and Hanukkah (Judaism), Ramadan and Eid al-Fitr (Islam), Diwali (Hinduism, Sikhism, and Jainism), and Vesak (Buddhism) are not. These holidays vary in their observances and dates and are often tied to lunar or solar calendars. That means the dates and the days of the week the holiday is observed may change from year to year.

If you observe a particular faith and it's important to you that your child also observes a holiday, make sure the days you feel are important are included in your child's parenting plan.

Secular holidays

Some important holidays aren't religious in nature but hold a particular significance to your family. These are called *secular holidays*, and if it's not designated with whom the child will spend their time, it's sure to cause confusion every time the holiday rolls around. The kids may also be off from school for these; if parents must work, special day care arrangements are necessary. That's why secular holidays are important days to consider adding to your parenting plan.

Following are some secular holidays to consider:

- New Year's Day (January 1)
- Valentine's Day (February 14)
- Mother's Day (mid-May) and Father's Day (mid-June)
- Juneteenth (June 19)
- Independence Day (July 4)
- Veterans Day (November 11)
- Thanksgiving Day (Fourth Thursday in November)

MOTHER'S DAY AND FATHER'S DAY

It's a standard procedure when designing a parenting plan to assign Mother's Day to Mom and Father's Day to Dad. When these days are forgotten, you may find the children spending Mother's Day with Dad and vice versa. This is bound to cause great dissension among the ranks!

Something else to consider is same-sex parents. Special arrangements must be made if both co-parents wish to celebrate Mother's Day and Father's Day with their child(ren).

When Marcy and Nikki broke up, they shared their time equally with their kids, the parents of Nathan and Lilly, and shared their time equally after the split. It was a cordial breakup, and although Marcy and Nikki did not celebrate all the holidays together, they did once celebrate Mother's Day jointly. Once Nikki met Louisa, and she moved in two years later, Nikki no longer wanted to celebrate Mother's Day with Marcy.

- Split the day.
  - Alternate Mother's Day each year.
  - Just as Christmas Day and Christmas Eve are often alternated, regard the Saturday prior to Mother's Day as Mother's Day Eve, and assign that day to one parent, and actual Mother's Day to the other.
  - Assign a completely different day each year for the other parent, like the second Sunday in whatever month they choose.

One solution would be to call it "Mother's Day Weekend" and alternate both the Saturday prior to Mother's Day as well as Mother's Day between the co-parents. So, the parenting plan could contain, "The children shall spend the Saturday prior to Mother's Day, 9 a.m. to the following Sunday at 9 a.m., with one parent on even years, and the other parent in odd years. The children shall spend Mother's Day at 9 a.m. Monday to school with one parent in even years, and the other parent in odd years."

Monday holidays

In a parenting plan, weekends are often designated as "Friday after school at 6 p.m. to the following Sunday at 6 p.m." When a holiday consistently falls on a Monday, it's common practice to attach the Monday to the previous weekend. It's therefore written in the parenting plan as, "Friday after school at 6 p.m. to the following Monday at 6 p.m.," thereby giving the parent who's assigned that weekend an extra day to spend with the children.

Monday holidays may also be alternated, say Memorial Day to one parent, Labor Day to the other, and then reversed the next year.

Here are the Monday holidays in the US:

- Martin Luther King Jr. Day (Third Monday in January)
- Presidents' Day (Third Monday in February)
- Memorial Day (Last Monday in May)
- Labor Day (First Monday in September)

Streamlining Exchanges

Exchanges are about the only time a child sees their parents together after a breakup. If those exchanges are stressful, their parents fight, or they bring their new significant other to antagonize their co-parent, a child will dread the exchange.

WARNING

Don't discuss anything that might erupt into a disagreement at an exchange. Exchanges aren't the time to discuss child support or why you didn't text back.

Keep exchanges free of stress so that the children look forward to going. The conversation at an exchange should be simple. Perhaps both parents cordially greet each other and then add something like, "Say hi (or goodbye) to Mommy! I love you, Mommy!" And then, "Have a great time! See you soon!"

Here's a common problem:

> Noah was 6. His parents were managing their breakup fairly well until Mom began bringing her new boyfriend, Johnny, to exchanges. Dad became sarcastic and irritable. At one exchange, the conflict escalated, the police were called, and Dad was nearly arrested in front of Noah. He was shaken, weepy all weekend, and when it was time to return to his mother, he pleaded to stay. "I don't want to go to Mommy's!" When asked why, he said only, "Johnny!"
>
> Dad assumed Johnny was abusing Noah and angrily accused Mom. She dismissed the claim, and another argument followed with Noah listening. Soon, both parents were in my office, each insisting Noah didn't want to go to the other home and each seeking more custody.

The issue wasn't preference or abuse. Noah was afraid of the exchanges. At six, he couldn't say, "Please stop fighting." All he could say was "Johnny," because that's who Dad argued with. It wasn't Johnny the person, it was Johnny the situation. The conflict frightened him, and asking to stay put was the only way he knew how to cope.

REMEMBER

You and your co-parent are your children's protectors. When kids are young, they can't tell you why they're hurt or exactly why they're frightened. You must read between the lines and do everything in your power to keep conflict to a minimum. That means that before you jump to conclusions or blame the other parent for wrongdoing, consult with them with your child's best interests in mind. Ask questions and listen to their responses, compare notes, and together make the necessary changes to keep your children safe.

Finally, accept that parenting plans can be adjusted as a child gets older or at any time if the plan simply isn't a good fit anymore. Each child is an individual with likes and dislikes and different temperaments to consider when designing a parenting plan that works for your family. Some kids roll with the punches and have no trouble going back and forth between their parents' homes. Other kids prefer to have a home base and sleep primarily in one bed.

REMEMBER

Try not to take it personally if your child tells you they prefer to sleep at Mom's or Dad's house, especially if things have changed dramatically after you decided to split. Your child isn't saying, "I like my other parent better than you." Your child is telling you, "I hate that you broke up. I like my bed. I like my stuff."

Addressing Separation Anxiety in Children

Separation anxiety is a normal stage of child development. It's observed in a child as early as 6 months but up to 2 years old, and sometimes even later. Simply explained, *separation anxiety* happens when your child becomes stressed when separated from a parent or caregiver. They don't understand that their loved one will eventually return and, as a result, they become fearful, act needier than usual, and cry when you or a trusted caregiver leaves the room.

At ages from 6 months to 2 years, this behavior is normal, and most children outgrow it when they realize the loved one that they depend on will return. But coping with separation anxiety may be challenging for estranged parents who no longer live together and don't agree on how to soothe their child when they become distressed during exchanges.

Helping your child understand separation

Ongoing conflict between parents can cause a child who seemed to be adjusting well to separation from the caregivers before the breakup to regress. Things to watch for are issues with potty training in a child who has been dry for months or years or who has trouble sleeping through the night.

Here are some ideas for coping with this new or regressed behavior:

- **Carefully explaining timeframes:** You may find yourself having to repeat explanations or develop creative ways to re-explain the same concepts you thought your children already understood. Concepts like time or days of the week are difficult concepts for preschoolers and youngsters to understand. When you say, "Don't worry. We'll see each other in a couple of days," make sure that they understand what "a couple of days" means.
- **Involving your child in documenting separations:** You may want to try things like purchasing a calendar and together crossing out the days you'll be gone. This practice is an easy way to relieve their anxiety about separating from you. And when done positively, it helps them to understand that time away from you isn't bad. Encourage them to enjoy their time with their other parent.

Approaching separation anxiety as a disorder

Although the behaviors associated with separation anxiety generally decline as the child gets older, in some cases, anxiety increases, advancing to a diagnosis of *separation anxiety disorder* (SAD) that requires intervention. SAD is marked by excessive crying or tantrums in toddlers. Older children may refuse to go to school, have nightmares, experience stomachaches, and be overly worried about the safety of their loved ones. Their anxiety significantly interferes with their daily lives, including social interactions, school attendance, and sleep.

Separation anxiety usually decreases as children develop and learn that separations are temporary. This isn't the case if your child is diagnosed with SAD. SAD can also be influenced by biological factors (like inherited tendencies toward anxiety), environmental factors (such as traumatic events or learned behavior from family members), and your child's attachment style.

REMEMBER

Breakups can contribute to but may not be the sole cause of SAD. It's easy for the guilt that parents harbor over the breakup to make them overly vigilant and prone to jumping to conclusions. Don't diagnose your own child. If the symptoms become extreme, seek professional help.

Understanding attachment styles

British child psychiatrist John Bowlby developed early childhood attachment theory. As Bowlby studied human behavior, he noticed that children became upset when separated from their parents, especially if a stranger was present or they were in unfamiliar surroundings, an important component to consider when developing a parenting plan for children after a parental breakup. Bowlby's observations helped him develop what's now referred to as childhood attachment theory. He wrote a pioneering series of books titled *Attachment and Loss*, published in 1969, 1973, and 1980.

Other psychological researchers have expanded Bowlby's theory over the years, but summarized, there are four primary attachment styles. Summarized, they're secure, avoidant, anxious, and disorganized. These styles develop in response to how a child is influenced by the individuals who surround them early in their development. The relationships they form later in life are based on those early interactions.

- **Secure attachment:** Represented by the ability to trust, find comfort in close contact, and the ability to seek support from a primary caregiver when needed. Those who are identified as having a secure attachment style have a positive view of themselves and others and have steady and fulfilling relationships.
- **Avoidant attachment:** Depicted as being emotionally distant, having discomfort with intimacy, and experiencing a tendency to quell emotions. Those with an avoidant attachment style often downplay the importance of forming long-lasting relationships.
- **Anxious attachment:** Portrayed by anxiety concerning abandonment, a desire for constant reassurance, and the potential for clinginess. Individuals with this attachment style may be needy, jealous, or overly dependent on their partners.
- **Disorganized attachment:** Frequently associated with trauma or inconsistent caregiving, leading to a paradox in behavior, combining the desire for intimacy with the fear of being close and the fear of abandonment. Individuals with this style may have difficulty trusting others and may exhibit inconsistent or unpredictable behavior in relationships.

You can see how a secure bond formed early in life can positively affect long-term mental health and the resilience of children. This is why it's so important for co-parents to learn to interact collaboratively and to keep conflict to a minimum. A positive and secure attachment makes all the difference to your child having positive outcomes later.

Coping with the whole family's anxiety

Here's a real distress call from a family dealing with separation anxiety.

> My co-parent and I parted ways about a year ago. I know that studies have shown that children adjust better to a breakup when both parents stay involved, but I watch my kids, and they are not doing well.
>
> About a day before it's time to go to the other home, each one of them gets weird in a different way. My youngest gets weepy and clings to me for dear life, my kindergartener gets whiny and will only drink chocolate milk, and my 8-year-old hardly speaks.
>
> Is this what separation anxiety looks like? I feel like crying myself. We all need help!

By stating "We all need help," I'm thinking that means both parents and children. Breaking up isn't easy for anyone, and your whole family is going through it and doing their best to cope.

The behaviors described in this real-life scenario do ring true for separation anxiety, but they're not exclusive to children whose parents have broken up. Any change takes adjustments. Even children who live with both parents in the same home may get nervous anticipating their first day of school or going away to camp for the summer. Both situations separate them from their parents and take time to get used to. How you prepare yourself and how you prepare your children for the changes will make the difference.

Proactively dealing with separation anxiety

Parents often believe they're the preferred parent when they hear that their children don't want to return to the other parent's home. They secretly think, "Obviously, he likes me best." Or "He likes it here best because he doesn't want to go back." But that may not be the case. There are lots of reasons why your child may not want to return, from not wanting to be in the middle of battling parents to not wanting to leave their new puppy.

WARNING

Don't pride yourself on being "the preferred parent." And don't try to appease your child by saying things like, "Don't worry. You'll be home soon." That sort of comment undermines your child's time with their other parent by implying that they're only at home when they're with you. That can increase your child's anxiety about being away rather than calm them. Remember, your child now has two homes. One isn't "better" or more real than the other.

Use the ideas in this list to help the whole family deal with separation in a positive way:

- **Practice brief separations.** You can start out with short visits and gradually increase the time spent apart.
- **Create positive goodbye rituals:**
  - Try giggling and kissing a toddler on each cheek.
  - Offer a wink and a secret handshake for older children.
  - Use a parting phrase on which the children can depend, like "Love you!" (initiated by parent or child), followed by "Love you more!" (from the other).
- **Support your child's time with their other parent.** Your children need time with both of you to be well-adjusted and feel secure.
- **Allow your child to take a comfort object with them when they go between your homes.** A comfort object is something that offers a child a sense of security during times of stress or change.

REMEMBER

Comfort objects can be anything that makes a child feel safe — from stuffed animals and blankets to specific items with unique textures, smells, or sounds. A comfort object helps children regulate their emotions by feeling more grounded when grasping the object, especially when transitioning between different situations or environments.

- **Be consistent with custody exchanges and circumstances.** Stick to routines and keep your promises. Subscribe to the adage, "Do what you say, say what you mean." Your kids must be able to depend on you.
- **Be kind to your co-parent in front of your children, particularly at exchanges.** Don't argue, snipe, or discuss anything that may erupt into an argument.

Making an Honest Assessment of Your Current Parenting Plan

Often, after a breakup, parents are so concerned with their own adjustment that they miss the clues their children are sending. The answer to a problem may be right in front of your nose, but it's not the answer you want to consider, so you ignore it. The following story explains this firsthand.

Leo and Sarah have been divorced for a year. Their daughter, Sami, seemed to be adjusting well, so they decided to slowly add additional time with Dad with the ultimate goal of reaching a 2-2-5-5 equally shared parenting plan. All seemed fine at first, but out of the blue, Sami started to struggle with sleeping through the night. Because they'd made what they felt was just a small change — a Wednesday night was added every other week to Sami's time with Dad — Leo and Sarah had trouble zeroing in on what the problem was. Both parents dismissed that "such a small change" could cause sleep problems.

Two days a month may not be a problem for an adult, but for a child attempting to adjust to their parents' breakup, even a small change to an already established parenting plan can affect their ability to comfortably settle in. Dad wouldn't even entertain returning to the previous schedule. This was now "his time," and he wasn't going to budge.

Understanding "time"

Every parent I've ever met wants more time with their children. And a breakup just adds to the anxiety parents feel about their contribution to uprooting their children's lives. Therefore, jealousy over "time" becomes a bone of contention.

REMEMBER

However, parents must remember to keep *time* in the proper perspective. It's not *your time* with your children vs your co-parent's time with the children. It's your *children's time* with you. Your child now struggles to share their one life with two parents. *Their* life is now split in half, not yours. Consider that when arguing about "time," and do what you can to prevent your child from feeling as if they're being pulled in two directions.

Examining how your children are adjusting

Here's a checklist to help you assess how your children are adjusting to the changes in their lives after your breakup:

- Is my child sleeping well? (Sleep disruptions are an indicator that something is wrong.)
- Is my child eating well? (A change in appetite is an indicator that something is wrong. This could be either eating too much or eating too little.)
- Is my child moody?
- Do they seem to be down, or are they sleeping all the time?
- Are they anxious, snappy, uneasy?

- Have they stopped enjoying things they used to enjoy?
- Does my child invite friends over? (Wishing to share their environment is an indicator that they're readjusting.)

All these things are symptoms of depression or anxiety, particularly in teens. In younger children, depression and anxiety look like uncharacteristic clinginess, whining, sleeping problems, headaches, or stomach aches.

If the answer to any of the questions in the previous list is yes, it's time to do three things:

- **Do some soul searching.** Ask yourself, "Is this the right parenting plan for my child?" If it's not, make the change. Your child needs you to be their advocate. Don't make them live with a parenting plan that works for you but not for them.

  Would you like the parenting plan you're expecting your child to live with? If not, consult your co-parent and make the appropriate changes, realizing that it's not about which of you has more time; it's about *what we can do to make this lifestyle more comfortable for our children.*
- **Reach out to a professional for help.** It may be time for therapy. Parents, trying to be conscientious after a breakup, often put their children in therapy immediately after the split. But sometimes people need some time for the dust to settle before therapy is helpful.
- **Do your best to create an environment where your children feel comfortable telling you how they feel.** Don't deny their feelings when they confide in you, even if you disagree with their observations. Listen and look for solutions together. Most of all, try not to take their objections personally — and remember to share your insights with your co-parent. Both parents must be advocates for positive change in the best interests of their children.

IN THIS CHAPTER

» Understanding the purpose of child and spousal support

» Determining how both child support and spousal support are paid

» Managing negative emotions

Chapter 8
Child and Spousal Support

When couples separate, finances often become the emotional lightning rod for all the anger, disappointment, and fear left over from the fractured relationship. Even couples who were amicable during the breakup can find themselves in heated debates when the subject of money arises.

That's because money, especially after separation, isn't just about numbers. It's about fairness, control, and trust. When you mix those with heartache, you have a recipe for conflict.

Yet the purpose of support, both child and spousal, isn't to punish or reward either parent. It's to stabilize both homes so the children can feel safe, secure, and loved. Support allows parents to maintain a predictable lifestyle for the children and ensures that both adults can rebuild after a separation without one falling behind.

Who pays what depends on a variety of factors: each parent's income, time spent with the children, work history, and living expenses. Courts aim to level the playing field so that both homes can meet the children's needs. In collaborative co-parenting, parents discuss these realities together, agree on a fair plan, and approach money not as "mine versus yours" but as "ours for the children." This is a difficult concept for estranged co-parents to grasp. Few accept it as reality immediately after a breakup and spend precious time agonizing about having to pay, not equating that the cash is for the children's benefit.

In this chapter, I discuss why spousal support and child support are paid, who pays them and why, and what to do if payments are delinquent. I offer suggestions about the necessary mindset to both give and receive support. Finally, I remind you to approach all disagreements with C.A.R.E.

The Purpose of Child Support

Child support exists for one simple, powerful reason: to make sure that children continue to have their needs met in both homes. It's not optional. It's not a favor. It's a legal and moral obligation designed to protect the children from the financial fallout of divorce or separation.

Too often, parents think of child support as a reflection of the relationship between the adults: "He doesn't deserve my money," or "she's taking advantage of me." But the money has nothing to do with either parent. It's set aside for the children. It's their roof, their shoes, their meals, their lights and water, and their sense of stability.

REMEMBER

Parents should do their best to keep their children from experiencing a sharp contrast between one home that feels stable and another that feels "less than." Financial support smooths those differences and allows children to move between homes without anxiety or embarrassment.

How's child support calculated?

Child support isn't just an arbitrary monetary amount calculated by an angry ex-spouse. It's based on state guidelines, which usually consider each parent's income, the custody schedule, and any special expenses such as health insurance and childcare. A computer program, which varies per state, calculates an amount by considering all these factors. These formulas may feel cold and impersonal, but they provide structure and consistency.

In a collaborative setting, parents often supplement the formula with common sense. If one parent earns significantly more, they might agree to cover extracurricular activities or medical costs even if the formula doesn't require it. Or if one parent has a more flexible schedule, they might contribute extra time in place of financial support during transitions.

Here's an example:

> Both John and Lucy were teachers, but John taught at a university, and Lucy taught second grade. Their salaries were vastly different. When John decided to move closer to the university, it added an hour to the commute to pick up the children. He ended up doing all the driving, and it took a toll on his back. It also affected how much time he could spend with the children. So he proposed a compromise. He asked Lucy to meet him halfway in the commute and offered to pay for a tank of gas a week. Lucy wasn't obligated. John had made the move, and the court found him responsible for all the transportation, but their personal negotiation helped them both: John received the extra help, and Lucy was grateful for the gas money.

Who's obligated to pay?

Both parents are obliged to support their children financially. That's true whether the children live primarily with one parent or divide their time equally.

This responsibility doesn't end when the relationship does. Supporting your children financially is part of continuing to love them after the breakup.

When does the court get involved?

If parents can't agree on a reasonable plan, the court steps in. Judges rely on financial disclosures and state formulas to determine an appropriate payment. But every family is unique, and no formula can capture the nuances of shared parenting.

That's why parents who can collaborate often have better results than those who let the court decide. The court's order will likely be fair on paper, but it may not reflect the emotional reality of your family.

> Samantha and Almanzo couldn't initially agree on support. Samatha feared Almanzo would underpay; Almanzo worried that Samatha would misuse the funds. After months of court hearings, they ended up with a strict order that left both feeling unheard. Eventually, with the help of a mediator, they learned to communicate directly. They created a shared spreadsheet, agreed to review expenses quarterly, and used direct deposit so payments were automatic. Their relationship improved dramatically once they took the power back from the courtroom.

What are the consequences for nonpayment?

Child support payments can be made directly or through a state enforcement agency. Using the official system to protect both parents, there's a clear record with less opportunity for conflict.

When a parent falls behind, consequences can be severe: wage garnishment, suspension of licenses, tax refund interception, and even jail time. But those legal repercussions pale compared to the emotional damage that befalls the children when they hear the stories about unpaid support.

Imagine a child overhearing, "Your mom still hasn't sent the money," or "Your dad says he can't afford to help this month." Those statements shift adult burdens to a child's shoulders. Children internalize the guilt, believing they're somehow the cause of the problem. "If I weren't around, Dad would have more money . . ."

REMEMBER

When support is treated as a parenting responsibility rather than a bargaining chip, children are spared the emotional confusion.

The Purpose of Spousal Support

Spousal support, also known as *alimony*, is designed to create fairness during the financial transition after separation. It's not meant to punish the higher-earning spouse or to reward the other. It's a tool to ensure that both parties have the resources to reestablish stability once they no longer live together.

For example, if one spouse stayed home to raise children or supported the other through graduate school, the law recognizes that this contribution has economic value. Spousal support can bridge the gap while the stay-at-home parent reenters the workforce or completes their education.

What is the basis on which spousal support is paid?

Courts determine spousal support based on several factors:

- Length of the marriage
- Each person's income and future earning capacity

- Age and health of both spouses
- Contributions to the marriage, both financial and domestic
- Standard of living during the marriage

Support can be temporary or long-term, depending on the circumstances.

Who is obligated to pay?

Once ordered or agreed upon, spousal support is a legal obligation. Nonpayment can result in enforcement actions just like child support. However, cooperative co-parents often manage payment directly and flexibly, understanding that the goal is independence, not dependency.

When approached with maturity, spousal support becomes part of the closure process, helping both parents transition from "us" to "me" without bitterness.

When does the court get involved?

While child support is formulaic, spousal support is more discretionary. Courts may step in when spouses can't agree on terms, but mediation or collaborative negotiation is almost always a better route to take.

Couples who determine their own plan, deciding an amount and conditions for termination, typically comply more consistently because they created the agreement together. Don't be afraid to ask for the help of an attorney to mediate your agreement. An attorney can advance the negotiation and then file the agreement with the court, eliminating a costly battle in court when parents don't agree.

What are the consequences for nonpayment?

Spousal support can be paid directly or through wage withholding. Failing to pay can lead to liens, contempt of court, or damage to credit, but the emotional cost is even higher. Continued conflict over support keeps both parties tied to the past.

The most successful co-parents view compliance as a matter of character. When your children see you honor your commitments, even to someone with whom they know you're in conflict, they learn integrity, respect, and self-control.

REMEMBER

EACH STATE IS DIFFERENT

Each state has its own rules and formulas for determining support. Some use strict guidelines; others rely on judicial discretion. For example, California bases child support on income and time share, while other states factor in education costs or health care more heavily.

Every court has a child support office that can answer questions and help you formulate a plan. What remains constant is the focus on the child's best interest. No matter where you live, courts expect parents to contribute according to their means and to prioritize stability for the children.

If you move to another state, be sure to update your order and verify enforcement policies. A family law professional can help ensure compliance across jurisdictions.

Dealing with the Bad Stuff: Resentment, Anger, and Nonpayment

Money often symbolizes power, and losing control over it can fuel resentment. The key to moving forward is transparency and mutual accountability. Share information, agree on boundaries, and review your plan regularly.

Always be mindful of who the support is for. Take this example:

> Louis struggled each month after making his child support payments. He resented sending money to his child's mother, convinced she was using it for herself. After one particularly frustrated call, I spoke with him privately.
>
> "What do you picture when you send the money?" I asked.
>
> "Her smirking," he said. "Like she's got me over a barrel."
>
> I asked how she used her car, the one he believed his payments funded.
>
> "To work, to pick up the kids, soccer, gymnastics," he admitted.
>
> That was the shift.
>
> "Then when you send the money, picture your kids, not her," I told him. "See them at practice. Remember who it's for."
>
> He tried it. Later, he called back.

"It helped. I'm not over it, but it didn't ruin my day."

Focusing on his children, not his ex, changed everything.

REMEMBER

If you're paying support, remember that your contribution helps your children directly. If you're receiving it, respect that it's difficult for the other person as well. Simple appreciation and acknowledgment can go a long way.

Managing anger

Anger is natural after separation, especially when finances are involved. But when anger guides financial decisions, it poisons your ability to successfully co-parent. Using money as a weapon, refusing to pay, overspending, or controlling through finances harms the children most of all.

When anger flares, pause, reflect, and use C.A.R.E. to cope:

- **Communicate** calmly about what's needed.
- **Accept** what the law requires and what you can't control.
- **Respect** each other's roles. Your co-parent isn't your enemy.
- **Empathize** with each other's position and your child, who is desperate for their parents to coexist calmly and wants their parents to get along.

TIP

Reach out for help. Discuss it. It's not about you. It's about your children. Your willingness to communicate can turn a crisis into an opportunity to model collaborative problem-solving for your kids.

Addressing nonpayment

The term *deadbeat* is thrown around frequently when a parent fails to pay child support, but it's extremely derogatory and oversimplifies the issue. Some parents refuse to pay out of spite, while others can't pay due to unemployment, illness, or financial collapse. Both situations demand accountability, patience, and empathy.

Here are some simple bits of advice to deal with what can be a difficult situation:

- **If you're owed support, enforce the order through the legal system, not through your children.** Don't make the kids carry the emotional weight of the badmouthing and poor communication.

» **If you're behind, face it head-on.** Contact your co-parent, make partial payments, and show effort. Work together. Courts are far more lenient with parents who demonstrate good faith.

REMEMBER

Spousal and child support aren't punishments or prizes; they're the framework that allows families to rebuild after divorce or separation. They ensure that children feel secure and that both parents can move forward with dignity.

Handled with C.A.R.E. (communication, acceptance, respect, and empathy), financial support becomes less about transactions and more about transformation. When parents fulfill their responsibilities with grace and honesty, they not only protect their children's future; they model integrity that helps their children grow into compassionate adults.

In the end, that's what collaborative co-parenting is all about: turning what could be a battlefield into a bridge with one honest conversation, one payment, one act of respect at a time — for the children.

IN THIS CHAPTER

» Choosing to see your co-parent as a teammate

» Coordinating parallel intentions

» The steps to becoming a team

» Overcoming the two-against-one dynamic

» Rebalancing the team

Chapter 9 Forming Your Co-Parenting Team

When two adults bring a child into the world, they create a lifelong coalition, and the quality of that coalition shapes their child's emotional landscape. A child doesn't care who left whom, who was right, or who has the strongest legal argument. They care about feeling loved and supported and living each day with predictability and freedom from their parents' emotional crossfire.

Teamwork is the antidote to that conflict. It lowers tension for all concerned and protects the child from loyalty binds. It also restores order to a system that might otherwise feel erratic and unpredictable. But teamwork is different from friendship. It's not dependent on forgiveness, reconciliation, or even emotional closeness. It's a professional-grade partnership that requires maturity, clarity, boundaries, and the willingness to put the child's needs above adult emotion.

Children read the emotional temperature of the adults around them, particularly if those adults are their parents. When that temperature is scorching with resentment or icy with avoidance, children internalize the tension. They may become anxious, withdrawn, or feel overly responsible for managing adult feelings. But when the temperature is warm, consistent, and predictable, when the parents behave like a team, children relax into their lives again. They feel safe moving between homes, expressing their feelings, and developing relationships with new people who may enter the family system.

In this chapter, I encourage you to evaluate your mindset, switching your thinking from an autonomous ex to a collaborative co-parent. I explore parallel intentions, which refer to co-parents having the same goals for their child but achieving those goals in diverse ways, and how those parallel intentions can be better aligned. Finally, I look at how to become a co-parenting team, how adding a partner can create the two-against-one dynamic, and how to get back on track.

Developing the Team Mindset

Co-parenting teams aren't born. They're built. They're formed through deliberate choices: choosing patience over pride, solutions over blame, bridges over walls. Some days the bridge wobbles, and other days it feels unbreakable. What matters is that you keep the bridge open and available to cross at any time you want.

Becoming a co-parenting team doesn't begin with shared schedules or perfect communication. It begins with an internal shift. You must decide inwardly and deliberately that you'll show up as a partner in raising your children, not as an advisory to your ex or someone so wounded they can't put their children first. That commitment is the foundation on which every step rests. When you choose to approach co-parenting with clarity, integrity, and purpose, your behavior starts to reflect that decision, your tone becomes steadier, your expectations become clearer, and your interactions become more focused on your child than on your past. From that internal commitment, the outward work of building a team, creating structure, defining how you'll communicate, identifying shared intentions, and coordinating your efforts becomes possible.

Here's an example of someone coming to realize the importance of the team mindset:

> "I just wanted to let you know that we are going to Disneyland this weekend." I thought it was the right thing to do to give my daughter's father a heads-up since we would be 400 miles away.
>
> "But it's my weekend," he said. "I was looking forward to seeing her."
>
> My heart sank into my stomach. I hadn't checked with him. I hadn't even mentioned it, and we had been planning it for weeks. I was so wrapped up in my own life of work, blending families, children, and coordinating efforts with my husband's ex-wife, I forgot the other side: my own daughter's father.

And now I was bulldozing him, notifying him at the last minute that he wouldn't be seeing his only child. To his credit, he didn't lose his temper because he could see that I was truly embarrassed by my own insensitivity, but he had the right to.

"Geezus," I said, "What can I do? I've made a horrible mistake. I can't tell her she can't go."

"No, you can't," he said sadly. "And I wouldn't do that to her."

I should have called him. I should have asked, not told him. I should have planned the trip around our daughter's time with him. I was simply overwhelmed by all my other responsibilities and should have reached out for help, but after years of not getting along and avoiding talking to each other, he was the last person I thought of. He should have been the first.

REMEMBER

The most successful co-parents understand that teamwork isn't about erasing the past. It's about designing a future where your child feels whole, secure, and loved in both homes. Every respectful exchange, every calm conversation, every moment of grace strengthens your co-parenting relationship. The team stays intact, the child stays centered, and the family, however reorganized, remains strong.

Parallel intentions: A bridge from rivalry to teamwork

When co-parents conflict, they often focus so intently on their differences that they miss one of the most stabilizing truths of post-separation parenting: Most estranged co-parents have parallel intentions. *Parallel intentions* are the underlying goals that run side by side beneath the surface disagreement. They're not identical strategies, and they don't require identical personalities or parenting styles. They simply reflect that both parents have the same goal but have different ways to get there. Those differences prevent them from seeing that they actually agree.

In mediation, parallel intentions show up everywhere. One parent may insist on strict routines because they believe structure creates emotional safety. The other may resist rigidity because they want the child to feel relaxed and understood. On the surface, these intentions look contradictory — routine versus flexibility — but when you look more closely, both parents are trying to promote the same outcome: a secure and emotionally healthy child. When parents realize that the argument isn't "my way versus your way" but rather "two approaches aimed at the same emotional goal," tension drops and cooperation becomes possible.

REMEMBER

Parallel intentions are powerful because they transform the narrative. Instead of assuming the other parent is undermining you, you start to see that they're moving toward the same horizon, just along a different path. This reframing doesn't erase the need for communication or compromise. But it restores dignity to both parents and redirects the focus to the child. Teams form when parents recognize that shared intention is more important than identical methods.

The work, then, isn't to force uniformity but to uncover the intentions that run beneath the conflict. Once those intentions are visible, parents can generate solutions that honor both perspectives while centering on the child's needs. Discovering your parallel intentions is the moment when rivalry softens, empathy returns, and genuine collaboration becomes possible. Consider this example:

> Lena and Katherine share custody of their teenage son, Marcus. Katherine is punctual to a fault; Lena is creative and spontaneous and often runs late.
>
> Their arguments over time and schedules were legendary. Marcus once said, "I hate Mondays. They're the day you two fight about Fridays."
>
> During a co-parenting session, I asked the parents to list what they each valued most. Both wrote the same words: Marcus's happiness and confidence. Once they realized they wanted the same outcome, or better explained, had parallel intentions, they began using short weekly texts to confirm schedules instead of emotional phone calls. The change was simple but powerful.
>
> Marcus later noted that he saw a difference in his parents, saying, "You two finally act like my coaches instead of rival teams."
>
> Lena and Katherine didn't become best friends, but they became reliable teammates.

TIP

Here are 12 questions co-parents can ask each other to discover their parallel intentions:

1. **What am I truly trying to accomplish for my child in this situation?**

   This question strips away the argument and forces clarity about the underlying goal. Is our intention the same?

2. **Why does this matter to me? What personal experience, fear, or memory is driving my approach?**

   Parallel intentions often hide beneath unresolved history.

3. **What might my co-parent be afraid of in this situation?**

   Parents in conflict often share the same fear. They just express it differently.

4. **Which part of my approach is about protecting my child, and which part is about protecting myself?**

   Parallel intentions become clearer when parents separate self-protection from child protection.

5. **If I remove my frustration with my co-parent, what do I actually want for my child right now?**

   This question isolates the intention from the conflict.

6. **What outcome do I hope my child experiences because of the choice I'm advocating for?**

   When parents articulate the desired child outcome, intentions often match.

7. **What do I assume my co-parent is trying to accomplish? And could I be wrong?**

   Answering these questions opens the door to empathy and reduces defensiveness.

8. **If my co-parent and I had the same intention, how would that change the way I interpret their behavior?**

   This question reframes the entire dynamic.

9. **What does my child need most right now? And could both our approaches be trying to meet that need in different ways?**

   This is where alignment usually becomes visible.

10. **What strengths does my co-parent bring to this moment that I might be overlooking?**

    Parallel intentions often hide in complementary skill sets.

11. **Where do our intentions intersect, even if our methods do not?**

    This is the heart of parallel intentions.

12. **Which behavior of mine would change if I honored the idea that we might want the same thing?**

    This question is where cooperation begins.

The team philosophy in action

Your team's philosophy shows up in small moments. Things like:

- A calm message sent before an exchange: "She's tired today. Practice ran late."
- A brief check-in after a dentist appointment: "No cavities! So much better than last time!"

» Allowing your child to call the other parent without tension.

» Staying flexible when unexpected circumstances disrupt the schedule.

Take baby steps first. Eventually, you'll learn to run.

Taking the Steps to Becoming a Co-Parenting Team

Successful co-parenting requires a self-imposed transformation that starts with a positive intention and grows through consistent, respectful action. Each step you take toward teamwork, no matter how small, creates stability for your children and rebuilds a sense of order after the upheaval of separation. The following eight steps outline how two parents can move from conflict to collaboration, forming a true partnership centered on their children's best interests.

1. Define your mission: "The children come first"

A co-parenting team needs a unified mission statement. Agree that every decision, schedule modification, and disagreement will be filtered through one question: "Does this benefit the children?"

When tension rises, the mission resets the tone and shortens arguments. It also separates preference from priority. What a parent prefers is second to what the children need. Revisit this mission after big events (moves, school changes, new partners) to keep both paddles rowing in the same direction.

2. Identify your niche

Each parent has strengths. Maybe one is the homework helper, and the other manages sports and appointments. Define who does what so you can stop duplicating efforts or stepping on toes.

3. Choose how you'll communicate

Some co-parents do best with text messages or a co-parenting app that keeps conversations focused on the child. Others can handle short phone calls. Whatever method you pick, keep it businesslike: brief, respectful, factual. Remember the "business-meeting" tone discussed in earlier chapters; it keeps emotion from hijacking the message.

This reduces ambiguity and minimizes emotional spikes.

4. Rebuild trust

Trust doesn't return just because it should. It returns because you create a predictable pattern of truthfulness and reliability. This happens when you start from scratch: Share child-related information consistently, like school updates, medical concerns, behavioral changes, new outlines, injuries, emotional shifts, and any relevant changes in your home. Make a pact. There will be no more secrets. Do what you say you'll do.

5. Use C.A.R.E. to communicate effectively

As I've discussed throughout this book, the C.A.R.E. principles are vital:

> **Communication:** The ability to problem-solve together is the lifeline of your team. Keep communication timely, relevant, and child-focused.
>
> **Acceptance:** Two homes will differ; align where it matters and allow autonomy where it doesn't.
>
> **Respect:** Interact with dignity, even when you don't agree. Avoid sarcasm, name-calling, and scorekeeping.
>
> **Empathy:** Stay curious about how your co-parent and your children are experiencing the situation.

6. Address problems immediately

Teams make mistakes, but a strong team corrects them early. Acknowledge missteps without defensiveness ("I didn't flag the schedule change soon enough"), apologize when necessary, clarify expectations, and restabilize the plan. Children feel safer when parents repair problems quickly. Avoid blame. Focus on solutions.

7. Develop consistency across households where it matters

When we talk about consistency between homes, we're not talking about identical parenting. We're talking about consistency in results, not methods:

> **Results** are the outcomes children need to feel safe and grounded, such as getting enough sleep, completing homework, taking medication correctly, arriving at school prepared, and following basic safety rules. These are the anchors that reduce stress because the kids know what to expect, no matter which home they're in.
>
> **Methods** are the way each home achieves those outcomes. Methods can differ based on personality, culture, routines, or household rhythms. One parent might use a structured bedtime routine with reading and lights-out; the other might offer a broader bedtime window with quiet play. Both can achieve the same result — adequate sleep — even if the path looks different. Identify which outcomes (results) should stay consistent across both homes and allow each parent to use the approach (method) that fits their home best.

Examples of areas to align:

- Bedtime ranges
- School expectations
- Discipline philosophy
- Device usage
- Medication
- Health and hygiene
- Safety rules

8. Celebrate wins

Progress strengthens the team, and small successes matter. Recognize improvements, such as better transitions, calmer communication, smoother scheduling, or a child's increased comfort. Celebrating positive patterns reinforces the behaviors that keep the team functioning.

Managing the Team for the Long Run

Managing the co-parenting team over the long run requires a commitment to flexibility. Children grow, schedules evolve, and families change in ways you can't always anticipate. What works for a preschooler may fall apart by third grade; what feels fair during the early stages of separation may need adjusting when new partners, new schools, or new jobs enter the picture.

REMEMBER

Flexibility doesn't mean giving up your values or abandoning consistency; it means staying open to recalibrating the plan when your child's needs shift.

Teams that thrive long term don't lock themselves into rigid patterns. Instead, they check in periodically, evaluate what's working, revise what's not, and allow each parent the freedom to adapt their methods while protecting the shared mission. Long-term success is built on the ability to pivot without hostility, update agreements without resentment, and meet change with cooperation rather than conflict. You see these skills in action in the following example:

> When their daughter, Harper, was six, Alex and Morgan followed a strict 2-2-5-5 schedule (see Chapter 7). It fit their work hours, and she transitioned well. But by middle school, it began to fall apart. Homework stretched across days, sports ran late, and she needed more time with friends. Moving every two days left her feeling rushed.
>
> Harper told each parent she felt "rushed all the time," especially on transition nights. At first, each assumed the other needed to adjust. But when they compared notes, they realized the issue wasn't either home. It was Harper. She needed longer stretches to feel settled.
>
> They reviewed the school calendar, compared schedules, and created a new plan: week-on/week-off, with mid-week dinners to stay connected. It wasn't either parent's preference, but it fit Harper's needs, and both adjusted.
>
> Two months later, Harper said transitions felt "so much easier." The success wasn't the schedule. It was their willingness to adapt. Alex and Morgan didn't cling to what used to work. They changed it, together, as their child's needs evolved.

Creating boundaries to protect the team

Every effective team relies on clear limits or boundaries, what's acceptable, what's off limits, and what keeps communication respectful and productive.

A boundary isn't a line in the sand to control your co-parent. A boundary clarifies *your* expectations. Boundaries are guidelines that keep interactions predictable, respectful, and focused on the shared goal of raising well-adjusted children.

Here's an example.

> Two parents agree to meet at Starbucks at 6 p.m. on Fridays to exchange their six-year-old child. When it's his weekend, Dad wants to have dinner with their son, so he asks Mom not to feed him. Mom agrees. But Dad is often late, sometimes by as much as 30 minutes. Their son, hungry and tired, becomes fussy after about 10 minutes of sitting in front of a place filled with food he knows and wants.
>
> Mom sets a clear boundary: "I will never keep our child from you, but I cannot sit in front of a restaurant while he cries waiting to be fed. If you are more than 10 minutes late, I will return home. You can pick him up there."
>
> Dad never crosses that boundary again. He understood the parameters and made concessions on his end to be on time.

Extending family balance

Children thrive when their environment is predictable. The way adults greet each other, exchange updates, and handle events creates that predictability. Even a simple wave at a school event can ease a child's internal stress.

A working relationship doesn't require friendship. It requires behavior that sends the message, "You're safe to love everyone in your life."

> Sasha and Jordan shared custody of their twins. Jordan's parents were very involved, often picking the girls up from school. At first, Sasha felt pushed aside. But instead of reacting, she spoke with them directly, set clear boundaries, and expressed appreciation for their help. The tone shifted. The twins felt more at ease, no longer worried about hurting anyone's feelings.
>
> In contrast, Jessica's divorce from Miguel strained the entire family. They shared a son, Isaiah, and Jessica's father, Leo, had always been close to Miguel. After the breakup, Jessica, still bitter, forbade her father from maintaining that relationship. This disrupted a long-standing tradition: an annual camping trip with Leo, Miguel, and Isaiah.
>
> Miguel planned to take Isaiah alone, and Jessica reluctantly agreed. But on the way, they picked up Leo and told Isaiah not to tell his mother. The trip went well, but Isaiah returned home anxious. He was carrying a secret he wasn't equipped to handle.
>
> When Jessica found out, she was furious, especially with her father. But the deeper issue was the position Isaiah had been put in. Asking a child to keep adult secrets creates stress they cannot manage. Isaiah broke down, caught in the middle of a conflict that was never his to carry.

Relationships continue after a breakup, even though you may not want them to. But, more importantly, these relationships intertwine. Leo was not only Jessica's father but also Isaiah's grandfather. And, after years of being related through marriage, Leo was remarkably close to his former son-in-law, Isaiah's father.

Considering these relationships from each person's perspective helps clarify the weight of Jessica's request. There are times you must hold your position as a parent, especially when your child's safety is involved. But when personal interests drive decisions, it's time to reset. Your reference point should always be your child's best interests.

In situations like this, setting the right example means allowing each relationship to stand on its own. Jessica let her anger with Isaiah's father influence her judgment, creating an impossible situation for her child. It starts with the co-parents. When co-parents strengthen their co-parenting relationship, the other relationships fall into place, and children are free to love everyone in their lives.

Supporting your co-parent

The importance of supporting your co-parent is often underestimated, yet it can be an exceptionally powerful way to reinforce your team dynamic. Supporting doesn't mean approving of everything your co-parent does; it means acknowledging their role in your child's life. Each expression of goodwill reinforces the message that your child is free to love both parents.

When one parent thanks the other or apologizes for wrongdoing, the entire atmosphere shifts. A quick text that says "Thanks for helping with homework" or "I appreciate that you switched the weekend so I could attend the concert" costs nothing and pays huge dividends in the trust department.

At each session, I ask the co-parents I work with if they applied some of the principles that week that we discussed in the previous session. Better communication starts with baby steps.

> One mother noticed her son's baseball glove was missing during her parenting time. Instead of accusing her co-parent of being irresponsible, she sent a simple message: "Hey, I think his glove might be at your house. Please check before tomorrow's game?" She later said the question mark was intentional. "It made it sound like a request, not a demand."
>
> The father replied, "It's here. I'll drop it off on my way to work." The exchange took less than a minute, but it mattered. "We're rarely that kind to each other. This was new."

Their son noticed. He told his father he used to dread games when both parents were there because the obvious tension embarrassed him. That's when it clicked for his father. The problem wasn't just the conflict. It was how visible it had become to their child. "To be honest," the father confided. "It never registered that we were so disagreeable that we might embarrass our son. *That* is what was embarrassing."

When parents choose cooperation over conflict, children notice. They feel supported, secure, and free to enjoy just being kids instead of running defense for their parents.

Responding when children test allegiances

"Mom says I don't have to do that at her house," or "Dad doesn't make me finish my dinner before I get dessert." Children naturally test loyalties, and they'll test the team. Since we all love our children, imagining that they might play one home against the other is sometimes unfathomable. "Not my child. They'd never lie to me."

Yes, they would. They're human. Children lie to get what they want or to avoid getting into trouble. They tell Mom one thing and Dad something else to advance their cause, or they might do it because they don't have the whole story. Sometimes it's not malicious. Sometimes kids think they understand, but their parents have left holes in the explanation. It's human nature to fill in the blanks. Then the kids pass on that information, and it's wrong.

When this happens, avoid criticizing your co-parent and let your child know that you and their other parent will discuss it and get back to them. Using that approach, co-parents remain equals. One isn't the boss, and the other asks permission. Discuss the issue with your co-parent, and then let your child know, "We have discussed it, and we have decided . . ."

Here's a great example of when something like this can easily happen. In this case, Mom used a lighthearted approach to check in. It broke the ice.

> Seven-year-old Max told his mom, "Dad lets me stay up until ten!" Mom wanted to snap back, "Your father is so irresponsible!" Instead, she paused and said, "Every home is a little different. In our home, bedtime is 8:30. Sounds like Dad and I need to get on the same page." Max quickly added, "Please don't tell Dad!"
>
> After Max went to bed, Mom called Dad. "I'm hearing bedtime at your house is 10 p.m." Dad laughed. It had been a one-time movie night. Max wasn't lying, just stretching the truth.

A quick conversation prevented a blowup and showed Max that his parents communicate and make decisions together. He stopped playing one home against the other because he knew they compared notes. This is team behavior in action.

Children are also sensitive to imbalance. They sense when one parent feels outnumbered or disrespected, and they may try to correct the imbalance by siding with whoever seems emotionally vulnerable. Or they may side with the stronger team to avoid conflict. Neither is healthy.

TIP

The way to protect your child is to ensure the team structure stays solid. Neutral responses help, such as these:

- "Let's ask your dad/mom about that together."
- "I want to understand this better. Let me check in with your dad/mom."
- "You don't need to take sides, honey. We've got this."

Adding new team members

As families evolve, new adults join the child's world: new partners, bonus parents, extended family members, coaches, mentors, trusted friends, and sometimes even neighbors who become part of daily routines. These "new team members" can strengthen the child's support system, or, if not integrated carefully, create tension, confusion, or emotional overload.

TIP

Explain to children that new partners or relatives, like grandparents, for example, don't replace anyone; they simply add to the number of people who care about them. Keep introductions gradual and communication transparent. It helps to remind yourself and your co-parent that this is about inclusion, not intrusion.

A father once said, "My wife is great with my kids, but my ex won't speak to her." I suggested that he and his co-parent agree that communication about the children remain between the biological parents. Over time, as trust was rebuilt, his co-parent began to include his wife in group texts about school events. No one forced the issue; respect opened the door naturally.

The most delicate transition: Adding a new partner

Introducing a new romantic partner can be tricky and must be done with planning and patience. I know firsthand because I was the new partner. The kids easily accepted me, but their mother, not so much. That took far longer than being accepted by the kids.

Years ago, when I began my journey as a new wife and bonus mom, I found myself reading *Working Mother Magazine*. In the magazine was a column called "Family Matters." Supposedly, the column rotated each issue between a biological mom, a bonus mom, and a single mom. This article was written by a *bonus mom* (formally referred to as a *stepmom*), and the question that was posed asked how she might solve a family problem.

The advice given was, "Just make the decision and do it." I was shocked. That was so far from the correct answer that I feared it would incorrectly guide other women in that position. No conscientious bonus parent would make a blanket decision for her bonus children without consulting both biological parents first. (Unless she was empowered to do so, or one of the parents was not in the child's life. Then it would be a moot point.) A bonus parent is a diplomat, even a mediator at times. But you get my point. I called the magazine and told the editor. After a lengthy discussion, I was surprisingly hired for my first writing gig. I wrote the "Family Matters" column for *Working Mother Magazine* for five years.

The truth is that new partners often want to help. They may offer opinions, step into decision-making, or try to solve problems. While their intentions may be good, misalignment can create unnecessary conflict. And that is why all the players must be very clear about their roles and responsibilities. New partners get their direction regarding parenting from the biological parents. New partners support the parenting team; they don't disrupt it.

Your team's mission statement

It may help to create a team mission statement, something that clarifies the family's goals and how they will achieve those goals. It can be written out and signed, or, for our purposes here, it can simply be discussed between family members, so everyone is clear on their roles and responsibilities.

"As a parenting team, our goal is to raise our child(ren) in a way that is safe, stable, and supportive, allowing them to feel secure and free to love everyone in their lives."

Once the goal is clear, define the roles. What part does each adult play? What decisions belong to the co-parents? Where can a bonus parent be helpful, and where should they step back? This must be clear. Many conflicts in remarried families come not from the problem itself, but from confusion about roles and authority.

Introducing another piece to the puzzle

And that introduces yet another layer, or piece to the puzzle–when co-parent's new partners have children of their own. Now, you're not just dealing with two parents. You're coordinating efforts between two co-parenting systems, each shaped by its own agreements.

Although you may hear that things should be the same in both homes, that's difficult when you're coordinating multiple family systems. It helps to understand that the goal may not be to make every home identical. It's to decide what must be consistent for the children you share and what can be different. When decision-makers agree on those points, the stress of going back and forth is reduced. Parents are calmer, and all the children, yours, mine, and ours, can relax into the rhythm of their same, but different lives.

REMEMBER

New partners support the parenting team; they don't disrupt it. New partners get their direction regarding parenting from the biological parents.

The only time this isn't a steadfast rule is if the new partner also has children. Then, it's even more important to coordinate efforts between homes.

WARNING

There can't be different rules for the new partner's children and your children. That is sure to prompt feelings of favoritism, and the family will split into factions. Look at the dynamic: me and my kids against you and your kids. Your co-parent will most likely unite with you as well. So, then you have co-parents living in separate homes uniting with their children who live in both homes, against their new partner and their children who live in the same home as your co-parent. It's an impossible scenario.

Following are some healthy boundaries for new partners:

- They can support daily routines, but primary parenting decisions remain between the parents.
- They can comfort the child but shouldn't discipline too soon. They may be empowered to discipline when the parent isn't present, at the discretion of the parent.
- They should avoid speaking negatively about either parent.
- They should follow the established house rules and family values.

Managing Situations When the Team Doesn't Agree

Co-parenting teams often begin unevenly. One parent may be emotionally ready for teamwork while the other is still grieving or reacting to the past. But sometimes the imbalance becomes more complicated. A new partner enters the picture, and suddenly decisions feel like they're coming from "two against one," extended family aligns with one side, or your child begins echoing an opinion that doesn't sound like their own. The emotional weight of the parenting system seems to shift, and not in your favor.

This is one of the most painful and confusing experiences for parents, even those deeply committed to collaboration.

REMEMBER

But here's the foundational truth: A coparenting system isn't a democracy. It's a partnership. And partnerships aren't determined by headcount. They're determined by structure and shared intent and united by a common goal or mutual interest: the children. Ultimately, a partnership thrives on the understanding that success depends on collaboration over control.

No matter how many adults surround your co-parent — their parents, their new partner, their sister, or their brother, or even their friends who have their ear — your role as a parent is never diminished. There must be an established hierarchy, or pecking order, to keep priorities straight and the homes running smoothly. That pecking order is that Mom is mom and Dad is dad. The other players are helpers, not decision-makers.

Understanding the two-against-one dynamic

In every co-parenting system, alliances naturally form. When those alliances aren't managed thoughtfully, they can create a two-against-one dynamic that undermines trust and stability. Sometimes it's one parent and their new partner aligning against the other parent; other times, a parent may unintentionally (and sometimes intentionally) align with the child against their co-parent. Regardless of how it happens, this imbalance shifts the focus from teamwork to competition, leaving children caught in the crossfire.

Understanding and addressing this dynamic is essential to maintaining a balanced, cooperative co-parenting team. True collaboration means ensuring that neither feels ganged up on, dismissed, or excluded from the important decision.

The moment a partnership turns into a majority vote, the children lose the sense of unity they need to feel safe and secure.

This dynamic can occur for many reasons:

- A co-parent aligns tightly with a new partner out of insecurity or comfort.
- A new partner wants to help but unintentionally oversteps.
- Extended family members come on strong, offering opinions or judgments.
- The child aligns with the more permissive or more emotionally expressive household.
- One parent becomes the "identified responsible one," while the other becomes the "fun one."

None of these scenarios means the team is broken. They mean the team needs rebalancing.

Rebalancing the team

Rebalancing the team means pausing to assess what's working, what's not, and how to realign your efforts toward your shared goal: raising healthy, secure children. It's not about assigning blame. It's about fine-tuning. Schedule regular check-ins to review communication patterns, routines, and responsibilities.

Sometimes, rebalancing becomes necessary when a new partner enters the picture and takes an overzealous approach, offering unsolicited parenting advice, overstepping boundaries, or attempting to "fix" co-parenting dynamics they don't fully understand. When this happens, both parents can reaffirm their core agreement: The parenting team consists of two parents. The new partner can support the team but doesn't steer it. Calmly restating roles and expectations protects the stability of the co-parenting structure and prevents unnecessary tension.

When parents address these shifts directly and with empathy, they model healthy boundaries and demonstrate to their children that love can expand without replacing or undermining anyone's place in the family system.

"Wait a minute," a new partner asked. "Are you saying I don't have a say in my own home?"

That's an understandable question. The answer is yes *and* no.

Of course, new partners make decisions together about their own home and how it runs. However, new partners must be sensitive to the co-parenting relationship that was in place before they arrived. I always explain it like this:

REMEMBER

Think of the children as a country. The parents are the presidents of that country; the new partners are the vice presidents. The vice president may not decide policy without the authorization or direction of the president. However, once that presidential decision is made, the vice president has full authority to make decisions within those parameters.

Dealing with extended family overstepping

Family and friends may also test your allegiance. Relatives often carry residual anger from the breakup and may gossip or criticize. Set clear boundaries: "I appreciate your concern, but we're both working hard to co-parent respectfully." You may even have to backtrack because you vented negatively in the past, and they're expecting agreement. Simply explain, "I know what I've said in the past, but we saw what our behavior was doing to our child. We vowed to stop it, and we'd like you to support us in that." Every time you defend the team, you're putting your child first.

> When Tenisha noticed her ex's mother texting her children directly about school and scheduling, she felt undermined. Instead of reacting emotionally, she texted her co-parent:
>
> "I'd prefer if all scheduling information came through us. It keeps everything clear for the kids. Can you handle this on your side?"
>
> Her co-parent responded positively. The system realigned.

TIP

When there's a problem initiated by a relative on your side of the family or by your friend, it's your responsibility to make the boundaries clear to them. It's your co-parent's responsibility to do the same with their side of the family or their friend.

Making repairs after team breakdowns

Every well-oiled machine experiences a breakdown at some point. You're driving down the street, hit a bump, and the tire blows. What do you do? You repair the tire. Miscommunication, disagreements, and emotional flare-ups are just bumps in the road. They're not failures; they're invitations for repair.

A "repair conversation" starts with either of these statements:

- "I didn't handle that the way I wanted. May we talk?"
- "I think we misunderstood each other. Let's do a reset."

The key to successful problem-solving with your co-parent is preparation. Have a clear, productive way to address problems before they arise. Think about it this way: Every workplace, large or small, has a process for handling grievances. You're told how to handle a disagreement before there's ever an issue. If it's a small company, you probably go to the owner. If it's a large corporation, you're instructed to go to HR. The point here is that there is something in place prior to solving the problem.

Co-parenting is no different. Have a plan in place for when a problem arises, so you know exactly how to handle it.

If you are going to have a serious conversation with your co-parent, hopefully, it will be some form of face-to-face discussion. Video call or meeting in person, some way that you can see each other, read each other's expressions, and hear the inflections in your voices.

Conducting the meeting

Use a clear structure to keep the conversation from spinning out of control. This is the same Problem-Solving Model used in previous chapters. It works for just about every type of discussion.

1. **Identify the problem.**

   State the issue clearly and keep it focused on the child.

   "It appears Jillian has missed the bus three times this week."

2. **Suggest a child-focused solution.**

   Come prepared with at least one idea that supports a solution in the best interest of your child.

   "Jillian has to be at school by 7:20 a.m. I know you leave your house at 7. I don't go to work until 9. How do you feel about my swinging by and taking her to school in the morning when she's with you? She'll be alone for 15 minutes at the most. She's 9, she can handle it, and she'll be at school on time."

3. **Negotiate.**

   This is the most important step of problem-solving. Negotiation means finding a solution together that both can accept — guarding against an immediate, "No!" That means, if you don't agree with your co-parent's suggested solution, *make a counterproposal*. "I don't feel comfortable with her being alone even for 15 minutes. Can you come a little before 7?"

4. **Compromise.**

   A compromise is when each person gives a little to reach a solution that works. Conceding to reach a compromise is easy when it's done in the name of your child. Look for an answer that works, even if neither of you gets everything you want. "That's a little early for me, but yes, I can do that."

TIP

You can find the Four-Step Problem-Solving Model Using I Messages document at `www.dummies.com/go/coparentingfd`. You can also find this on the Bonus Families website at `www.bonusfamilies.com/4StepModel`.

Nurturing Team Trust and Transparency

Trust is the foundation of every healthy co-parenting relationship — and the hardest thing to rebuild once it's been broken. Divorce or separation often shatters the illusion of certainty, and in its place comes a fragile mix of suspicion, fear, and self-protection. But to form a true co-parenting team, trust must be redefined not as blind faith, but as consistent, transparent behavior over time.

When parents are hurt, they often expect the other to earn their trust again while forgetting that both share the responsibility to build it. You can't control whether your co-parent acts with integrity, but you can control your own transparency. The more open and predictable you are, the safer the environment becomes for both of you and, most importantly, for your children.

Starting small

When it comes to building trust, you must start small. That means you follow through on commitments and respond to texts or emails about the children promptly, even when the answer is "I'll get back to you." Let your co-parent know about doctor appointments, report cards, and upcoming events without being asked.

REMEMBER

Transparency is the antidote to suspicion; it replaces wondering with knowing.

After years of conflict, Sarah and Daniel decided to try a shared online calendar for their kids' activities. At first, they used it reluctantly — each suspecting that the other would misuse the information. But over time, they began adding more details: homework deadlines, field trips, even reminders for picture day. Within months, the small act of sharing schedules reduced misunderstandings dramatically. "I stopped assuming he was hiding things," Sarah said, "and started realizing he was actually showing up."

Transparency doesn't mean oversharing or forfeiting boundaries. It means sharing enough to keep your co-parent informed and your children protected from miscommunication. You're not reporting to each other; you're coordinating for your child's well-being.

As you rebuild trust, remember that it's not a one-time decision; it's a daily practice. Every civil text, every timely exchange, every time you resist the urge to assume the worst, you're adding another layer of stability to your child's emotional foundation. Over time, those layers become a bridge strong enough for both parents and their children to cross safely.

Parents build trust in the following ways:

- Showing up when they say they will
- Keeping exchanges calm
- Sending updates promptly
- Being consistent with rules and expectations
- Avoiding blame and accusation
- Repairing quickly when things go wrong

Taking inventory

Transparency amplifies trust. When parents share relevant information, such as school notes, mood changes, illnesses, upcoming events, and new routines, the child feels protected, and the co-parenting relationship becomes smoother.

TIP

Consider a weekly check-in to assess the team strategy and how your child is progressing. You can prepare by listing three pieces of information your co-parent would benefit from knowing this week. Try sharing one of them today in a calm, neutral message.

Adjusting When Another Breakup Occurs

Modern families evolve. Even after the initial separation, new relationships form and sometimes end. Each transition brings ripple effects for everyone involved, especially the children. How you and your co-parent navigate another breakup — yours or theirs — can either reignite old wounds or demonstrate how far you've both come.

When a new relationship ends, it's easy to retreat into old patterns: blame, defensiveness, or "See, I told you so." But your children need something different from you this time. They need stability and empathy.

REMEMBER

If your co-parent is hurting, supporting them doesn't mean you're reuniting; it means you recognize that they're human. Children learn compassion by watching how their parents treat each other, especially when it's least convenient. Take this example:

> When Liam's ex-wife, Rachel, ended a two-year relationship, their daughter was heartbroken. She'd grown close to Rachel's partner and felt confused about losing yet another adult she loved. Liam resisted the urge to gloat or withdraw. Instead, he told their daughter, "It's okay to miss him. You can talk about him anytime." He also sent Rachel a brief text: "I'm sorry you're going through this. Let me know if we should adjust schedules while things settle."

That small gesture reminded everyone — especially their daughter — that empathy still existed between her parents.

Children form emotional attachments to the people their parents date. When those relationships end, kids can feel abandoned or unsure of how to grieve. Co-parents who handle those transitions thoughtfully help children understand that love can change form without disappearing.

New partners sometimes become important figures in a child's life. When those relationships end, children may feel confused, sad, or guilty. They may wonder:

- "Did I do something wrong?"
- "Will I ever see them again?"
- "Is this my fault?"

If you're the one experiencing another breakup, understand that children don't need details; they need reassurance that stability remains. Both parents must be steady during this time. The goal is not to explain adult details, but to maintain predictability.

TIP

Helpful responses include:

- "Adults make decisions about relationships. It isn't because of anything you did."
- "You're allowed to feel sad. I'm here to talk whenever you want."
- "Our routines stay the same. You're safe."

Following are two examples of how a bonus breakup (the breakup of two people, one or both of whom had children prior to their getting together) was handled.

When 13-year-old Ava's bonus dad left abruptly, she felt abandoned. Her mom, Claire, was devastated, too, but she protected Ava from absorbing that grief. Claire kept routines stable, encouraged Ava to talk with her father about her feelings, and ensured the adults stayed united. Claire also paved a path for Ava to continue to talk to Chris, her bonus dad, if she felt the need to stay in touch. She did, and at 17, they have a loving friendship to this day.

Ava later said that the consistency between her parents and her ability to remain in contact with Chris made the loss easier to process.

In this next example, the parents made their decisions based on their wants and needs — not the child's.

When 14-year-old Austin's bonus mom, Jenny, left their home in Santa Cruz, California, she mentioned that she felt it was important to break the news to Austin together and let him know where she and his 6-year-old bonus sister could be contacted. Jenny and Austin's father were together for six years, and Austin had grown close to Jenny and her daughter, Arianna. Austin's father said, "I'll tell him, and I'll have Austin contact you."

But the call never came. Jenny thought Austin was angry, and that's why he didn't reach out. She didn't want to reach out to Austin's father; the breakup was nasty. But Austin actually blamed himself for the breakup since no one would tell him what happened.

Three years later, Austin got up the nerve to ask a neighbor where Jenny had gone. On a weekend, he was supposed to be with his mom, and with his mom's permission, he tracked Jenny down through the neighbor and traveled almost 80 miles, ending up on her front porch. Jenny had married her new partner, and she was pregnant with their first child.

Austin explained to Jenny that his father told him nothing. When he learned the truth, he was so angry with his father that he refused to return to his home. Once back in Santa Cruz, Austin lived exclusively with his mother. Neither Jenny nor Austin told Austin's father about the visit.

This approach was unhealthy for a few reasons. For starters:

- Alex was kept in the dark, and because he had so little information, he filled in the blanks, blamed himself for the breakup, and carried feelings of guilt for years. He was furious with his father for keeping a secret and for offering so little explanation. This set the stage for dishonesty in his future relationships, especially with his father.
- The mother's decision to keep the child's desire to see his bonus parent a secret and to support a meeting between Jenny and Austin without the father's knowledge also reflected questionable judgment.

In the end, this wasn't about the breakup. It was about how the adults handled it. When communication breaks down and information is withheld, children are left to create their own version of the truth. That version often includes blame, guilt, and confusion. Co-parenting isn't about avoiding hard conversations. It's about handling them in a way that keeps your child informed, reassured, and out of the middle.

3 Finding Balance

IN THIS PART . . .

Create homes that feel grounded, stable, and responsive to the child's needs

Understand how your breakup may be affecting your children and learn how to help them through it

Manage your own stress so you can communicate effectively with your co-parent

IN THIS CHAPTER

» Breaking down the elements of safety

» Communicating safety concerns

» Coordinating safety in both homes with C.A.R.E.

» Making decisions about leaving children alone

» Handling suspicious injuries and other warning signs

Chapter 10
Making Both Homes Safe Places

"I didn't want you to be mad."

Eight-year-old Avery sat at the kitchen counter quietly peeling the label off her water bottle. Her mom noticed she was unusually tense. When she finally asked what was wrong, Avery whispered, "I don't want you to be mad at Dad."

Nothing sends a warning signal to a co-parent faster than a child feeling the need to protect one parent from the other. After a breakup, children instinctively pick up on the tension between their parents and often become emotional messengers. Avery had been worried about a loose back gate at her father's home. It wasn't that unsafe for panic, but it was unsafe enough for her to notice. She didn't speak up earlier because she didn't want to cause trouble.

REMEMBER

This is why safety in co-parenting must include more than physical protection. True safety is emotional, relational, and developmental. It allows a child to speak freely without fearing conflict, judgment, or loyalty traps.

This chapter focuses on helping co-parents create homes — plural — that feel grounded, stable, and responsive to the child's needs. Homes where children don't carry adult stress. Homes where their concerns can be heard without causing a storm. Homes where both parents and their children know what to expect and whom to trust.

Defining a Safe Environment

When parents live under one roof, they have at least the sense that they know what's happening to their children, who's coming in and out, what the routines look like, and how the day unfolds. But once the family separates and children begin moving between two homes, there are inevitable stretches of time when one parent simply can't see what's going on. Add in the distrust, suspicion, and raw emotion that often accompany separation or divorce, and it's no surprise that parents worry about their children's well-being. Those concerns can intensify when an ex-partner introduces new friends, a new social circle, or a new romantic relationship. Children feel this shift too; transitions already stir up anxiety, and many children quietly worry about their own safety just as much as their parents do.

How do you know when to worry and when to relax?

It's an excellent, complicated question, especially when you're unsure about your co-parent's judgment and find yourself wondering whether the kids are truly safe when they're out of your sight. A safe environment in co-parenting includes four essential pillars:

- Physical safety
- Emotional safety
- Relational safety
- Developmental safety

Physical safety

Physical safety encompasses these key elements:

- **Secure housing:** The home must be structurally sound with doors and windows that lock, offering children protection from harm and unauthorized entry. Roommates, if necessary, are properly vetted prior to moving into the home.

- **Sanitary living space:** Cleanliness is essential to a child's health. This includes tidy rooms, clean bathrooms, and surfaces free from debris or pests.
- **Age-appropriate supervision:** Children should be watched according to their maturity. What works for a teenager isn't appropriate for a toddler.
- **Safe sleep arrangements:** Every child needs a proper bed or sleep space, free from hazards, to ensure restful, safe sleep.
- **Functional utilities:** Heat, running water, and electricity are essential. Working appliances aren't luxuries; they're foundational to safety and daily living.
- **Basic hazard prevention:** Common dangers such as sharp objects, toxic chemicals, stairs, and weapons must be secured or removed from a child's reach.

Emotional safety

For a child to feel emotionally safe, these requirements should be met:

- **Predictable adult reactions:** Children feel secure when they can trust the adults in their lives to respond to stress consistently and appropriately.
- **Calm exchanges:** This includes exchanges between parents and other caregivers. Peaceful transitions between homes reassure children that they're not caught in the middle of a conflict.
- **Freedom to talk without fear of reprisal:** Kids should feel confident expressing thoughts or feelings without worrying they'll get someone in trouble.
- **Routines that reduce anxiety:** Predictable schedules like bedtime, mealtime, and study time create a calming structure during uncertain times.
- **Low conflict:** Minimizing arguments, especially in front of the children, protects their emotional well-being and preserves trust.

Relational safety

Relational safety involves children's relationships with their parents:

- **No loyalty binds:** Children should never feel forced to pick a side or hide love for one parent to please the other.
- **No negative talk about the other parent:** Badmouthing or criticizing the other parent makes children feel torn and unsafe; they internalize those messages deeply.

» **No emotional fines:** "You hurt my feelings by having fun over there." Guilt trips and emotional punishment for enjoying time with the other parent create confusion and stress.

» **Consistent reassurance:** Children thrive when both parents actively affirm that it's okay to love and enjoy time with everyone in their family.

Developmental safety

Developmental safety requires these standards:

» **Age-appropriate routines:** A preschooler needs early bedtimes and a safe space, while a teen needs privacy and space for independence.

» **Boundaries that protect growth:** Limits on screen time, chores, or social activity shouldn't restrict development. They should guide and support it.

» **Structure that supports school, sleep, and hygiene:** Daily expectations around homework, bedtime, and personal care help kids feel confident and cared for.

» **Balanced expectations:** Parents should align expectations across households so that children don't feel confused by extremes like strict rules at one home and no rules at the other.

WHAT SAFETY LOOKS LIKE DAY TO DAY

Safety is communicated through small, consistent actions:

- There are predictable bedtime routines.
- Parents or other adult caregivers communicate about school and health issues.
- Children understand the rules.
- There are consistent meal patterns.
- There are calm exchanges.
- Feelings are allowed.

Noting Safety Concerns with Your Co-Parent

When parents separate, they often carry emotional residue — hurt, distrust, disappointment, fear. These emotions can make it difficult to determine whether a concern about the other home is legitimate or fueled by anxiety. Many parents swing between overreacting — "Everything is unsafe over there!" and underreacting — "I'm probably imagining it." Neither extreme protects the child.

Learning to observe objectively

Instincts often run ahead of the facts. Fear tells one story, frustration tells another, and before you know it, a minor incident feels like a major threat. Learning to observe objectively means slowing down and looking at what's actually happening, not what you're afraid is happening. And there are different kinds of concerns:

- A *safety concern* is any condition that poses a reasonable physical, emotional, or developmental risk.
- A *difference* is a variation in routine that doesn't harm the child.
- A *trigger* is an emotional reaction rooted in your past, not your child's present.

Learning to distinguish between the three is an essential co-parenting skill.

Responding to a safety concern

When you identify a legitimate safety concern — something that poses a reasonable physical, emotional, or developmental risk — respond with calm urgency. Document what you've seen, talk with your co-parent using neutral language, and offer a specific solution. For example:

> "I noticed the medication wasn't given to Josh yesterday. What do you think about creating a shared log so we can both stay on top of how much medication he's receiving?"

If the concern is serious or recurring, involve professionals (pediatrician, school counselor, mediator) to ensure the child's safety without escalating conflict.

For example:

> When three-year-old Adele wasn't eating consistently at Dad's, Mom grew concerned. When the doctor used the term "failure to thrive," she panicked. Dad disagreed. "She's just thin. I'm thin. She takes after me."
>
> Mom came home with reports pointing to a problem. Dad felt blamed. "The doctor is reacting to what you tell her. You say she's not eating at my house, and it becomes my fault."
>
> The solution was simple: attend appointments together. Hearing the same information firsthand allowed them to follow a plan without blame or debate.

Responding to a difference

When something is simply a difference in approach — say, bedtimes differ, or screen-time rules aren't identical — respond with flexibility. Remind yourself, "Different doesn't mean dangerous." Accepting variation between homes is part of the back-and-forth lifestyle.

Responding to a trigger

When you realize you're reacting to a trigger — something from your past, not your child's present — respond with self-reflection rather than reaction. Pause, breathe, and ask, "Is this about my child or about me?" Seek clarity before speaking to your co-parent. If needed, talk it through with a therapist, life coach, or trusted friend.

REMEMBER

The wise response is curiosity, not a demand for correction, because triggers require understanding and healing.

Responding properly when your co-parent doesn't see the problem

When one parent believes something is wrong and the other dismisses it as "no big deal," communication can get tense quickly.

In moments like this, it helps to pause and look beyond the disagreement. The worried parent isn't overreacting; they're responding to a pattern they're seeing. And the relaxed parent isn't uncaring; they may genuinely interpret the behavior differently. Instead of arguing about who's right, shift the focus to the child's experience. That shared lens turns a potential standoff into teamwork.

TIP

Try these strategies to communicate your concerns:

- Explaining the child's struggles factually without blaming
- Asking your co-parent's opinion about what you notice
- Offering tools (calendars, reminders, routines)
- Sharing input from teachers or doctors
- Sticking to short, neutral messages

WARNING

Avoid lectures, sarcasm, or dramatic warnings, especially if you feel your co-parent isn't taking the issue seriously. Those approaches usually backfire, turning the conversation into a power struggle rather than a problem-solving moment.

A calm, straightforward message — free of digs or ultimatums — keeps the focus where it belongs: on helping your child feel secure in both homes.

Determining Real Safety Concerns

Legitimate safety concerns fall into the following categories:

- **Physical hazards:** Broken windows, unsafe play area, unsecured pools, or dangerous adults in the home
- **Supervision issues:** When a child is left alone too long, or caregivers are inattentive or impaired
- **Hygiene and health:** Ongoing neglected hygiene or repeated untreated illnesses
- **Emotional instability:** Exposure to chronic conflict, yelling, or inconsistent moods
- **Developmental risks:** Routines so chaotic that they affect sleep, schoolwork, or emotional regulation

These patterns don't have to be extreme to matter. Subtle, repeated disruptions can slowly chip away at a child's sense of stability.

Defining child abuse and neglect

It's natural for separated or divorced parents to run their households differently. One parent may serve healthier food, drive a safer car, or maintain a tidier house. These variations are common in the back-and-forth lifestyle. But there's an important distinction between less-than-ideal parenting and actual abuse or neglect. The boundary can sometimes feel blurry, especially when emotions are high, so it helps to begin with clear definitions.

Physical abuse

Professionals — physicians, psychologists, social workers, and law enforcement — typically group child abuse into four broad categories, and a single case may include more than one. The first and most widely recognized is physical abuse. Professionals strongly discourage all forms of physical punishment, including spanking, slapping, hitting, kicking, forceful shaking, and striking a child with an object such as a belt or wooden spoon. These methods are not only ineffective but harmful. They can escalate behavior problems over time and, more importantly, cause lasting psychological injury. When parents say, "I was spanked, and I turned out fine," I acknowledge their experience and then remind them that many children don't "turn out fine," and physical punishment harms far more than it helps.

That said, not every instance of physical punishment meets the legal threshold for abuse. There's no federal law against spanking, and definitions vary widely from one jurisdiction to another. In some places, Child Protective Services uses stricter standards; in others, the threshold for intervention is higher. Understanding how physical injuries are evaluated and which types raise concern can help parents recognize when a situation may be crossing that line.

WARNING

It has been my experience that CPS draws the line at scratches and bruises, so if you're leaving marks when you discipline, that may be recognized as physical abuse.

Emotional abuse

On the other end of the spectrum is emotional abuse, and it's by far the most difficult to prove because emotional abuse leaves no bruises or scars. Emotional abuse affects the psyche and often stays with a child long after bruises or scars heal.

Separation and divorce already strain children's emotional well-being, with effects that can last a lifetime. During this turbulent period, parents are often exhausted, anxious, depressed, or overwhelmed — hardly the conditions under which adults do their best parenting. Emotional abuse may involve yelling, belittling, ostracizing, threatening, blaming, or emotionally withdrawing from a child. It also includes exposure to violence between adults in the home. And while some behaviors fall into a gray area between poor parenting and true emotional abuse, others are unmistakably damaging.

Consider this example:

> Nine-year-old Evan comes home excited to show his father a science fair ribbon. Before he can speak, his father snaps, "Why are you bothering me? I've had a long day." Evan tries again. "Second place? Figures. You never finish strong. If your mother hadn't babied you, maybe you'd win something worthwhile. Go to your room."
>
> Later, when Evan confides he's hurt, his father dismisses him. "Stop being so dramatic. If you cry, I'm not taking you next weekend."
>
> Over time, Evan learns his feelings will be mocked, his efforts aren't enough, and nothing is ever good enough. That message is the hallmark of emotional abuse.

Sexual abuse

The possibility of sexual abuse is every parent's nightmare. It can be difficult to detect, which fuels anxiety in separated families where trust is fragile. Sexual abuse doesn't always involve physical contact; it can include exposing a child to sexually explicit material or behavior.

Any child can be sexually abused. But some children face a higher risk. Studies show that girls are abused more frequently than boys. Children with developmental disabilities are more vulnerable than their typically developing peers. Children of single parents, especially when those parents are coping with major stressors, are at higher risk. Household conflict, whether between parents or between a parent and child, can contribute to vulnerability as well. Equally important is what doesn't increase risk: Sexual abuse doesn't discriminate by race or socioeconomic status.

On the other hand, some things that understandably alarm parents are normal development and don't indicate sexual abuse.

> Jillian walked into her daughter's room to find 4-year-old Becca and her stepbrother, Juan, also 4 years old, naked from the waist down. Becca was crouched over Juan's penis, staring at it intently.
>
> "Oh my God, Becca! What are you doing?"
>
> "I'm looking at Juan's thing, Mommy."

Children are inquisitive; they experiment. Two 4-year-olds looking at each other's "privates" would most likely not be of concern to Child Protective

Services, but it would be strongly suggested that the parents not leave the children unsupervised. In contrast, an adolescent of 14 "experimenting" with a child of 3 or 4 would be of concern.

Investigating sexual abuse is complex due to its sensitive and legal nature. Some medical professionals are specially trained as certified medical examiners (CMEs) and are the preferred providers when available. A pediatrician or emergency clinician may also conduct the exam. Credible concerns should always be evaluated by the most qualified provider in coordination with Child Protective Services and law enforcement.

WARNING

Be aware, however, that physical examinations to prove sexual abuse can be extremely invasive and frightening for a child. Don't approach these examinations frivolously.

If you suspect sexual abuse, your instinct may be to ask your child detailed questions. Who, what, when, and where? As difficult as it is, do your best to resist that impulse. Children's memories are more fragile than most adults realize, and repeated or leading questions, such as "Was it your mother's boyfriend?" can distort their recollection and jeopardize the credibility of their statements.

REMEMBER

It's also important to remain as calm as possible. A frightened child may shut down entirely or simply agree with you for fear of making you angry. CMEs are trained to ask developmentally appropriate nonleading questions and document responses in ways that will hold up in court.

Even then, it's frustratingly common for sexual abuse exams to be inconclusive. Examinations are often performed after the fact, when evidence has since been washed away or has healed. Plus, many forms of sexual abuse leave no physical trace. But the absence of physical evidence doesn't prove that the abuse didn't occur. The child's statement, when obtained correctly, is often the most critical piece of information necessary for a conviction.

Neglect

Neglect is failing to meet the child's basic physical, medical, nutritional, or developmental needs. Emotional neglect falls under emotional abuse, but the impact is intertwined. Some cases of neglect are subtle; others are unmistakable and demand urgent intervention.

"Something felt off, but I couldn't put my finger on it."

When Michelle picked up her 7-year-old son, he looked exhausted. He fell asleep in the car, something he never did. Her imagination started to run. Instead, she asked gently, "Rough night?"

He yawned. "Dad had friends over. They were loud."

Not dangerous. Not neglect.

But a pattern Michelle wanted to keep an eye on.

She sent a brief, neutral text to his dad.

"He was really tired today. Maybe we can both watch how late he stays up on weeknights."

Clear. Calm. Child-focused, and it didn't instigate a sarcastic reaction. Dad simply replied, "Agreed." The next time they spoke, they refined what that meant. Bedtime on school nights would be 9 p.m. at both houses. They'd reserve loud, friendly get-togethers for the weekends — not because either of them was judging the other's behavior, but because their child needed a quieter environment during the week so he could do well in school.

Not every parenting difference is a safety issue, although in the early stages of co-parenting, it can certainly feel that way. Some concerns are really about discomfort, not danger:

- They don't fold laundry the same way.
- He eats too much junk food over there.
- Her house is messy.
- They allow more screen time.
- Their bedtime is later.
- They don't enforce chores.

These differences can be frustrating and may even challenge your personal standards, but they don't rise to the level of safety concerns unless they create consistent harm or emotional distress for the child. The goal is to distinguish true risk from everyday variation, so your energy is focused where it truly matters: your child's well-being.

TIP

It can help to ask yourself: "Is this dangerous, or is it just different?"

Watching for patterns

Patterns reveal truth more than isolated incidents. One or two late bedtimes aren't a crisis. Five late bedtimes in a row might indicate a supervision issue. One missed meal is human error. A hungry child every Sunday is a pattern. One scraped knee is childhood. Repeated injuries with vague explanations deserve attention.

Safety concerns should be:

- Observed calmly
- Documented neutrally
- Communicated peacefully

REMEMBER

Patterns, not individual moments, drive decisions.

TIP

Here's an exercise to help you discern if something is a pattern or a preference, or if you're responding to a trigger. Note if any of the following are true.

The concern is . . .

- A one-time situation
- A repeated occurrence
- Emotionally triggering to me
- Affecting my child's functioning
- Truly unsafe
- Something we just do differently
- Needing clarification, not confrontation

Then, finish these statements:

- One step I can take that focuses on my child's well-being, not my frustration, is __________________________________.
- The positive action I can take is __________________________.

Creating Two Safe Homes

Parents can create two safe homes by treating safety as a shared project, not an individual competition. The first step is agreeing on the basics: stable housing, adequate supervision, a safe place to sleep, and routines that support the child's well-being. Even if the homes look different, both parents commit to meeting the same essential needs. This means talking openly about concerns without shaming or micromanaging. "Can we check in about bedtime? He seems overtired on school mornings, and that seems to be an easy fix," rather than, "You never put her to bed on time."

Next, co-parents should share information regularly and proactively. This may seem strange for some, but sincerely think about it. How will it really hurt to be open and transparent about your child? Safety requires both homes to stay updated about medical issues, new medication, behavior changes, school concerns, and emotional shifts. A quick text, "The teacher mentioned he's a little overwhelmed; let's both reinforce breaks while doing homework," keeps both parents moving in the same direction. This is done to reinforce teamwork, not blame or call out the other parent for having a lackadaisical attitude about doing their job. When information flows freely, problems are caught early, and neither parent feels blindsided.

REMEMBER

When a disagreement does arise, the goal is to problem-solve, not prove a point. Responding with C.A.R.E. can make all the difference.

Coordinating safety concerns using C.A.R.E.

Talking about safety with an ex is rarely simple, especially when emotions are high, trust has taken a hit, or one parent is more relaxed than the other. But safety conversations don't have to turn into power struggles. Using the C.A.R.E. model — communication, acceptance, respect, empathy — keeps the discussion grounded, child-focused, and productive, even when the relationship between households is strained.

What follows is how C.A.R.E. works when you need to talk about supervision, injuries, medication, or any other issue that directly affects the child's safety and well-being.

Communication: Keep it clear, neutral, and safety-based

When safety is involved, your goal is to communicate information, not accusations. Toxic or tense dynamics often lead parents to over-explain, defend, or blame. That instantly shuts down cooperation.

Instead, use:

- Short, factual language
- One concern at a time

» Questions instead of assumptions

» A calm tone, even when you're nervous

Here are examples of neutral statements that keep the focus on the child's immediate safety needs, not the co-parent's mistakes:

» "She mentioned that she fell at recess. Did the school contact you?"

» "The inhaler was empty when he arrived. Can we coordinate refills so that he always has one?"

» "I noticed the new skateboard. Do you have pads there, or should I send ours?"

Acceptance: Acknowledge differences in style without letting them derail safety

Acceptance means recognizing that parents rarely approach safety the same way. One may run a tighter ship; the other may be more relaxed. That doesn't automatically make either household unsafe.

What matters is this:

» Different is okay. Unsafe is not.

» Acceptance keeps conflict from escalating by allowing both parents to:
  - Acknowledge different comfort levels
  - Identify the specific safety concern
  - Look for a shared solution instead of a moral debate

Example:

"I know we handle screen time differently, but when he stays up past midnight, his anxiety spikes. Can we agree on a consistent bedtime on school nights?"

This isn't about trying to control the other home. It's about accepting differences while still protecting the child from predictable struggles.

Respect: Use boundaries that support collaboration, not control

Respect shows up through tone, timing, and boundaries. When discussing safety, respect means:

- » Sticking to child-focused facts
- » Not using safety as a disguise for criticism
- » Staying within the agreed-upon communication plan (text, app, email)
- » Limiting how often you reach out
- » Responding within reasonable timeframes

Example:

> "I'll send the medication instructions in writing so that nothing gets missed. If you need clarification, let me know."

This approach respects the other parent's ability and their space. It also protects you from over-functioning, micromanaging, or communicating impulsively out of fear.

Empathy: Keep the child's experience at the center of the conversation

Empathy is where safety conversations become meaningful. Instead of focusing on what the other parent "should" do, shift to what the child feels when parents disagree or fail to coordinate.

Ask yourself:

- » "If our child listened to this exchange, would they feel safer or more anxious?"
- » "What does this issue look like through my child's eyes?"
- » "What change would genuinely help them right now?"

Example:

> "When he gets two different messages about helmets, he gets confused and stops wearing one at all. Can we both reinforce the same rule so that he feels secure about what's expected?"

Empathy unites co-parents around the child, even when the adults don't see eye to eye.

Putting C.A.R.E. into practice

Using C.A.R.E., safety conversations shift from adversarial to cooperative — even if the relationship between parents remains delicate.

- **C** (communication) keeps the tone calm and factual.
- **A** (acceptance) reduces power struggles by acknowledging differences.
- **R** (respect) sets boundaries that stabilize communication.
- **E** (empathy) brings the focus back to the child's experience.

Safety becomes a shared priority, not a battleground.

Finally, co-parents must agree that safety is nonnegotiable. If one parent notices a hazard, lack of supervision, unsafe driving, or medication errors, they agree to bring it up respectfully and listen to the other parent's perspective. Instead of assuming bad intent, they collaborate on fixes: adding reminders, adjusting routines, seeking professional input, or consulting a mediator if needed.

REMEMBER

When both parents consistently show that they'll address problems rather than deny them, the child benefits from two homes that aren't identical but are aligned in their commitment to protection, stability, and care. These small but steady steps build trust over time.

Dealing with home comparisons

Parents often compare homes to evaluate "equality," but children evaluate homes based on familiarity and emotional comfort, not necessarily furniture or swimming pools. If a child mentions creature comforts, it may be that the parents are openly comparing, "I'm so sorry I don't have as nice a car or house as your dad/mom." Or it could be as simple as the parents not allowing the children to bring their stuff back and forth. "That tablet stays here. Your mother/father can buy one for their house." The parent has now openly called the children's attention to the difference in creature comforts. If the child wasn't comparing them before, they are now.

I've seen parents demand that their children take off their clothes at the door before they return to the other home. "I bought those jeans. Take them off before you go back." That kind of parenting is about the parents, not the children.

They've lost sight of the communication, acceptance, respect, and empathy it takes to properly co-parent, and it calls attention to the differences between homes.

If you're looking for a child to feel safe in both homes, calling their attention to the differences isn't the way to do it. That forces them to compare. Homes don't have to match in material ways, but they should match emotional rhythm, if possible. That happens when parents put the needs of the children — not their own vendettas — first.

Recognizing true housing safety concerns

REMEMBER

Housing becomes a true safety concern when:

- Utilities are repeatedly disconnected.
- The home is structurally unsafe.
- There are exposed hazards.
- There's chronic filth that affects health.
- The child can't sleep safely.
- Dangerous adults live in or frequent the home.
- The parent can't supervise due to a questionable environment.

Unstable living arrangements lead to chaos. Occasional clutter doesn't make a home unsafe. A broken toy bin isn't unsafe. A mattress on the floor isn't unsafe. Safety concerns arise from patterns that compromise health or stability. A parent transitioning between homes or trying to create a new lifestyle during hard times isn't unsafe if handled responsibly. Consider this example:

> Michael and Denise were recently divorced. Michael moved out of the family home into an apartment and had very little left over after bills to buy furniture. Denise was furious that Michael was taking so long to get organized. He had the bare necessities but no beds for the kids when they came over.
>
> She threatened to take him back to court until Lisa, their 6-year-old, came home with a story about how much fun she and her siblings had when they camped out in front of the TV at Daddy's house. They ate popcorn and watched fun movies, and Daddy was right there with them. Denise realized it wasn't about furniture, but that Michael was doing his best to spend time with the children. She stopped her threatening and began to look for ways to support his parenting of the children they both loved.

COMMON MYTHS ABOUT HOUSING

Myth 1: Each child must have their own room in both homes.

Reality: A child needs a safe, comfortable sleeping space. Private rooms are ideal but not required.

Myth 2: If one home is "nicer," the other is inadequate.

Reality: Children evaluate emotional tone, not granite countertops.

Myth 3: Frequent moves automatically make a home unsafe.

Reality: Moves can be stressful, but children do well when adults communicate clearly and keep routines steady.

Myth 4: The parent with more financial resources provides the "better" home.

Reality: Safety, not wealth, is the determining factor.

Leaving Children Alone: Proper Supervision and Readiness

Few safety issues spark more disagreement between co-parents than supervision. Questions come up constantly:

- How long can I leave them alone?
- Is it okay if I run to the store?
- Can my teenager babysit the younger child?
- Why did he leave them alone when I never would?

These concerns are understandable. Supervision touches on judgment, trust, and each parent's sense of what "safe enough" looks like. When two households have different comfort levels, even small decisions can feel like big risks.

How parents' backgrounds shape perceptions

Supervision disagreements may arise not because one parent is careless, but because they come from different childhood experiences, hold different comfort levels, live in neighborhoods with varying levels of safety, or simply rely on different parenting styles. Sometimes the conflict is fueled by a misunderstanding of what's developmentally appropriate; what feels like "too much freedom" to one parent may be entirely normal for a child at that age. Recognizing the roots of these differences helps co-parents approach the conversation with empathy rather than accusation, making it easier to find common ground.

For example, a parent who was raised in a tightly supervised home may see constant oversight as loving and necessary, while a parent who grew up with more independence may believe that freedom builds confidence. If your childhood included chaos and unpredictable adults, you may be hyper-aware of possible dangers; if your childhood felt stable and nurturing, you may assume most environments are safe unless proven otherwise.

These invisible histories can collide when co-parents try to agree on supervision. Understanding that each parent's lens was shaped long before the child was born allows the conversation to shift from "You're too strict" or "You're too lax" to "We came from different worlds. How do we combine what's best for our child now?"

Deciding when children are ready to be left alone

Children become capable of short periods alone gradually, based on maturity, not age alone. A 9-year-old who's cautious, calm, and communicative may be safer than a 12-year-old who's impulsive or anxious.

Look for these signs of readiness in your children:

- Ability to follow safety rules
- Comfort being alone
- Ability to call a parent
- Understanding emergency steps if they feel threatened or unsafe
- Not engaging in risky behavior
- Emotional stability

The environment also plays a role in deciding if children can be left alone. Consider these factors:

- Safe neighborhood
- Locked doors and windows
- No unsafe adults around
- Functioning phone
- Short time periods

Using state age guidelines

In the US, there's no consistent law nationally that determines how young a child can be when left alone, and requirements vary by state. Several states offer clear laws or recommended ages when children may be left alone.

For example, Illinois prohibits children under 14 from being left alone. Georgia advises that children 8 and under should never be left unsupervised, and those 9–12 may be left alone for less than two hours. Maryland and North Carolina provide statutory age guidelines, while Tennessee and Washington recommend a minimum age of 10. Kansas suggests that children ages 6–9 may be left alone briefly, with older children allowed more independence as maturity increases. Colorado, Connecticut, and Mississippi commonly use age 12 as a benchmark for being left alone.

Many states have no set legal age for leaving a child home alone. Instead of relying on a number, these states expect parents to use sound judgment, and they allow Child Protective Services to get involved when supervision falls short. If a child is left in a situation they aren't capable of handling or one that could reasonably endanger them, CPS can investigate even when no specific statute has been violated. The takeaway: No law doesn't mean no accountability. Authorities can still act when they believe a child's safety is at risk.

Allowing siblings to supervise

Talking to so many children over the years, the consensus regarding babysitting siblings seems to be that they don't mind it occasionally, but not on a regular basis — and it's greatly resented if a teen is *expected* to babysit and not asked.

Although sibling supervision can be positive, as older siblings learn responsibility and younger siblings feel supported, it becomes unsafe when:

» The older sibling feels forced.

» The younger child has high needs or is disabled.

» The older sibling lacks maturity.

» Too much responsibility shifts to a child.

Recognizing Suspicious Injuries and Other Warning Signs

Nothing spikes a co-parent's anxiety faster than a bruise, cut, or unusual mark on their child. Injuries are part of childhood. Kids run, fall, crash, climb, jump, and bump. Yet after a breakup, injuries often become emotionally charged. Parents may fear the worst or assume negligence when the explanation seems unclear.

For the record, a suspicious injury isn't just an injury; it's an injury accompanied by:

» Inconsistent explanations

» Repeated patterns

» Fear or hesitation when describing what happened

» Injuries inappropriate for the developmental stage

» Explanations that don't match the child's abilities

» Emotional behavior that doesn't fit the story

Understanding the context is just as important as the injury itself.

Identifying normal childhood injuries versus warning signs

Children get bumps and bruises as they grow. That's part of the territory. Skinned knees from running too fast, bruises across the shins from climbing or scooter mishaps, and the occasional scratch from rambunctious play are all developmentally expected. You'll also notice the predictable elbow or forearm bruise from slipping off a bike or misjudging a jump. These injuries typically come with confident, straightforward explanations because they make sense in the context of a child's age, activities, and abilities.

But other injuries should make parents pause. Repeated marks in the same location, bruises or abrasions in places usually protected by clothing, or injuries that appear to have a distinct shape or pattern are worth a second look. So are explanations that don't match a child's developmental stage, or statements like "I can't remember" or "I'm not allowed to tell you."

WARNING

Most concerning is when a child looks scared or shuts down when you gently ask what happened. Those moments are red flags, not because they confirm wrongdoing, but because they signal that something in the environment — physical or emotional — may not be safe.

A normal injury paired with an unusual story is something to monitor, but a strange injury combined with fear deserves your full attention. Children rarely tell the whole truth if they feel their honesty will spark conflict, get a parent in trouble, or violate a "don't tell" message they've been given. They may feel embarrassed, confused about the details, or unsure of how you'll respond.

REMEMBER

In fact, children often protect their parents by softening the truth, even when it puts their own well-being at risk. This is why your demeanor matters. When you stay calm, steady, and grounded, you give your child the safety to speak freely. When you react with alarm or anger, they may retreat, edit the story, or shut down entirely — exactly the opposite of what you're hoping for. Your ability to regulate your own emotions makes it easier for your child to share theirs, and that's where real understanding and protection begin.

If injuries increase during times of conflict, your child may be overwhelmed, not unsafe. When warning signs arise, they don't always point to abuse. More often, they reflect issues with supervision: things like a distracted caregiver, a new partner in the home, age-inappropriate play, or simply a household running in a chaotic rhythm. These kinds of supervision problems typically show up as repeated minor injuries, inconsistent explanations, unexplained marks, excessive tiredness from late nights, or uncertainty about who was responsible for watching the child at a given time.

REMEMBER

When these patterns appear, the most effective response is a collaborative one. Approaching the other parent with curiosity and concern rather than accusation creates space to improve supervision without escalating conflict or defensiveness.

Sometimes the warning signs point not to physical safety but to emotional distress. Children under stress may act out, cling for attention, regress in behavior, develop nervous habits, or become noticeably clumsier. Emotional strain can disrupt their sleep, concentration, and coordination — factors that naturally lead to more bumps, scrapes, and mishaps.

When you notice an increase in injuries during periods of family tension or parental conflict, consider that your child may be overwhelmed rather than unsafe. Understanding the emotional context helps you respond with support and stability, focusing on what your child is feeling instead of assuming the worst about what may have happened.

Asking your child about questionable incidents

"I object, Your Honor! That's leading the witness."

If you've never been to court, you've at least heard that phrase on TV. It's an objection when an attorney asks a witness a question by suggesting the answer. Leading your child to respond the way you would like them to can prompt the wrong answers and fill your child with anxiety. Plus, if you try to use the conversation as proof in court, you may be accused of coaching your child. If that's the outcome, you won't be taken seriously.

Avoid questions like:

- "Did your Dad/Mom do this?"
- "Did something bad happen?"
- "Is someone hurting you?"

Instead ask:

- "Tell me what happened."
- "Where were you when you got hurt?"
- "How did you feel afterward?"
- "Is there anything you want me to know?"

These are open-ended questions that encourage honesty without planting fears and possibly giving you erroneous answers.

Deciding when to seek help

Sometimes, simply observing or asking questions isn't enough, and it becomes wise to bring in professional support. When an injury is serious, when concerning patterns start to repeat, or when a child shows fear about returning to the other home, additional guidance may be necessary. The same is true when explanations remain inconsistent, when new adults enter the child's life, and the stories around them feel unclear, or when you notice a sudden decline in your child's behavior, mood, or functioning. Chronic supervision concerns — when you repeatedly feel the child is being left without adequate oversight — also warrant more than a casual check-in with your co-parent.

When you do reach out for help, think in terms of a team rather than a crisis response. A pediatrician can assess injuries or developmental changes. A school counselor or therapist can help interpret behavioral shifts or emotional distress. And when the situation involves safety questions that can't be resolved between homes, consulting with a mandated reporter, mediator, or parenting coordinator can offer structure and direction. Each of these professionals brings a different lens, but all share the same purpose: keeping your child safe.

REMEMBER

Seeking help isn't an attack on your co-parent. It's not about building a case or punishing anyone. The goal is to remain focused on your child's safety and well-being. When adults stay focused on that, even difficult situations can be handled with clarity, responsibility, and care. The goal is safety, not punishment.

Calling Child Protective Services

Parents may call CPS in retaliation or out of concern, but what remains is that a parent may not have to call for help at all. Many of the professionals that work with your children — teachers and their aids, childcare workers, doctors, nurses, and therapists — are "mandated reporters." That means, by law, they must alert Child Protective Services if they suspect neglect or abuse. If they sweep their suspicion under the rug, they could lose their license.

You must remember, however, that things you find to be questionable may not be of concern to CPS. A child who misses a shower or has dirty hair occasionally will most likely not lead to a CPS finding of abuse. Even lice in your child's hair may not rise to a CPS finding. But there may be a finding of neglect if there's no running water or no electricity. Then a child would be unable to wash or stay warm. Also, spanking your child isn't illegal. So if you don't agree with your co-parent's form of discipline, one spanks, the other doesn't, and you report it, CPS will rarely make that judgment call. They will, however, substantiate physical abuse if the child has cuts or bruises because of discipline. In some states, custody orders state that spanking as discipline is reserved for "an open hand on a clothed bottom."

A CPS investigation alone isn't a determiner of guilt. It just means there was an investigation. As a result of that investigation, there are various levels of findings:

- **Unfounded** means there was an investigation, and it was determined that the allegation didn't happen or didn't rise to the level that a determination needed to be made.
- **Inconclusive** means that after the investigation, they couldn't zero in on the truth. Say there were contradictory explanations reported, so there was no finding. This doesn't mean the incident didn't happen. It means they couldn't substantiate the findings.
- **Substantiated** means the allegation was found to be true after an investigation.

If there's an investigation, the following may happen:

- Dismissing the case if the social worker finds no evidence of neglect or abuse
- Ordering the family to participate in services to address specific issues
- Placing the child in foster care if the agency deems it necessary for their safety

WARNING

Never threaten to call CPS in anger as a form of retaliation against your co-parent. Investigations can be extremely invasive because the child is asked questions that may scare or traumatize them. It can also prompt invasive examinations that a child may remember throughout their life. For your child's sake, call CPS only if it's needed, not as a weapon.

Knowing When Substance Use Is a Co-Parenting Safety Concern

Few topics generate more fear or conflict between co-parents than alcohol or drug use. For some, it's a non-issue: responsible, moderate use that never affects parenting. For others, it's a recurring concern rooted in history, behavior patterns, or real impairment.

The challenge is separating controlled, appropriate adult behavior and occasional poor judgment from chronic misuse that threatens your child's safety.

Not all use is abuse. Not all concern is control. But when substance use affects supervision, routines, emotional stability, or decision-making, it becomes a safety issue, not a moral disagreement.

Recognizing the signs of substance-related risk

Concern becomes legitimate when substance use leads to the following:

- » Slurred speech while supervising children
- » Falling asleep or "checking out" during parenting time
- » Missed pickups or late arrivals
- » Unsafe driving
- » Emotional volatility or unpredictable moods
- » Financial instability affecting care
- » Unsafe adults entering the home
- » Children reporting fear or confusion
- » Refusal to discuss safety concerns
- » Repeated hangovers that reduce functioning

These behaviors compromise a child's sense of security and predictability.

For example, when 11-year-old Ethan told his mom, "Dad smelled funny when he picked me up," she felt a surge of panic. Instead of accusing, she simply texted this:

"Hey, Ethan mentioned smelling alcohol today. Everything okay?"

His father admitted that he had a beer with lunch but felt fine. The next week, Ethan said it again. And the next.

This wasn't a one-time misstep. It was a pattern. Patterns matter.

The co-parents agreed to:

- Avoid drinking before exchanges
- Designate a backup driver when needed
- Communicate openly about concerns

This prevented escalation and kept Ethan safe.

Deciding when to seek help

TIP

Seek outside support in the following situations:

- The co-parent is impaired regularly.
- The child reports fear.
- Driving under the influence occurs.
- Safety agreements are ignored.
- New adults in the home contribute to substance use.
- Emotional volatility destabilizes routines.
- The parent refuses to address concerns.

"You know why I don't like it when my parents drink too much?" a 10-year-old client asked me. "Who will take care of me?"

The goal isn't punishment of the parent; it's protection of the child.

IN THIS CHAPTER

» **Assuring kids that the breakup isn't their fault**

» **Identifying the signs of stress by age**

» **Helping kids grieve**

» **Practicing calm through the storm**

Chapter 11
Helping Your Children Cope with Your Breakup

Adults often underestimate the emotional earthquake a family split can create for a child. You may feel justified in your decisions, confident in your timeline, or even relieved after an extended period of conflict, but your children may have a harder time. Their story doesn't begin the day you tell them you and their other parent will no longer be living together. The security they once took for granted suddenly has edges, and their world feels more fragile. Even if your intentions are good and your plan is carefully crafted, the breakup changes the terrain beneath their feet, and you and your co-parent will need to become the emotional engineers who help rebuild their new, two-home landscape.

In this chapter, I discuss how your children may be feeling while facing your breakup, the dangers associated with stress in children by age, how they may or may not be adjusting, and how you can walk them through what they're feeling.

Seeing the Breakup through Your Child's Eyes

Children don't only evaluate breakups based on the reasons adults give them or the history that led up to the decision. They evaluate breakups based on how their own life changes and how the adults behave afterward. They accepted the turmoil prior to the breakup as the status quo. What else could they do? But a breakup makes it real, forever. A child can withstand enormous change if the adults around them remain predictable, responsive, and calm.

In contrast, even a relatively "amicable" separation can become emotionally destabilizing if communication breaks down, exchanges are tense, or the children sense hostility simmering beneath polite smiles. The good news is that children are profoundly resilient, but resilience doesn't appear out of nowhere. It grows in the presence of adults who teach them how to manage emotions, understand changes, and trust that the adults are, as I often say, "the captains of the ship," even if the waters are rough.

Parents often believe that protecting their children from the truth is the same as protecting them from the pain. While the details of adult conflict should remain out of children's earshot, the facts of the breakup and the emotional ripple effects that follow shouldn't be minimized or ignored.

Children often assume responsibility for events they don't understand. When no one explains the changes, kids' imaginations fill in the blanks. Some children conclude they weren't "good enough," and that's why their parents split. Others decide they should have been more obedient, less moody, or more helpful. Still others assume one parent is the villain and the other is the victim — not because parents say so, but because children may choose a side to make sense of the chaos.

When parents offer age-appropriate explanations and consistent reassurance, children learn that the breakup was an adult decision driven by adult issues, not a reflection of their worth or loyalty.

Grieving After the Breakup

And yet, even with all that reassurance, grief doesn't disappear overnight. Many children go through transitional stages remarkably like the grief stages seen in adults. This is a simplified version of the five stages of grief, introduced by Dr. Elizabeth Kübler-Ross in her book *On Death and Dying*.

1. Shock or denial
2. Sadness
3. Anger
4. Bargaining
5. Acceptance

When an adult faces grief of some sort, these stages don't unfold in a predictable pattern. Children can experience a stage, jump a stage, and then revisit a stage. A 6-year-old may show sadness today and curiosity two years from now. A 14-year-old who seems unfazed at the time of the breakup may suddenly feel resentment when a new partner enters the picture.

Grief has no expiration date, and you may find yourself reexplaining something you know you explained years before. Why? Because kids really didn't understand it years before, even though they said they did. Now they're older and can process the information, so they ask you once again for an explanation. Part of helping your children cope is understanding that they'll revisit the breakup emotionally at different ages, each time trying to make a new sense of it.

How stress shows up in children

Not all stress is bad. It's also a learning tool. Without small stresses, children don't learn or develop as they should. A toddler may fall when learning to walk, a 5-year-old may struggle with a bad dream, a teen may face their first dance. In each case, the stress of the event is a tolerable and teachable moment. As a parent, you help your children cope in different ways. You may offer words of encouragement, a story where you faced the same thing, or possibly a hug to ward off the boogie man.

A child will rarely go to a parent saying, "I'm stressed about the custody schedule," or "I'm having trouble processing this transition." Stress reveals itself in behaviors, attitudes, sleep patterns, school performance, appetite, and, for younger children, play. When parents know what to watch for, they can respond before stress becomes overwhelming or misinterpreted as disorganization, defiance, or "acting out."

Infants and toddlers

You may think your infant is too young to experience stress, but if you broke up soon after they were born, they, too, can feel the tension or the anxiousness that parents or extended family feel as they try to maneuver the back-and-forth. What looks like cholic could very well be your child's response to your anxiety.

A "failure to thrive" diagnosis or an infant's inability to keep food down could be their response to your ongoing conflict with your co-parent.

Toddlers don't understand the meaning of a breakup, but they deeply sense changes in tone, tension, and routine. A toddler may cry more during exchanges, become clingier at bedtime, or regress in potty training. They may wake more frequently during the night or startle easily. It's important to remember that none of these behaviors signals blame. They're signals of disruption. Young children rely entirely on predictable scaffolding: the rhythm of feeding, sleeping, and playing, and the emotional steadiness of caregivers. When these rhythms become uncertain, their nervous system protests.

I often remind parents that children this age benefit far more from stable routines than lengthy explanations. They don't understand the words, but they do understand warm arms, consistent schedules, and calm adults. If you can keep the transitions smooth and the emotional climate steady, these little ones adapt quickly. You don't need them to understand the breakup. You just need them to feel safe within it.

Preschool-age children

Preschoolers live in a world where imagination and reality blend. When you tell them about the separation, they may respond with magical thinking. "If I'm really good, you'll get back together." "Maybe if we buy a bigger house, Daddy will move back in." They may express fears through play. Watch for dolls arguing, stuffed animals leaving home, or superheroes performing rescues. Some preschoolers develop separation anxiety, refusing to leave one parent or fearing that the parent who leaves for work won't come back.

Behaviorally, stress shows up in irritability, tantrums, sudden aggression, or reverting to baby-like behaviors. Preschool kids may become more controlling because their world feels out of their control.

Your role during this stage is to ground kids this age gently in reality. Short explanations, spoken with calm consistency, help them feel anchored. "Mom and Dad live in different houses now, but we both love you." "You didn't cause this. Nothing you did made this happen." You repeat the message as many times as kids need, calmly, compassionately, and without shifting the emotional burden to them.

School-age children

School-age children are the truth-seekers. They want reasons, timelines, and explanations. They may not need graphic details, but they certainly need clarity.

Without explanations, they often fill the gaps with self-blame or resentment. Stress at this age is often revealed as stomach aches or headaches, and academically by difficulty concentrating, forgetfulness, slipping grades, or frequent visits to the school nurse.

School-aged children may also become focused on rules and fairness. They want to know the custody schedule down to the minute, who's picking them up, when homework will be done, and whether both households will follow the same rules. They crave order because order makes chaos feel manageable.

But children don't always show us what's wrong in obvious ways. Sometimes, very different struggles can look exactly the same on the surface. I often hear from divorced parents who are convinced their child needs medication because they're disorganized, distracted, and not following through. "He can't keep track of anything," they'll say. "He's all over the place. I think he has ADHD."

They may be right. But not always.

The behaviors they're describing, forgetfulness, lack of focus, poor follow-through, can just as easily be a child's response to the upheaval of a breakup. When parents separate, children's worlds shift overnight. Routines change. Homes change. Emotional tone changes. The adults they rely on may be stressed, distracted, or on edge. Even in the best of circumstances, that's a lot for a child to absorb.

And sometimes, what we see as disorganization is actually something else. Take forgetfulness. A child with ADHD may forget because the brain has difficulty holding onto information long enough to act on it. The intention is there, but attention slips before anything sticks. A child who is struggling emotionally, who may be experiencing depression or simply feeling overwhelmed, can look exactly the same. They forget assignments, lose track of what they're supposed to do, and seem checked out. But in this case, the issue isn't that their attention is being pulled away. It's because their mental and emotional energy is depleted. They may be preoccupied, worried, or just trying to adjust to a world that no longer feels predictable.

From the outside, both children look distracted. Internally, they are having very different experiences.

The same is true for motivation. A child with ADHD may not start because they don't know where to begin or feel overwhelmed by the steps. A child reacting to a breakup may not start because everything feels heavy, uncertain, or out of their control.

One is struggling with regulation. The other is struggling with emotional load.

When we assume a child's behavior is a disorder, we move quickly toward fixing it. When we understand that behavior may be a response, we slow down and ask a different question: What is this child dealing with right now?

This doesn't mean your child's behavior should be dismissed or ignored. It means we have to be careful not to label a child too quickly when the context tells an important part of the story.

Divorce is a major life transition. Before deciding that a child's disorganization is a condition that needs to be treated, it's worth asking whether it might be a reaction that needs to be understood. If these behaviors persist or interfere with your child's daily life, that's when it's time to consult with qualified professionals who can sort out what's really going on. Getting the right support matters, but so does understanding the context.

Preteens

Preteens internalize stress differently. They may withdraw, become more sarcastic, or develop "I don't care" attitudes that mask deeper worry. Peer relationships take center stage during this developmental stage, and family change can make them feel painfully different from their friends. Preteens may worry about logistics, friendships, extracurricular commitments, or how they'll explain the custody schedule when asked to hang out.

Some preteens respond to stress by trying to take on adult roles, mediating between parents, comforting a heartbroken parent, and worrying extensively about finances. Others become quickly frustrated or impatient, expressing their stress through irritability rather than tears. Others say nothing at all and internalize their worry.

Here's an example from my archives that drives this home:

> Ten-year-old Lucas had always been an easygoing child — cheerful, curious, and flexible. His parents, Anna and Grant, separated after a long period of quiet tension. When they told Lucas, he nodded calmly and didn't ask many questions. Both parents assumed he was handling it well.
>
> Two months later, the school nurse called. Lucas had been in her office four times that week with stomachaches. He hadn't complained at home. But when the nurse gently asked if anything was worrying him, he whispered, "I'm afraid if I forget something at Mom's, Dad will think I like her house better."

That one thought told the whole story. Lucas wasn't acting out or resisting the schedule. He was anxious, trying to manage the emotional balance between his parents.

When his parents understood this, they changed their approach. Instead of saying, "Don't forget your homework," they began saying, "This is new for all of us. If you forget something, we'll figure it out." That shift removed the pressure. His stomachaches faded not because the breakup hurt less, but because he was no longer carrying it alone. Lucas' parents made a point of letting Lucas know they were communicating regularly. The responsibility for consistency shifted back where it belonged — with the parents.

Teenagers

Teenagers are balancing emotional independence with a profound longing for stability. They may act like they don't care, but in secret, that may not be the case. A family breakup can make them feel untethered. They may question relationships, loyalty, fairness, or the entire concept of commitment. Some teens become angry and oppositional. Others become overly compliant. Some throw themselves into activities to fill up their days and avoid feelings; others retreat into their rooms.

Teenage stress can also show up through risk-taking behavior, like drinking, vaping, using drugs, making impulsive decisions, or making abrupt changes in friend groups. It can also manifest internally through depression, anxiety, or self-doubt. Teens will call you out if your approach is inconsistent, hating the "do as I say, not as I do" form of discipline. It seems hypocritical to them, and if they see inconsistency, they'll meet you with out-and-out disrespect. Above all, teens need to know the adults are still in charge. They may criticize your decisions, but they feel safer when you make the decisions thoughtfully and consistently and are forthcoming with your reasoning.

Teaching Your Children to Cope with Stress and Anxiety

When children go through a family breakup, their nervous systems often operate on high alert. Even when they appear calm on the outside, their minds may be racing, their bodies tense, and their emotions disorganized. Children don't naturally know what to do with those internal signals. Some lash out; others shut down. Some, like Lucas from the previous example, worry silently. It can be difficult for parents to read the signs.

Teaching a child to cope isn't about eliminating their stress. It's about giving them a forum to talk about it with a trusted adult and helping them learn to regulate stress when they feel it.

Parents may assume that coping techniques must be complex and clinical. But the most effective strategies are simple, repeatable, and modeled by calm adults. Children learn best by watching, hearing, and practicing. A coping tool becomes useful only when the adults consistently weave it into daily life. You can't teach a child to calm themselves if you only introduce the idea during a crisis. Practice these tools in neutral moments so they feel familiar when stress hits.

Naming your emotions

If there's one universal truth about helping children cope, it's this: It's difficult for children to manage feelings they can't name.

When a child says, "I don't know," it often means, "The feeling is too big," or "I don't have a word for it." Naming emotions brings the intensity down. It gives structure to chaos. It turns something overwhelming into something understandable.

When you say to a child, "You seem worried about tomorrow's schedule," you're not putting words in their mouth. You're modeling emotional recognition. Children feel seen when their emotions are named gently, without judgment. Giving kids an emotional vocabulary — sad, worried, shy, angry, frustrated, overwhelmed, disappointed, relieved — offers them a toolkit they can carry between homes.

REMEMBER

Naming an emotion doesn't make it worse; it makes it manageable. When a child's internal experience earns a safe place in conversation, their body calms. Their shoulders lower. Their breathing steadies. They begin to feel that their inner world matters enough for adults to try to understand how they're feeling.

Practicing breathing techniques

Has anyone ever told you to "Take a breath" when you're upset? Although that phrase is now regarded as somewhat sarcastic, there's a reason people say it. Breathing techniques are the cornerstone of emotional regulation, and the earlier a person learns to use them, the better.

When a child is stressed, their breathing becomes shallow. Their heart rate rises. Their body prepares to fight, flee, or freeze. Teaching a child to breathe deeply helps them regulate their physiology. Every age can do it.

You can practice breathing in fun, child-friendly ways. Younger children can pretend they're smelling a flower or blowing out a candle very slowly.

Older children can count slowly, inhaling through the nose and exhaling through the mouth. *Box breathing* is a simple technique you can teach children when their emotions start to feel too big. They breathe in slowly for 4 seconds, hold that breath for 4, breathe out for 4, and pause for 4 before starting again. That steady rhythm gives their body a signal: They're safe. They can calm down now. For many kids, having something concrete to count and repeat helps them shift from overwhelm to control. When co-parents use and reinforce the same technique in each home, children learn that managing strong feelings is a shared skill — not a punishment — and that both parents are working together to help them feel steady during stressful moments.

Understanding cognitive behavioral therapy strategies for kids

Cognitive behavioral therapy (CBT) sounds clinical and difficult, but in truth, it's quite simple to do. CBT guides children and adults to understand how thoughts, feelings, and behaviors are connected. It isn't about analyzing every emotion. It's about teaching children how to challenge the thoughts that create unnecessary distress.

When parents incorporate CBT concepts at home, they teach children to evaluate their feelings rather than drown in them. Children experiencing a family breakup develop anxious thoughts that feel true even when they're inaccurate.

> "Dad will be lonely without me."
>
> "Mom will be mad if I tell her I miss Dad."
>
> "If I forget something at the other house, that means I love that parent more."

These worrisome thoughts attack a child's core, making them anxious. CBT helps children examine these beliefs gently.

Kids learn to distinguish between a feeling and a fact:

> A feeling says, "I'm scared."
>
> A fact says, "Both my parents love me and want to keep me safe."

You can make it into a game. When your child confides a worry or you can tell that they're struggling, ask, "Feeling or fact?" and explore which one it is. Once children learn to challenge their thoughts, anxiety loses its grip. CBT doesn't remove sadness, but it prevents sadness from turning into fear, fear into panic, and panic into shame or even depression. It teaches children to become better observers of their own minds.

Parents certainly don't need to be therapists to use CBT tools with their children or incorporate them into their own lives, but you can certainly consult a therapist if you need additional guidance. The key is to help you and your children slow down enough to understand what their thoughts are telling them and question whether those thoughts are true or part of their anxiety about the changes that go along with a breakup.

Incorporating predictability and structure

I mention predictability throughout this book because it's the one thing children depend on during their adjustment after their parents split up. Children thrive on predictability. With all the changes they're facing, predictability becomes their anchor. Even small uncertainties, such as knowing where the toothbrush goes, when bedtime is expected, or who will pick them up from school, help them settle emotionally. Predictability also reduces anxiety. Children don't ask for rigid control; they ask for clear rhythms.

When routines fall apart, even unintentionally, children experience stress in their bodies before it manifests in their behavior. A child who becomes overly tired, overstimulated, or emotionally taxed may not say, "This schedule is too inconsistent." They may simply melt down. They may argue, refuse to cooperate, become inattentive at school, or fall apart during exchanges. Predictability is the background structure that allows their emotional systems to rest.

Developing emotional predictability

An adult's brain has the benefit of a fully developed frontal cortex, which means adults can regulate their emotions, pause before reacting, and think problems through. Of course, not all adults do that, but they are far more capable of it than children. Children's brains rely more on the amygdala, the part of the brain that responds quickly and emotionally, because the prefrontal cortex, where reasoning and self-control live, is still under construction.

Research shows that the prefrontal cortex isn't fully developed until someone is in their mid-20s. That's why children react impulsively and feel things so intensely. They're not being dramatic; they're being developmentally appropriate. And they need the adults in their lives to help them slow down, make sense of their feelings, and learn how to think things through before reacting.

After separation, parents often worry about what the other household is doing. This is understandable, but children don't benefit from a parent interrogating, criticizing, or comparing homes. When parents avoid negative talk, children relax. When exchanges are neutral, children move freely between homes. When adults problem-solve rather than argue, children learn that relationships can remain stable even during transition.

Staying in sync with your children

Parents who are attuned with their children notice when their shoulders slump, when their tone becomes tense, or when they begin to withdraw. They don't pounce with their questions. They offer support and might say, "You seem a little quiet today." When approached in that manner, the child is allowed to go to the parent on their own time.

Observant parents also know that children express stress differently in different homes. A child who cries at one house and shuts down at the other isn't necessarily being manipulative. They may be adjusting to the emotional energy at each house. Each home has its own tempo, and children adapt instinctively. Attuned parents understand this and avoid assuming their home is "better" or "worse." It's simply a different emotional space.

Addressing your children's spiritual needs

A family breakup often triggers questions that go beyond who picks up the children or what time dinner is served. Children sometimes experience spiritual confusion during transitions. They may wonder whether they're being punished, whether love is dependable, whether promises matter, or why good people sometimes stop being partners.

Spiritual needs can be religious, cultural, philosophical, or simply existential, but in plain language, this includes modeling things like affection, compassion, forgiveness, gratitude, a sense of self-worth, and, most importantly, love. How you approach these attributes may change as you go through a breakup, but the importance of modeling them for children remains the same both before and after a split with your co-parent.

Perhaps the most important thing to nurture in your children after a breakup is hope, the belief that life has meaning and purpose and can improve after facing challenges. If your children become depressed while you're facing trials, hopelessness can take center stage. Gently reminding your children that their life will continue to unfold, that they'll discover purpose and direction as they get older, can offer all of you a grounding sense of possibility.

If spirituality or faith traditions were part of the family before the separation, maintaining them can be stabilizing. Even if both homes practice differently, children benefit when parents speak respectfully about each other's beliefs. If one home is more spiritual than the other, it's still important to affirm the children's experience without dismissing or undermining the other parent's practices. Although parents inherently believe their way of thinking is correct, children faced with two diverse points of reference can find it unnerving. Spiritual safety means children can explore meaning without feeling caught between loyalties.

For some families, spiritual support comes through community, youth groups, cultural gatherings, and extended family traditions. For others, spirituality is found through nature, meditation, service work, or personal reflection. What matters is creating space for children to make sense of the world in ways that bring them comfort rather than confusion.

Finally, children may find comfort in traditions, rituals, or routines that connect them to something larger than their immediate situation, particularly if they participated in such traditions prior to your breakup. Believing in something greater than themselves may offer comfort when their world seems turned upside down. Lighting a candle before bedtime, saying a blessing before meals, keeping a gratitude journal, or practicing mindfulness can help children feel grounded. The key is to look for ways to keep both you and your children centered and continuing to feel safe in times of confusion.

Reacting When Stress Becomes Toxic

Most stress children experience during a family breakup is manageable when adults stay steady, nurturing, and predictable. But sometimes stress becomes more than a developmental challenge. It becomes toxic. Toxic stress happens when children's emotional load remains high for too long without enough buffering support from adults. It affects their body, mind, and nervous system. Children may become overly anxious, depressed, withdrawn, or hypervigilant. Their schoolwork and friendships might suffer. Their sleep may deteriorate. Their appetite may fluctuate. They may struggle with anger or impulsiveness, or they may shut down completely.

When stress begins to tip into the toxic range, your job as a parent and co-parent becomes twofold:

- Reducing conflict
- Increasing support

If you believe the stress between your homes has reached a toxic level, you may assume a dramatic intervention is immediately necessary. Truth be told, it is, but it's not as difficult as you might think to make changes. Children respond to how their parents act. Parents are the ones creating the toxic atmosphere. Change begins with consistent, intentional adjustments and small but meaningful shifts in the way the adults respond to one another, particularly in front of or within earshot of the children.

The more chronic the tension between homes, the more likely children are to exhibit symptoms. They may not articulate their worry because they can't, but they live it. Toxic stress thrives in environments where children feel helpless or responsible for adult emotions. That's why one of the most proactive things you can do is assure your child in tone, behavior, and consistency that you're the parent and they're the child. They don't have to fix anything. They don't have to carry your sadness on their shoulders. They don't have to keep the peace. That's your job, not theirs. And make sure you follow through.

Moving toward healing

Once the dust settles, the focus has to shift from what happened to what comes next. Healing comes from consistent choices that reduce conflict, increase stability, and help your child feel secure again. The steps that follow are where that begins.

Reducing conflict

The most effective first step is reducing the conflict. Children can endure the breakup. What harms them is the emotional fallout between the adults, so that must stop. If you can't envision interaction without conflict, it's time to take a proactive approach. Consider co-parenting counseling with a professional who will teach you how to break the negative thought/negative behavior chain and raise your children together. When you focus on cooperation rather than competition with your co-parent, your child's stress decreases. Even if only one parent is capable of calm communication, the child benefits. You control only your half of the dynamic, but your half matters tremendously.

Increasing the support

Next, assess whether the current parenting schedule truly supports your child's emotional needs. Schedules developed during high conflict may not be the best for your child's development. Co-parenting after a breakup isn't a fixed arrangement. It's a dynamic, evolving process that requires recalibration as your child grows. What felt manageable during the early months of separation may not fit once school, activities, friendships, or developmental milestones shift.

A child may need more time to settle during transitions, go to bed earlier, have a simplified routine, or establish a different rhythm between homes. Flexibility is the most powerful antidote to toxic stress that you can offer your child. When parents insist on rigid adherence to schedules simply to "win" or "prove a point," children pay the emotional cost.

I've said this to every co-parenting client I've worked with: "Look at the schedule and make your decisions in the best interest of your child. The court order is a default. It is put in place to eliminate parental disagreements; it is not written in stone."

If what's currently in place doesn't work for your child, change it. That shows you love them more than demanding your time and stressing them out. If parents agree, they can change anything in a court order. Do what's best for your child. That means the schedule may change, and you may spend less time with your child for now, but if that's what's best for them, make the sacrifice. "Time" can be addressed in many ways. You can reassign breaks or time in the summer or adjust weekends to end on Monday rather than Sunday. You can always find a solution when your primary motivation is your child's well-being.

Reaching out for help

You may not be able to do everything by yourself, both in a literal sense and in fulfilling your child's emotional needs. Your child will need the support of other caring adults, starting with their parents, of course, but extended family plays a huge part in keeping your child safe, stable, and properly nurtured. If you've reached the point where you can't offer all these things by yourself, others can help, beginning with your co-parent. Reach out to other caring adults, like grandparents, aunts, uncles, teachers, or your best friend. It's up to you and your co-parent to create a community of support for yourselves and your child.

Adjusting without overreacting

When a child expresses discomfort, parents sometimes respond with panic. "My co-parent must be doing something wrong!" But children often express stress during normal developmental transitions. The key is discerning whether the stress reflects the breakup or simply a normal developmental response.

If a child says, "I miss Mom at bedtime," the answer isn't to eliminate Dad's parenting time. The answer is to provide reassurance and routines that ease the child into both environments. From a practical sense, that may mean adjusting phone calls from Mom or Dad to a period other than bedtime.

If a child says, "I hate switching houses," the immediate solution isn't to reduce the transitions but to make the transition calmer, gentler, and more predictable.

Adjustment isn't about reacting to every emotional ripple. Overreaction won't reduce your child's stress. It's about observing patterns, noticing what helps, and responding with flexibility, patience, and a collaborative spirit.

Seeking therapy for your child

> "This breakup has really affected our son. One minute, he's withdrawn, and the next minute, he's oppositional. I think he needs to see a therapist."

I often hear this from concerned co-parents who have been court-ordered into co-parenting counseling. They continue to fight after their breakup and feel that the court will make a decision that will stop the other parent from doing whatever they feel is inappropriate. They reassure me that their child is unaware of the conflict, but in the same breath, they confide that their child needs therapy.

Children benefit from having a neutral adult who can help them understand their emotions without feeling caught between two battling parents. However, let this register: You're sending your child to therapy to cope with *your* behavior. You have control over that.

Therapists give children a safe space to say what they fear saying out loud at home, not because they don't trust their parents, but because children instinctively protect their parents' feelings. A trained therapist allows children to explore emotions without fear of upsetting anyone.

SIGNS YOUR CHILD MAY NEED PROFESSIONAL SUPPORT

A child may benefit from therapy if they exhibit:

- Persistent sadness lasting more than a couple of weeks
- Withdrawal from friends or activities
- Noticeable changes in appetite or sleep
- Excessive worry or fear
- Declining grades or concentration problems
- Frequent physical complaints without medical causes
- Aggression, impulsiveness, or emotional outbursts
- Statements of self-blame, hopelessness, or feeling unwanted

Parents should select a therapist experienced in working with children of separated families. Ideally, both parents should participate in the intake process, even if communication is strained. Never use a therapist as a weapon in a custody dispute, and don't pressure your child to side with one home or the other.

Good therapists teach children coping skills, help them understand the breakup in age-appropriate ways, and empower them to express emotions safely. They also help parents understand what children need. A therapist isn't a referee; they're a resource and a guide.

When therapy is used appropriately, children often feel lighter within a few sessions. They begin expressing emotions more freely, communicating needs more clearly, and recovering more quickly from stressors. Therapy doesn't erase the breakup, but it helps children integrate it into their story without letting it define them.

Many children attend therapy only briefly. Others benefit during key developmental stages. There's no shame in returning to therapy months or years later when new challenges arise. Healing isn't linear, and neither is development.

Helping kids thrive after a breakup

The breakup of a family doesn't doom children to emotional hardship. Children thrive not because their parents stay together, but because their parents remain devoted to creating stability, warmth, and cooperation within a changed family structure. You and your co-parent may no longer be partners in marriage, but you remain partners in raising a resilient child.

Helping children cope requires attentiveness, compassion, flexibility, and the willingness to grow alongside them. It's not about eliminating their sadness or shielding them from discomfort. It's about walking with them through it, showing them that love endures even in transition, and teaching them that families can transform without falling apart.

When parents communicate, coordinate, and attend to children's emotional world with steady hearts, children learn one of the most important lessons of all: Security comes from loving relationships, not from living in a single household.

Children won't remember every schedule change or every moment of stress, but they'll remember how you addressed their problems, how you treated them and your co-parent with respect, and how you helped them feel safe.

IN THIS CHAPTER

» Redefining yourself after a breakup

» Examining how stress complicates decision-making

» Identifying emotional overload when parenting and co-parenting

» Incorporating stress relievers into your daily routine

» Protecting your mental health

Chapter 12 Coping with *Your Own* Stress

Every co-parent I've ever worked with believes that their stress is invisible. They think they're holding it together well enough that the children don't see it, their co-parent won't weaponize it, and their friends won't judge it. But stress is never truly invisible. It shows up in the way you talk, the way you walk, the way you breathe, and the way you make decisions. It slips into the tone you use when you say goodnight, the tension in your shoulders when you pick your child up from school, and the way your mind races when you're trying to sleep. Stress becomes the background music of your life after a breakup, and until you name it, understand it, and address it, it can run the show without your permission.

This chapter discusses how stress shows up in co-parenting and how it affects both the brain and the body, why it interferes with clear thinking and calm communication, and why co-parents may react impulsively when tensions are high. It looks at the difference between chronic and situational stress, how each influences parenting decisions, and how these patterns may play out during transitions, disagreements, and problem-solving conversations. It covers practical techniques, such as breathing, grounding, mindfulness, and progressive relaxation, that reduce the body's stress load and allow you to respond rather than react. Finally, it walks through strategies for communicating under pressure and shows how using calm, thoughtful responses not only protects the co-parenting relationship but also helps children feel secure and supported in both homes.

Stress after a breakup isn't a flaw. It's a psychological and emotional response to loss, fear, uncertainty, and transition. Even if the separation was the healthiest option, even if you initiate it, even if you've been "emotionally done for years," your body and mind still process the end of a relationship as a major life event. You may feel sadness one hour and relief the next. Anger one moment and nostalgia the next. Some parents feel numb. Others feel raw. And some feel both, switching back and forth without warning.

Stress manifests differently for everyone. You may be irritable, hyper-productive, and forgetful. You may experience physical symptoms you've never had before and don't identify as "stress." Perhaps you feel like you're parenting underwater, moving slowly through molasses, trying to remain functional while your insides feel scrambled. Stress affects how you interpret your child's behavior, how you respond to conflict, and how you see yourself as a parent. It's the lens through which you interpret every interaction with your co-parent. Unless you understand that lens, you may misinterpret far more than you realize.

The Stress of Redefining Yourself

People tend to believe that all stress is bad, but a life completely free of stress would be a life without hurdles. Scaling those hurdles contributes to learning and growth.

Separation forces you to reevaluate who you are. You're no longer a partner in the same way. You may no longer be a daily parent as you once were. Your routines, financial stability, or identity markers are now different. The stress of reinvention is real. Even when you're managing well on the outside, on the inside, you may still feel disoriented.

You may struggle with coming home to a quiet house for half the week when you were once accustomed to constant activity. You may feel the stress of constant responsibility as you parent alone with no one to tag in. Perhaps you feel the stress of judgment, real or perceived. Or you fear the unknown: What will the holidays look like now? What will the future hold? What will dating be like? Will my children be okay?

Stress that goes unacknowledged becomes stress that controls you. When you deny your emotional experience, you're more likely to lose your temper, make impulsive decisions, isolate, or turn to unhelpful coping mechanisms. Stress demands attention, whether you give it willingly or it forces its way into your life.

Examining the trauma

Trauma doesn't always come from events that are violent or catastrophic. It can come from chronic emotional tension, years of conflict, the slow erosion of trust, or the collapse of the future you imagined. Trauma is what happens when your coping capacity is overwhelmed, and the emotional landscape of your life changes abruptly. Separation, even when necessary, is a form of trauma.

REMEMBER

Your trauma and your child's trauma aren't the same. You may be processing years of pain and disappointment. Your child may be processing the sudden shift in their daily life. You may feel relief. They may feel disorganized and confused. You may have had months or years to prepare emotionally. Even though they may have lived with the arguing for years, they probably learned to accept it as the status quo and were therefore unprepared for the breakup announcement.

Examining the trauma means looking at your emotional history with honesty and compassion. What was painful? Confusing? Still feels unfinished? What triggers strong reactions in you today? As much as moving forward and forming a new relationship as co-parents rather than exes is important, trauma doesn't stay in the past. It leaks into your reactions, your patience level, your communication, and your parent-child interactions. The more you understand your trauma, the less likely it is to shape your parenting in ways you never intended. Understanding it increases your likelihood of moving forward to form that new co-parenting relationship.

Exploring the impact of ongoing conflict

Many parents underestimate the impact of chronic conflict. Even low-level conflict that becomes acceptable — sarcasm, emotional withdrawal, passive-aggressive communication — can create a stress response that becomes automatic. Your nervous system learns to brace in anticipation. You prepare for the next argument before it happens. You interpret neutral messages as hostile. You may feel defensive even when no threat exists.

When you're living in that emotional posture, parenting becomes more difficult. You may discipline inconsistently, overreact to minor issues, or retreat emotionally when your child needs connection. Trauma steals your emotional bandwidth. It makes your world feel smaller, and your reactions feel bigger. Or you may check out, unable to respond as you would if you weren't overwhelmed by an unnamed emotion.

I often hear parents say, "I didn't know I was traumatized." The conflict had become so second nature, so status quo, that they didn't see the daily conflict they faced as trauma.

Coping with the fallout

The aftermath of separation is messy. Even when two parents work hard to keep the children insulated, fallout seeps in. You may feel lonely, overwhelmed, financially strained, or socially disoriented. Everything that once felt familiar now feels temporary. Even joyous moments feel empty.

> After the breakup, I found myself feeling guilty when I felt even a tinge of happiness or when I was having fun. I'd stand back and watch myself and think, "Is it okay that I'm laughing?"

Coping with the fallout means acknowledging the emotional residue. You may feel sadness, fear, resentment, longing, regret, guilt, relief, and anger, sometimes within a single day. Too often, parents try to push past these feelings, hoping sheer willpower will carry them through. But feelings are like children: Ignore them, and they get louder. Address them, and they settle.

Fallout also shows up in ways you may not expect. You may feel exhausted from making decisions alone. You may feel triggered by your co-parent's new behaviors or new partner. You may resent the custody schedule even if you agreed to it. You may feel overwhelmed by tasks your ex-partner used to handle and that are now on your shoulders. These experiences aren't signs of failure; they're signs of transition and change.

You may find comfort in this insight from Deepak Chopra: "All great change is preceded by chaos." When things feel especially difficult, I see it as a transition. And, being the eternal optimist that I am, I trust something better is on the other side.

Emotional Overload, Parenting, and Co-Parenting

Stress affects your emotional bandwidth. When you're overloaded, your patience shrinks. You may overinterpret your child's behavior, take their meltdowns personally, or assume their frustrations reflect your inadequacy. You may find yourself disciplining more harshly or, conversely, not disciplining at all because more conflict feels unbearable.

Fallout creates a ripple effect, a sort of catch-22. The term, described in John Heller's novel *Catch-22*, is a paradoxical situation in which the conditions or rules contradict each other. So, your reactions affect your child's behavior. In turn, your child's behavior affects your stress. And around and around it goes unless you make a concerted effort to interrupt the cycle.

When stress runs high, your demeanor shifts subtly at first and more drastically over time. You may find yourself speaking faster, losing your temper more easily, withdrawing into silence, avoiding eye contact, overreacting, making decisions impulsively, changing your mind frequently, or struggling with staying consistent.

Stress narrows your window of tolerance. Decisions made from fear, scarcity, exhaustion, or resentment rarely serve your long-term goals. Parents under stress may agree to schedules that don't work, make accusations they don't believe, or refuse compromises that would actually help. Stress makes you defensive. It makes you interpret questions as criticism. It makes you doubt your instincts.

Falling victim to decision fatigue

One of the most harmful effects of stress is something referred to as *decision fatigue*. Parenting alone, even part-time, means making dozens of decisions daily that you may not be used to making. Maybe your co-parent made them when you were together, and now, living alone or outside of that relationship, you have to make them yourself. But do you? You have a co-parent. You have help. Perhaps the stress of getting to a place where you realize you're a team makes the transition overwhelming. You don't want to decide because you just don't care right now.

When stress is high, it's common to become indecisive or overly rigid. You may choose based on the opposite of whatever your co-parent wants, not because it's best, but because you're overwhelmed. Stress makes logic feel like a luxury.

Try these techniques when decision fatigue sets in:

- **Notice the signs.** When you feel irritable, scattered, or oddly emotional over routine choices, pause and ask yourself: "Am I tired, or am I tired of deciding?"
- **Reduce the load.** Choose one simplifier for the week:
  - Create a shared routine with your co-parent so you make fewer decisions on the fly.
  - Send short, direct messages: "Do you want to decide this or should I?"
  - Hold nonurgent issues for a weekly check-in rather than answering instantly.
- **Divide; don't duplicate.** Identify one task you can trade or delegate to your co-parent. These might be things like school updates, activity sign-ups, or medical scheduling. Shared responsibility lightens emotional weight.
- **Use a reset phrase.** When fatigue peaks, try saying, "I'm overloaded. Let's revisit this later today or tomorrow." This protects communication from becoming reactive. The phrase I use is, "My motor just shut off." That tells my family that I'm done for the day and need to recharge.
- **Refill your battery.** Take a brief walk, stretch, journal for a few minutes, or simply sit quietly. Meditate for 15 minutes. Even small resets restore clarity and reduce the likelihood of harsh discipline or miscommunication.

Using inappropriate discipline

When parents are stressed, discipline can become distorted. Some parents become overly strict, creating harsh consequences for minor issues because they crave control in at least one part of their lives. Others become overly permissive or inconsistent, allowing inappropriate behaviors because they feel guilty, exhausted, or afraid of conflict. Extremes leave children confused.

Inappropriate discipline is rarely intentional. It's usually a sign that the parent's internal world is frayed. You may yell not because your child's behavior is severe, but because you feel pushed to your capacity. You may avoid consequences because you can't bear one more emotional challenge. You may rely on punishment instead of teaching, or excuses instead of boundaries.

The key is consistency, which is difficult when you're pushed to your limit. But children don't need perfect discipline. They need to be able to anticipate what's coming so they can weigh their behavior. Consider it a teachable moment for both you and your children. Be aware that when stress drives your discipline, your child feels the chaos even if they don't understand its source. Then you must weigh whether the discipline is really effective at that point.

STAYING CONSISTENT WITH DISCIPLINE

Ask yourself: "Is this discipline matching the behavior or matching my mood?"

If the answer is "matching my mood," follow these steps:

1. **Look at the child, not the offense.** Notice what your child's behavior may be communicating. Acting out, disobeying, and arguing are ways for a child who doesn't feel seen to demand attention. Are they overwhelmed? Hungry? Tired? Feeling ignored? Understanding why your child may be misbehaving prevents overcorrection.
2. **Reset with your co-parent.** Share a neutral observation: "He seemed frightened after last night's discipline. Let's compare notes and discuss what works for both of us."
3. **Choose one shared strategy.** Consistency reduces confusion. Try choosing one for the week:
   - **Short age-appropriate time-outs or breaks:** The rule of thumb is to match the time-out to the age of the child. 3 years old = 3-minute time-out. 5 years old = 5-minute time-out. Longer time-outs breed frustration and become ineffective.
   - **Loss of privilege:** Losing a privilege for a set amount of time works best with older children.
   - **Logical consequences that match the behavior:** Allow the child to make amends by apologizing or helping to fix something they broke.
4. **Revisit the strategy.** Did the consequence teach the child what you and your co-parent hoped it would? If not, adjust together. This cooperative approach may feel unnatural to estranged co-parents. But if you find it difficult to stay organized and are stressed to the max, imagine how your children feel. Whether you're a couple or not, you and your co-parent are responsible for raising your children the best you can.

Making your child your confidant

This is one of the most common and damaging stress responses after a breakup. When parents feel lonely, overwhelmed, or misunderstood, they may turn to their children for emotional support. They confide adult problems, express fears, or share frustrations about their co-parent. The child becomes the parent's emotional partner and often volunteers things they don't understand. Rather than make things clearer, children become more confused.

This dynamic is subtle at first:

> "I'm having a hard day."
>
> "Your mother makes things difficult."
>
> "I just wish someone understood how much I'm carrying."

The child, wanting to help, becomes hyperattuned to the parent's emotions. They take responsibility for adult feelings. They become the comforter rather than the comforted.

This role reversal creates an emotional burden. Children may feel anxious leaving that parent when it's time to go home with their other parent. They may fear upsetting that first parent or worry that they're lonely. They may hide positive feelings about the other home, feel guilty, or question their loyalty to one parent or the other.

A child should never be the emotional container for their parents' stress. Parents need adult support systems. Search out friends, a therapist, or spiritual communities, and protect your child emotionally.

Allowing your child to sleep with you

After a breakup, many parents allow their child to sleep in their bed. Sometimes, it's intentional as a temporary comfort. Maybe it's accidental: The child crawls in, and the parent, overwhelmed and lonely, allows it without thinking.

A child sleeping with you isn't inherently harmful. But when it becomes a pattern driven by parental stress rather than the child's need, it can create emotional entanglement. Children may feel responsible for soothing the parent. Parents may lean on the child for comfort that should come from adult support systems.

Bed-sharing can also complicate transitions. A child who sleeps with one parent but not the other automatically causes the child to compare homes. This may make them feel anxious, unsettled, or resistant — the exact opposite feelings you want them to have by sleeping with you. The message becomes, "I'm here to make you feel better," rather than, "Both homes are emotionally safe."

When bed-sharing becomes a coping mechanism for the parent rather than the child, it's time to examine what emotional need is being unmet and to find healthier alternatives.

Allowing your child to sleep with you can also complicate the transition into a new relationship. Co-sleeping is soothing and intimate; children often interpret it as special. When a new partner eventually enters the picture, the shift can feel abrupt and deeply personal.

If a parent suddenly says, "Taylor is sleeping over tonight, so you need to sleep in your own bed," a child may not hear a simple logistical change at all. What they hear is, "You're being moved out to make room for someone I like better." Their bed isn't just a new location; it feels like a demotion.

The emotional message lands harder if co-sleeping has been a longstanding habit, especially after a breakup, when children are already vulnerable, craving stability, and fighting fears of abandonment. That's why it's important to anticipate how these transitions might feel to a child and to shift sleep arrangements gradually and thoughtfully, rather than tying the change to the arrival of a new adult.

Stress and Domestic Violence (Perpetrator and Victim)

Not only is stress emotionally exhausting, but it can become dangerous when it escalates unaddressed. After a breakup, some parents find themselves teetering on the edge of behaviors they themselves acknowledge are questionable. Stress doesn't cause domestic violence, but it can exacerbate patterns already rooted in the relationship or create conditions where those patterns might worsen. According to data from the National Intimate Partner and Sexual Violence Survey (NISVS) published by the Centers for Disease Control and Prevention (CDC), one in three women and one in four men have experienced physical violence from a partner in their lifetime.

For the parent at risk of becoming the perpetrator

The stress of a breakup with your co-parent may make you feel angrier than usual. More reactive. More defensive. You may interpret every interaction with your co-parent as a provocation. You may feel wronged or misunderstood, and the intensity of those feelings may surprise you. When stress turns into aggression, it often starts small: a raised voice during an exchange, a threatening tone in a text message, a slammed door. These are the earliest signs that stress has pushed you beyond your emotional threshold.

Domestic violence is rarely an overnight transformation. It begins with control, rigidity, blame, or emotional volatility. If you recognize these tendencies in yourself, this isn't the moment for shame. It's the moment for intervention. Support groups, therapy, anger management programs, and accountability structures aren't punishments. They're lifelines. Be proactive. Seeking help at this stage is the greatest act of protection you can offer your child.

Children who grow up in environments with uncontrolled anger internalize fear even when the anger isn't directed at them. They learn that relationships are unpredictable. They learn to appease or to withdraw. Early intervention prevents your stress from becoming your child's trauma.

Following are ten steps to manage anger and frustration and prevent you from possibly becoming an abuser:

1. **Recognize your early warning signs.** Anger rarely comes out of nowhere. Notice the physical and emotional cues, tight muscles, pacing, irritability, clenched jaw, or the sense that you need to respond right now. Awareness is your first safety tool.
2. **Step away before you react.** A simple, calm phrase like, "I need a moment; I'll come back," protects everyone involved. Walking away isn't abandoning. It's responsible self-regulation. Distance breaks the escalation cycle.
3. **Regulate your body to reset your mind.** Anger is physiological. You can feel the adrenaline kick in when you start to get angry, and it can become addictive. Breathing slowly, grounding your feet, splashing cool water on your face, and taking a brief walk can reduce adrenaline and restore clarity.
4. **Question the story you're telling yourself.** Anger often builds on assumptions. "They're disrespecting," "I'm being pushed out," "I'm being ignored or not taken seriously." Pause and ask, "Is there another explanation?" Or "What would I tell a friend?" A small shift in perspective can prevent an overreaction.
5. **Delay important conversations until you're calm.** Agree with your co-parent that heated discussions will wait, whether that means later in the day or tomorrow. Many regrettable actions happen during escalated conversations; postponing them is a powerful prevention strategy.
6. **Use neutral communication tools.** If in-person conversation escalates, communicate through texts, email, or a co-parenting app. Written communication slows the pace, gives you time to think, and helps you choose calmer words.
7. **Build healthy outlets for stress.** Exercise, therapy, meditation, journaling, or hobbies that release tension keep your emotional pressure lower. Parents who regularly decompress are less likely to erupt under stress.

8. **Repair quickly when you slip.** If you raise your voice or react harshly, acknowledge it early:

   "I lost my temper. That wasn't okay. I'm working on it."

   Repair prevents shame from turning into more defensiveness or aggression.

9. **Practice safe, structured conflict-resolution skills.** Tools like iMessages, active listening, time-outs, and collaborative problem-solving keep disagreements from becoming confrontational. Structure reduces the risk of escalation.

10. **Seek support if patterns persist.** It's difficult to be proactive when you're right in the middle of a stressed reaction. Don't be afraid to reach out for help to break the cycle. Therapy, anger management, DV prevention classes, and co-parenting coaching are ways to understand triggers, replace harmful patterns, and reinforce safer behaviors. Reaching out is an act of protection for your child, your co-parent, and yourself.

For the parent at risk of becoming the victim

Stress can also make you more vulnerable to tolerating behaviors you would previously identify as unsafe. Isolation, exhaustion, and fear of conflict can distort your perception. You may convince yourself that the yelling was "because of the breakup" or that the threatening language was just "stress talking." These rationalizations make sense emotionally because your nervous system is trying to protect you, but they can be dangerous.

If your co-parent's behavior includes intimidation, monitoring, belittling, financial control, or any form of physical aggression, stress isn't the explanation; it's the fuel. And you're not responsible for managing their emotional state or preventing their outbursts.

Seek support immediately. Friends, family, therapists, mediators, and domestic violence resources exist to help you establish safety. Children exposed to domestic violence, even indirectly, experience long-term emotional harm. Protecting yourself is protecting them.

Are you a victim of abuse? Abuse isn't always obvious. At first, it starts with tension, criticism, or control, but it slowly grows into something that leaves you feeling small, afraid, or uncertain of your own judgment.

Use this quick self-check to clarify what you're experiencing:

1. **Ask yourself:**

   "Do I feel fearful, anxious, or on guard around my partner or ex?"

   "Do I change my behavior to avoid anger?"

   "Do I feel like I'm walking on eggshells?"

   If you feel unsafe often, that's a warning sign, not a relationship issue.

2. **Look at their behavior** and check any that apply:

   They insult, belittle, or humiliate me.

   They control my access to money, transportation, or communication.

   They isolate me from friends and family.

   They monitor my movements, devices, or social media.

   They threaten self-harm, harm to me, or harm to the children.

   They use force, intimidation, or physical aggression.

   Patterns of power and control, not occasional arguments, signal abuse.

3. **Track your reactions** and notice whether you freeze during conflicts, avoid bringing up concerns, feel confused about what's "normal," or apologize to keep the peace. These reactions often indicate a survival response, not a communication issue.

4. **Ask a trusted person for perspective.** If you don't check in with a trusted friend about your thoughts, it's a closed conversation with yourself. Share what's happening with someone safe and neutral. If you feel embarrassed or afraid to talk about it, that alone is meaningful information.

5. **Prioritize safety.** If anything you checked raises concern, consider speaking with a professional or hotline. You don't have to make the decision today; you only have to stay safe today.

The apps shown in Table 12-1 can increase your personal safety and provide options when you feel unsafe. They're supplements, not substitutes for emergency services.

These apps should be used in addition to, not instead of, emergency services. If you're in immediate danger, call 911. For confidential help and support, contact the National Domestic Violence Hotline at 1-800-799-SAFE or visit TheHotline.org.

TABLE 12-1 Safety Apps to Consider

App	What It Does
myPlan	A free, confidential app that helps users process safety decisions when experiencing abuse, offers links to local support services, and gives options for help.
Bright Sky	Developed by Hestia, this free and secure app provides information on domestic abuse, links to local support services, and options for help.
Aspire News	A disguised safety app that looks like a news platform but includes hidden resources, emergency contacts, and direct access to support for individuals experiencing abuse.
eBodyGuard	Voice- or touch-activated, this app sends your GPS location to 911 and a chosen contact while recording audio of the situation.
SafeTrek	Intended for personal safety during travel, but useful in abusive situations. Alerts emergency services or a trusted contact if the user fails to deactivate it.
bSafe	Offers voice or touch-activated SOS alerts, "Follow Me" location sharing, and a "Fake Call" function to help users exit uncomfortable or dangerous situations.
Hollie Guard	Created by Hollie Gazzard Trust, this app sends alarms and GPS location to designated contacts when activated.

The Connection between Trauma and Danger

After a breakup, many parents who face domestic violence in their past or present are ashamed to admit that it's their experience. They worry about losing access to their children or appearing unstable. But acknowledging it is an attempt to break the cycle before it harms the next generation.

Here's the difference between trauma, danger, and stress.

Trauma is what happened to you. It's the event, or *pattern of events*, that overwhelmed your sense of safety, dignity, or control. Trauma leaves emotional imprints based on past danger, and those imprints shape how you respond to triggers in the present.

Danger is what *could* happen next. It lives *in the current moment*. It's not about memory. It's about real, active risk. Danger requires a protective response, such as leaving, setting boundaries, calling for help, or seeking support.

Stress is what warns you to pay attention. It's your *internal alarm system*. Stress signals that something feels off, uncertain, or unsafe. The goal is not to ignore it, but to interpret it accurately. Consider: "Is this stress left over from trauma, or is it signaling actual danger right now?"

When parents learn to distinguish between trauma from the past, genuine risk in the present, and the stress that alerts them to both, they respond more effectively and keep themselves and their children safer.

Recognizing the difference between these three is the key to staying grounded and safe.

Protecting your mental health

Unchecked stress can induce or exacerbate mental health conditions in parents, including anxiety disorders, depression, panic attacks, and post-traumatic stress disorder. If you or your co-parent — or even your child — have a diagnosis that requires medication and you/they aren't med compliant or don't take the prescribed medication consistently, that can also prompt extreme reactions to stressful situations. Follow the suggestions of your doctor. Don't adjust medication yourself. It may contribute to shorter fuses and unpredictable reactions.

Even parents who have never experienced mental health concerns before may find themselves overwhelmed by intrusive thoughts, rumination, or sudden waves of fear.

Anxiety

Stressed-based anxiety is common after a breakup. You may fear the future, dread interactions with your co-parent, worry excessively about your children, or imagine worst-case scenarios. Anxiety reshapes your perception. What's manageable begins to feel catastrophic.

You feel anxiety in your body. It makes your heart beat faster and raises your blood pressure. Some even tell me their head starts to buzz. Almost everyone has trouble making decisions when they're struggling with anxiety. And those going through a breakup can easily go past feeling anxious to experience a full-blown panic attack.

Panic attacks may occur during high-conflict periods or transition points, such as exchanges or legal processes. Panic reflects a nervous system pushed beyond its limits.

A panic attack feels like your body suddenly believes you're in danger, even if your mind knows you're not. It comes on quickly and intensely. Many people describe a wave of fear or dread that hits without warning. Your heart may pound or race, your breathing may feel tight or shallow, and you may struggle to get enough air.

Some people feel dizzy, lightheaded, or shaky. Others notice tingling in their fingers or lips. Your stomach can flip, you may feel sweaty or chilled, and your chest may hurt enough that you fear a heart attack.

Emotionally, panic attacks feel surreal and frightening. You may feel disconnected from your surroundings, like you're floating or not fully inside your body. Some explain it as, "I feel like I'm in a dream." Your thoughts can race: "Something terrible is happening," "I can't control this," "I'm dying," or "I'm losing my mind."

Even though the episode is temporary, it can feel overwhelming and confusing in the moment.

Afterward, people often feel exhausted, embarrassed, or shaky for hours. Many describe a sort of "panic hangover" whereby they feel physically drained and emotionally raw.

REMEMBER

A panic attack feels dangerous, but it's not. You won't die from a panic attack. It's the nervous system reacting as if you're in danger, when in reality you're not. It's the fear of the sensations and physical reactions, not the reactions themselves, that creates the spiral.

Depression

What does depression feel like?

Depression can feel different for everyone, but Table 12-2 lays out some common emotional and physical experiences people often report.

TABLE 12-2 Symptoms of Depression

Experience	How It Manifests
Emotional numbness	Feeling flat or numb, where nothing feels joyful or fulfilling anymore. Things that used to bring pleasure no longer appeal to you.
Persistent sadness or emptiness	A deep feeling that doesn't seem to go away, no matter what you do.
Hopelessness	The feeling that things will never get better. No light at the end of the tunnel, so to speak.
Fatigue	Feeling drained, both mentally and physically, even when you haven't done anything. Basic tasks seem overwhelming. You may not get out of bed or off the couch.

(continued)

TABLE 12-2 *(continued)*

Experience	How It Manifests
Irritability of frustration	Short temper or frustration over small things, particularly if you weren't like that before.
Social withdrawal	You find yourself pulling away from friends, family, or activities you once enjoyed. It might feel pointless to interact with others.
Difficulty concentrating or making decisions	The brain feels "foggy," and it becomes difficult to focus or make decisions, no matter how simple they seem.
Physical symptoms	Depression isn't just mental. It can show up as aches and pains, problems sleeping (either not being able to sleep or sleeping too much), changes in appetite, or digestive problems.
Extreme feelings of guilt or self-criticism	A harsh inner critic can make you feel as if you're not good enough and never will be.

In severe cases, depression can lead to thoughts of self-harm or suicide, though not everyone with a depression diagnosis feels that extreme.

There's a difference between situational depression and chronic depression, and understanding the distinction reduces shame and improves coping. Table 12-3 differentiates the two.

TABLE 12-3 **Differences between Situational and Chronic Depression**

	Situational Depression	Chronic Depression
Feature	Situational: tied to an event	Chronic: ongoing regardless of events
Specific stressor	Trigger	Often no clear trigger
Duration	Improves as the situation resolves	Long-lasting or recurring
Treatment	Support, coping, problem-solving	Clinical treatment support
Outlook	Often temporary	Requires ongoing management

TIP

You can find plenty of information on your own about all the symptoms of depression, and it's tempting to self-diagnose. Don't do it. Talk to a mental health professional instead. If they diagnose you with depression, follow their directions.

Post-traumatic stress

Parents emerging from emotionally abusive or chronic conflict often carry post-traumatic symptoms into their co-parenting. Loud voices, certain phrases, or even text notifications can trigger physiological responses that feel disproportionate but are actually rooted in past harm.

Your mental health directly shapes your child's emotional world. A parent who's anxious, depressed, or traumatized needs support, not judgment. Children do better when their parents do better emotionally, physically, and mentally. This means if you feel overwhelmed, get help, not only for your sake, but for your children's.

Finding workable tools for dealing with stress

Coping with parental stress means building a toolbox on which to rely — not one perfect solution but a variety of small, reliable strategies that help you stay centered. The goal isn't to eliminate stress (that's impossible) but to manage it effectively so it doesn't seep into your parenting or shape your reactions.

Making small adjustments can help. The power of small emotional changes is often underestimated. A five-minute breathing routine. A ten-minute walk after dinner. A consistent bedtime. A "no co-parenting talk after 8 p.m." rule. These small changes interrupt the cycle of stress and provide the nervous system with the breaks it desperately needs.

Relaxation techniques

Relaxation techniques aren't luxuries. They're necessities. After a breakup, your nervous system remains on high alert for months. Relaxation techniques shift your body out of survival mode.

You can practice simple relaxation strategies daily.

- **Breathing.** Deep breathing calms you by changing what's happening in your body. When stress hits, your sympathetic nervous system speeds up your heart, tightens your muscles, and releases adrenaline. Slow, intentional breathing activates the parasympathetic nervous system — your body's calming system — lowering heart rate, reducing blood pressure, and slowing stress hormones like cortisol. It also increases oxygen to the brain, improving focus and helping you think clearly instead of reacting. At the same time, it relaxes muscles and reduces the lightheaded or shaky feelings that often come with anxiety. In simple terms, breathing signals to your brain that you're safe, helping your body shift out of fight-or-flight and back into balance.

» **Progressive muscle release.** Tensing and then relaxing different muscle groups resets the body's stress response. The nervous system interprets a muscle release as a signal of safety. This reduces physical discomfort, lowers heart rate, and helps the mind shift out of high-alert mode.

» **Mindfulness.** By focusing on what's happening right now — your breathing, your senses, or the task in front of you — you step out of ruminating about the past and worrying about the future. Staying present gives your brain space to regulate emotion more effectively.

» **Visualization.** Imagining a safe, peaceful setting, such as a beach, forest, or comforting memory, helps your brain shift away from stress triggers. Visualization "rehearses" calm responses, training your nervous system to react less intensely during future stressful moments.

» **Body-based calming.** Warm showers, stretching, grounding exercises like yoga or tai chi, and even a weighted blanket create physical sensations that communicate safety to your brain. When the body feels soothed, the nervous system becomes less reactive, making it easier to think clearly and reduce anxiety.

» **Meditation.** Meditation relieves stress by helping the mind and body shift out of survival mode and into calm awareness. As you meditate, your breathing slows, your heart rate steadies, and your nervous system moves out of fight-or-flight and into a restorative state. It interrupts spiraling thoughts, reduces the tendency to catastrophize, and lowers stress hormones. Over time, it trains your brain to notice stressful thoughts without getting pulled into them, creating more emotional space, clearer thinking, and a greater sense of control. In short, meditation gives your brain practice in settling down so that when stress hits, it can respond rather than react.

If you find it difficult to meditate, try guided meditation. *Guided meditation* is a form of meditation where a voice — either recorded or in person — walks you through each step of calming the body and mind. For people who find it hard to quiet their thoughts on their own, guided meditation offers structure, focus, and direction. The voice may lead you in slow breathing, visualizing a peaceful setting, relaxing specific muscles, or noticing sensations without judgment. Because you're following someone else's words, you don't have to "figure meditation out," which lowers frustration.

Support groups

Support groups provide something that no co-parenting book can offer: real-time shared experience. You reduce isolation when you sit with people, either face-to-face or via video chat, who understand the exhaustion, confusion, and emotional upheaval of a breakup and co-parenting after that breakup. You learn you're not alone. You learn you're not failing. You learn what has helped others. Most of all, you learn you're human.

Support groups come in many forms, from divorce recovery, single parenting, domestic violence, faith-based groups, and more. I even head a bonus mom/bio mom support group through the bonus families website to help counterpartners (moms and bonus moms or dads and bonus dads) better understand each other and work together more successfully.

Your child needs you to receive adult emotional support elsewhere so that you can remain their parent rather than their confidant. Perhaps the most important aspect of all these tools mentioned is the proactive model it offers your children. When they see you taking a proactive approach in confronting your stress, they'll follow in your footsteps.

Seeking therapy when needed

Therapy used to be thought of as the last resort when facing a problem, a stop-off place right before admitting there's no more help out there. Thank goodness therapy is now regarded as mainstream assistance when facing a psychological or emotional trial. Good therapy helps you understand your emotional patterns, break cycles of stress, and rebuild your internal world with clarity. Therapy doesn't erase the breakup, but it prevents the fallout from defining you.

For therapy to really work, you must be honest in session and dedicated to making the necessary changes to help yourself. A therapist can collaborate with you to identify your stumbling blocks and discover the best methods to address them, but they can't solve your problems or think for you. A good therapist is a resource for your recovery, but they can't do the work for you. That's up to you with their guidance.

4 Managing Special Occasions and Child-Centered Milestones

IN THIS PART . . .

Explore your new normal and celebrate child-centered holidays, milestones, and family rituals

Introduce a new marriage or formal commitment into an established co-parenting system

Support your adult children with steadiness and clarity when they commit or marry

IN THIS CHAPTER

» Maintaining reasonable holiday expectations

» Tailoring family traditions and rituals

» Managing gift-giving

» Observing religious traditions

Chapter 13
Enjoying Holidays and Child-Centered Milestones

Most holidays and milestone events exist to bring families together, to pause, take stock of blessings, and share moments that connect one generation to the next. But when a breakup or divorce reshapes the family system, these same occasions can feel bittersweet. Traditions that once felt automatic now require even more planning. How much will stay the same and how much will be different? Will you celebrate together or separately? Maybe you're close to your co-parent's Aunt Mary. Will she want to celebrate with you or with me? Will you go in together for presents for the kids, or should you get them something separately? Should you still buy presents for your co-parents' parents? Where will you and your co-parent sit at your niece's christening? At your son's bar mitzvah?

This chapter explores what your new normal might look like across a variety of situations, large and small. Every milestone offers a chance to reassure your child that their world is still whole, even if it's arranged differently.

The important thing to remember is this: Nothing about your holidays, milestones, or family rituals is fixed. You're allowed to adjust traditions, update rituals, and make changes that match your children's developmental needs and your co-parenting reality.

Holidays will feel different for a while, but different doesn't have to mean worse. In fact, many co-parents eventually find that planning and thoughtful communication lead to celebrations that are calmer, clearer, and more child-centered than they were before.

Having Reasonable Expectations for Holiday Celebrations

Almost no co-parent looks forward to the first major holiday after a breakup. The second or third may not be easy either. Even when parents do their best to "keep it light" for the kids, holidays often spotlight absences and what looks different. Setting reasonable expectations can help.

Trying to re-create holidays exactly as they once were usually results in frustration and disappointment. Instead, aim for moments of connection and child-focused decision-making, not scorekeeping.

Think of this season of life as a transition period. Some old traditions will still work beautifully. Others may need gentle revision or retirement. None of this signals failure; it signals a family healing and adapting.

THE SPECIAL OCCASION LITMUS TEST

A litmus test is a quick way to see what's going on beneath the surface. Here, the test is simple: watch your children during special occasions. These moments amplify emotions and reveal what everyday routines can hide.

- Is your child relaxed or tense?
- Are they excited, or worried about upsetting one parent?
- Do they feel free to enjoy the moment, or are they managing everyone else's feelings?

Ask yourself what decisions you are making to help your child feel supported. When support guides your choices, guilt eases, tension softens, and children experience holidays and milestones the way they're meant to — with excitement, comfort, and the freedom to enjoy the moment without carrying adult emotions.

The celebration may not look the way it once did, but with intention and cooperation, it can be just as meaningful — sometimes even more so.

Setting the example for the children and the extended family

Children take cues from the adults around them. When co-parents maintain courtesy, keep conflict low, and model flexibility, extended family usually follows suit.

Your children and other relatives watch how you interact. Whether a holiday feels tense or warm is determined by the tone you set, not the parenting plan, schedule, or gifts.

Setting the example means speaking positively about your co-parent, even when you disagree; maintaining boundaries without pettiness; refraining from guilt-inducing comments; prioritizing your child's comfort above your own pride or preferences; and communicating plans clearly so everyone knows what to expect.

Keeping a family feel for all occasions

Keeping a family feel after a separation is about showing children that what mattered before still does. The message remains the same: You still belong to a family system that cares about you.

Here are practical, child-centered steps you can take to preserve that feeling across two homes.

- **Honor continuity before creating change.** Before discarding old traditions, look at how you can adjust them. A holiday dinner might move to a midafternoon supper. A bedtime ritual may happen on different nights. The goal isn't duplication, but reassurance.
- **Keep the child out of the middle.** Nothing erodes co-parenting trust more than children acting as messengers, translators, or emotional buffers. Direct communication between co-parents, even when limited or businesslike, allows children to stay in their rightful role: kids.

» **Speak respectfully about the other home.** Children build their identity from both households. When one home is criticized, a child feels internally divided. Neutral or kind language, especially when emotions run high, protects a child's sense of wholeness. You don't have to agree with your co-parent to acknowledge their role.

» **Let traditions evolve naturally.** Some rituals will fade, and new ones will emerge. Invite children into the process: "What feels important to keep?" or "What would you like to add here?" When children have a voice, transitions feel collaborative rather than imposed.

» **Reinforce the bigger picture.** Children need to hear, repeatedly and calmly, that families can change shape without disappearing. Two houses don't mean two families competing for loyalty. They mean one family learning how to function differently.

A family feel isn't housed in one living room or defined by one calendar. It lives in predictability, emotional safety, and the steady message that love and care don't end just because their parents now live in two homes. When co-parents focus on adjustment rather than abandonment, children learn that change doesn't have to mean loss.

Taking sides

After a breakup, it's common for family members to take sides. Family loyalty can become tangled with grief, anger, or a need to protect, and people may retreat rather than risk saying the wrong thing. For the parent in the middle, this can feel like a second rupture layered on top of the first, leaving you isolated at a moment when support is needed most.

When no one is talking, the most constructive step is often to lower the emotional volume rather than raise it. Resist the urge to defend your version of events or recruit allies. Instead, lead with steadiness and clarity. A simple, non-accusatory outreach opens a door without demanding anyone walk through it immediately. Focus on shared values, especially the well-being of the children, and be willing to tolerate discomfort while relationships recalibrate. Some family members will come back slowly, and others may not. But modeling calm, respectful boundaries protects your emotional health and shows your children that conflict doesn't have to mean permanent division.

Many co-parents are surprised to discover that extended family often becomes more cooperative when they see parents treating each other with dignity. Your model cues everyone else to adjust their tone as well.

Celebrating separately or together

Ask most children about holidays, birthdays, and school dances after a breakup, and you'll often hear sadness in their voices. These are the days children feel most aware that their parents live in separate homes.

Celebrating together can work beautifully when you and your co-parent share a low-conflict, predictable relationship. Boundaries are clear and respected, communication is calm, and both adults understand their roles. There's no guessing, power struggles, or unspoken tests. When everyone knows what to expect, children are free to enjoy the moment.

This balance is especially important when new partners are part of the picture. When expectations are discussed ahead of time and honored, new partners aren't left to wonder where they fit or how they're supposed to behave. Most importantly, the children aren't placed in the middle, pressured to perform happiness, manage adult feelings, or prove loyalty. Instead, they experience the celebration as comfortable, relaxed, and centered on their well-being rather than the adults' unresolved history. They're free to form new memories without pressure.

Celebrating together should never be attempted because someone feels guilty or pressured, feels it's what you're supposed to do, or is trying to "put on a show." It should only happen if the parents' communication is stable and the experience will genuinely lower, not increase, the child's stress. Celebrating together should be the natural order of things. If it's not, don't attempt it.

For many families, celebrating together simply isn't realistic. Two calm celebrations are far healthier than one awkward, tense gathering.

Togetherness isn't a requirement of healthy co-parenting, but it can become a possibility when the foundation is calm, predictable, and child-centered. Shared celebrations only work when they grow out of trust, clear boundaries, and a shift away from conflict. Audry's parents didn't rush ahead of their emotional readiness; they responded to a moment their child offered because their co-parenting relationship had matured enough to hold it. When co-parents create space for choices that once felt impossible, children feel the difference.

Adjusting Traditions and Family Rituals

Traditions are what families do. Rituals are how families do them. Many co-parents feel thrown off balance when familiar rituals no longer make sense. When the cast of characters or the setting changes, rituals can feel hollow or incomplete.

Tradition versus ritual: Why it matters

Learning the difference helps co-parents make good decisions. Traditions can often remain the same (such as visiting the same pumpkin patch or attending the same Christmas Eve service), though rituals may need adjustment (such as who lights the candles, who reads the story, or who opens the first gift).

Breakups change the cast but don't need to erase the tradition itself. The question becomes: What part of this tradition matters most to our child, and how can we preserve that meaning in a new way? If a ritual becomes painful or feels forced, families can create new ones that honor both the past and the present. This isn't betrayal. It's growth.

When to modify traditions

A tradition might need revision when it excludes one parent unfairly, triggers conflict or competition, depends on roles that no longer exist, causes distress for the child, or no longer reflects your current family structure.

Knowing when to modify a tradition is less about loss and more about readjusting your perspective. Traditions are meant to create comfort and connection, not tension or loyalty conflicts. Adjusting a tradition doesn't erase its meaning; it honors the purpose behind it. By approaching change thoughtfully and keeping your child's emotional safety at the center, you show them that families can adapt without breaking.

When to start new traditions

Families consider creating new traditions when the old ones no longer fit. After a split, each home settles into a new rhythm. If your family deeply loves a tradition but can no longer carry it out in the same way, you can adjust it. By reshaping familiar rituals to match your current lifestyle, you preserve what matters while making room for what's *now*. Taking a little from the past and a little from the present is often how families gently create a future that feels both meaningful and emotionally safe. The purpose of a tradition isn't only to preserve the past, but to create continuity, meaning, and emotional security. Traditions help friends and family feel connected across time, even as circumstances change.

Remembering the child's experience

When traditions are duplicated across two homes, they stop being comforting and start being comparative. Whose morning was better? Whose gifts were opened first? Even when no one says it out loud, children are put in the middle. Copying traditions in both homes can unintentionally turn holidays into a quiet contest.

Adjustment removes competition. Sometimes holding on to the tradition works, but if the tradition is adjusted or something new is created, celebrating is still meaningful, still intentional, without trying to match or outdo it. The child doesn't have to compare. They just get to belong.

The form of a tradition may need to adapt, but its purpose is still to strengthen connection and help family members feel grounded.

Creating Smooth Transitions for Children during Milestones

Children are already sensitive to the back-and-forth cadence of co-parenting; holidays and milestone events can feel even more intense. Your goal is to make transitions predictable, calm, and guilt-free.

Plan ahead, way ahead

Parents often underestimate how much pressure children feel when the plan changes repeatedly or isn't clear. Whenever possible, try to confirm times in advance, pack bags the night before, share contact expectations, and avoid last-minute bargaining about time.

Everyone operates best on routines, especially when emotions run high.

Saying goodbye without the guilt

Children should never feel that their happiness in one home causes pain in the other. Transitions are already emotionally loaded moments, especially around holidays and special occasions. When a parent expresses sadness, loneliness, or loss in a way that leans on the child for comfort, the child may internalize the message that enjoying time away is a betrayal. Even subtle comments can leave children torn between excitement and guilt as they move from one home to the other.

This doesn't mean parents must hide their feelings or pretend that separations are easy. Adults should manage their own emotions so that children don't have to. A child's job is to celebrate, relax, and feel free to love both homes without emotional consequence. When parents communicate goodbyes with reassurance and steadiness, they communicate that the child can move between homes with confidence rather than worry, setting the stage for healthy transitions and a sense of security that lasts long after the holiday ends.

Use C.A.R.E. to guide holiday negotiations

Holidays have a way of magnifying old wounds, which is why structure and intention matter so much when negotiating time. Using the C.A.R.E. framework (communication, acceptance, respect, and empathy) keeps conversations grounded and prevents celebrations from becoming battlegrounds.

Communication works best when it's brief, neutral, and child-focused. Lengthy explanations or emotional backstories tend to reopen conflict rather than resolve it. Stick to logistics, timelines, and what the children need to feel settled and secure.

Acceptance is often the hardest step. Divorce means no one gets every holiday exactly as they imagined, and holding out for "fair" can quietly turn into a power struggle. Letting go of perfection makes room for workable solutions.

Respect requires resisting the urge to keep score about who had last year, who gave up more, and who owes whom. Holidays shift over time, and flexibility today often builds goodwill for tomorrow.

Empathy asks you to step out of adult disappointment and into your child's experience. Children don't measure holidays by equity charts; they measure them by emotional tone. The ultimate goal isn't to win a date on the calendar or to prevent holidays from being used as leverage, but to protect them as moments of connection for both parents and their child(ren) rather than conflict.

HOLIDAY GROUND RULES

Holidays have a tendency to bring out both the best and the worst in our family members, particularly when co-parenting. When emotions run high, it helps to have a few simple guidelines to keep the focus where it belongs: on your child. These principles can help you move through the season with less conflict and more intention.

Communication: Keep conversations short, neutral, and focused.

Acceptance: You may not get everything you want, and neither will your co-parent.

Respect: Avoid scorekeeping. Next year may look different.

Empathy: Try to see the holiday through your child's eyes.

The goal isn't to "win" a holiday. It's to avoid using holidays as weapons.

Gift-Giving

Gift-giving becomes complicated after a breakup because emotions creep into decision-making. Jealousy, guilt, competition, and nostalgia can influence what should be a simple, joyful experience.

Presents for the children

> "I bought Eli a drone," his mother told me. "His dad knew about it and went out and bought the exact same thing, only bigger and more expensive. Now Eli feels awkward, and I feel tricked."
>
> When I spoke with the father, Lance, he admitted he'd felt insecure. "I panicked," he said. "I wanted Eli to be excited about coming to my house. I wasn't trying to compete. I just didn't want to feel less important."

This is a classic example of parents letting their own fears guide their decisions. When insecurity takes the lead, well-intentioned gestures can quickly turn into quiet competition, and the child becomes the one left holding the emotional weight.

Eli didn't just receive a gift; he received a dilemma about how to react, who to please, and what his excitement might signal to each parent. Thoughtful communication about presents and an honest awareness of the emotions driving those choices help keep children out of adult dynamics. Gifts are meant to be expressions of care, given freely and received without pressure.

A healthier approach involves these strategies:

- **Coordinating big gifts:** Coordinating big gifts can mean alternating large gifts or coordinating support gifts. For example, one parent gives the child the drone, and the other parent gives something to be used with the drone. A variety of drone accessories are available, including batteries, cameras, launch pads, controllers, custom props, and protective cases. Coordinated giving demonstrates firsthand that the child's parents are supporting each other's parenting, not competing.
- **Splitting costs when appropriate:** Agree on who gives what.

Gift-giving becomes much easier when both parents agree on a simple rule: "No competition. The giving is for *our* child(ren)."

When children live far away

Distance complicates everything. A long-distance co-parent often worries about not knowing what their child likes anymore.

Trying to stay in touch with a child who lives far from you is a challenge, but that's why it's important to keep communication open with the parent they live with most of the time. Many retreat and figure they have no ally, but the solution is straightforward: Cultivate better year-round communication so that when you must rely on the other co-parent's take on something, it feels collaborative, not exposed admission. You can do this by doing the following:

- Asking your co-parent for ideas
- Asking your child directly
- Choosing gifts that support connection (journals, photo books, video-chat-friendly activities, or special outings together)

TIP

If the child has a phone or tablet, or if you want to buy the child a phone or tablet as a present, ensure that both homes agree on expectations for use. The device isn't the problem; conflicting rules are.

Presents for co-parents

Sometimes co-parents maintain a level of friendliness in which giving each other small gifts feels natural. For other couples, that is wildly uncomfortable.

Appropriate gifts might be coffee, tea, chocolates, a small candle, a plant, or a neutral gift card. These items communicate goodwill without crossing emotional boundaries.

Inappropriate gifts would be anything romantic, anything symbolic of the past relationship, anything that hints at criticism, or anything that could unsettle a new partner. Keep the gesture simple and supportive.

Presents from the children

Supporting children in choosing or making a gift for their other parent is one of the most powerful ways to demonstrate co-parenting maturity:

> Jared, a bonus dad, recalled the first time he took his partner's daughter, Mila, to buy something for her mother.

"She knew just what she wanted: a silver bracelet with little leaves. She marched right up to the counter like she'd been saving her whole life for it. When we wrapped it, she looked so proud."

Jared told me that the shopping trip changed everything.

"It wasn't about her mom or me. It was about Mila. I realized supporting that connection didn't diminish me. It made all of us feel steadier."

If your co-parent asks you to take the lead

If your co-parent asks whether you could take the kids to pick out something for their mom (dad), it's not an insult or a burden. Instead, it means they trust you, they want the children to feel connected, and they know you're capable of supporting the child's relationship with their other parent without letting insecurity or jealousy interfere.

Children feel secure when both homes treat the child's love for the other parent as something to be respected, not feared.

Gift-giving with extended family

Grandparents, aunts, uncles, and long-standing family members don't stop loving a child simply because a marriage ends. In many co-parenting families, their continued presence provides familiarity and reassurance. But gift-giving is often where underlying tensions surface. Gifts are visible, memorable, and easily interpreted.

For parents who were genuinely close to their former in-laws, gift-giving can quietly reopen grief. You may hope or expect that the relationship you built will continue. When gifts become less frequent, more formal, or routed exclusively through your ex, it can feel deeply painful. What you're grieving isn't divided loyalty, but the loss of a relationship you believed stood on its own.

That sense of betrayal is rarely spoken aloud, yet it's common. A change in gift-giving can signal that the bond was more conditional than you realized. This realization can feel like a second, quieter loss layered on top of the divorce itself.

A similar and often more intense reaction can arise when your own parents are involved. Gift-giving makes their choices visible. When they give generously to your ex, coordinate gifts jointly, or remain warm and inclusive during exchanges, an instinctive protest may surface: "You're my parents. Your allegiance should belong to me." A breakup can strip away a sense of protection you didn't realize you were still leaning on, and gift-giving can become the moment you feel that loss most sharply.

Gift-giving often unintentionally places children in the emotional middle. Comments such as, "This stays at our house," or "You don't need to tell your other parent about this," can turn a present into a secret. The child is no longer simply receiving a gift; they're asked to manage adult relationships.

Former in-laws and sometimes grandparents on your side may also use gift-giving to hold onto a connection when they fear their role is shrinking. Larger gifts, more frequent gifts, or gifts that seem to compete with the other household may feel reassuring to the adult, but they often feel heavy to the child. Children sense when generosity comes with expectation.

From a co-parenting perspective, the goal isn't equal gifts or perfectly coordinated holidays. The goal is freedom without guilt. Children should never feel that accepting generosity from one side of the family requires emotional repayment to the other.

Healthy co-parenting allows room for grief without passing it on. It recognizes that a parent may feel hurt when gift-giving highlights shifting loyalties — whether with former in-laws or their own parents — while still protecting a child's right to continuity and connection. Creating emotional boundaries for yourself may be necessary. Asking a child to carry those boundaries is not.

When adults handle gift-giving with clarity and restraint, children learn that love doesn't have to be rationed, that relationships can change without becoming unsafe, and that caring about many people doesn't require betraying anyone.

In co-parenting families, gift-giving works best when it remains what it was always meant to be: an expression of care, not a test of allegiance. Children free from managing adult loyalties are free to experience the joy of being loved by many people at once.

If extended family members want to maintain a relationship with the co-parent, it should be respectful, appropriate, and child-centered. A simple strategy is to frame extended-family gifts as either from the children or for the children's use. This allows relationships to stay warm without giving the impression that relatives must pick a side.

The only time extended-family gifting becomes harmful is when it's used to exclude one parent, to undermine a relationship with a relative or a co-parent, or to use the child to send political or emotional messages. If that happens, boundaries with kindness are necessary.

Taking Holiday Photographs

Holiday photographs, especially those used for cards or shared with extended family, may seem like a minor detail, but when co-parenting or in bonus families, they often carry more emotional weight than anyone anticipates. A photograph freezes a moment in time, and for children, that image can quietly communicate who belongs where, who's connected to whom, and whether the adults in their lives understand the family they're asking the child to navigate.

In co-parenting families, photographs can become surprisingly complicated. Parents who no longer share a household still share children, possibly traditions, and extended family expectations. Remarriage adds another layer, bringing new partners, bonus siblings, and grandparents who may or may not understand the current family structure.

Here's a helpful guide to make the placement of all the players easy to understand:

- **Co-parents:** If co-parents are in the same picture, it's best to put the children between them.
- **Bonus parents:** When parents have remarried or have a new partner, bonus parents may also be included in the photo. Inclusion, however, doesn't mean rearranging relationships. Bonus parents belong in the picture when they're part of the child's daily life, but their placement shouldn't blur or replace biological roles. When parents have children from previous relationships, those children are most comfortable standing near their own parent.
- **Extended family members:** Extended family members often want to be included, especially during the holidays. When they appear in photos, arrange them in a way that reflects reality rather than sentiment. Grandparents naturally gravitate toward their adult child and that child's children. Bonus grandparents may stand alongside their partner. No one needs to be hidden, but no one needs to be repositioned to make a point, either.

REMEMBER

In families where former partners are present for holiday gatherings, it's especially important to avoid placements that create discomfort or confusion. Divorced or separated parents don't need to stand next to one another in photographs, and a current partner shouldn't be positioned between two people who were previously married. Position the bonus parent on the side of their partner without making the photo look rigid or staged. Using different levels — some people sitting, others standing — or creating natural groupings often results in more relaxed photos. What matters isn't symmetry, but intention.

Managing Holidays

Holidays can be some of the most challenging times for co-parents and their children. They carry expectations, traditions, and emotions that don't simply disappear after a breakup. What once felt natural may now require planning, flexibility, and intention. As you move through each holiday, the goal is not to re-create the past, but to create new experiences that allow your child to feel secure, supported, and free to enjoy the moment. Let's begin with Halloween, often the first holiday during the "holiday season" that tests how this new dynamic will work.

Halloween

Halloween carries more weight for children than it does for parents. It brings a mix of excitement and anxiety. Rooted in neighborhood familiarity, children want to walk the streets where their friends live and see houses they recognize. When parents live in different communities, the question becomes, "Which neighborhood makes the night feel most like Halloween?" The answer is found by seeing the evening through your child's eyes.

Not every decision is about fairness between adults. Often, the emotionally safe choice is the one that preserves the child's sense of belonging, even if it means adjusting parenting plans or long-standing expectations.

Thanksgiving

Thanksgiving can feel heavy after a breakup because it symbolizes home, history, and togetherness. For many families, the holiday spans generations, recipes passed down, predictable seating arrangements, and relatives arriving from distant places. When a separation occurs, the familiar architecture of the day fractures, and parents must ask themselves not only how to divide time but how to preserve the spirit of gratitude in unfamiliar circumstances.

Ultimately, shifting perspective can help. Rather than imagine Thanksgiving as one sacred day that everyone must cling to, reframe the holiday as a season. Start a new tradition. Perhaps another day in the same week or month could be when your family gathers to celebrate Thanksgiving.

Hanukkah

Hanukkah often provides more flexibility than other holidays because it spans eight nights rather than one. Still, that flexibility can create tension when parents disagree about how to divide the time. Some families alternate nights; others share the full eight days every other year; and some choose to celebrate portions of the holiday separately.

What matters most is that the lighting of the menorah remains peaceful and meaningful for the child. If co-parents are worried about losing the majority of Hanukkah nights, perhaps some nights can be celebrated individually in each home, and two nights can be shared occasions, where the other parent stops by to light candles together, exchange small gifts, and create a short moment of unity. Then, the other parent leaves, while the other continues to celebrate.

It's not a return to the way things once were, but it honors the shared symbolism of the holiday and reassures the child that both homes value the same tradition.

Christmas

Christmas can be one of the most emotionally charged holidays for co-parents because it comes with imagery of "perfect" families, nostalgic memories, and deeply ingrained rituals. When the parenting schedule means children will be in one home on Christmas morning and in the other next year, children often internalize the idea that they're letting one parent down, no matter where they wake up.

The most common misstep parents make around Christmas is unintentionally placing emotional responsibility on the child. Telling a child, "This holiday won't feel right without you," isn't the affirmation it may be intended to be. It becomes a burden for the child. Children thrive when parents treat Christmas not as a single day but as a week or season filled with opportunities to connect. This approach allows them to look forward to a full week of fun and magic, not just one night.

When both parents approach the holiday season with flexibility, children stop feeling like they're carrying the weight of two households. They begin to feel loved in more than one place.

Eid

For Muslim co-parents, Eid can be a complex holiday to navigate because of its profound cultural and religious meaning. Eid al-Fitr marks the end of Ramadan, a month of fasting, prayer, and community. Eid al-Adha follows several months later. The timing of both holidays shifts each year based on the lunar calendar, which can lead to unexpected scheduling issues.

Many Muslim co-parents tell me that Eid is the holiday they most want to spend with their children because it reflects not only celebration but spiritual identity. That desire is completely understandable. It's also why it's so important to plan ahead and acknowledge that both parents may feel emotionally attached to the day.

Perhaps you could create a tradition in which you, your child, and co-parent attend the morning prayer service together, even though you arrive and leave separately. Afterward, perhaps your child goes with your co-parent to a family celebration, and the next day, the child spends time with your side of the family. Approaching Eid as a cluster of meaningful moments spread across two days, instead of a single day, can preserve the essence of the celebration without forcing the child into an impossible emotional choice.

Valentine's Day

Valentine's Day may not carry the same cultural weight as Christmas or religious holidays, but it brings an emotional complexity all its own. It can stir up nostalgia, unresolved feelings, or the temptation to send "just one little card" that seems harmless but carries unspoken meaning.

A Valentine, even a simple one, comes with romantic undercurrents. It's usually best to skip it. If children want to make a Valentine for a parent, encourage them to do so. Let it be their creation, not an adult's symbolic gesture.

In co-parenting, some days are for looking back. Valentine's Day is more wisely used as a day for looking forward.

Mother's Day and Father's Day

Mother's Day and Father's Day stir a unique kind of vulnerability. Each parent wants to feel valued, recognized, and included. When the parenting schedule doesn't align with the holiday, emotions can run high. But these days are most meaningful when adults prioritize the child's experience over the calendar.

I once spoke with a father who was upset that his weekend with the children did not fall on Father's Day. His instinct was to "hold the line." But when he pictured his children ten years from now, he realized they wouldn't remember the schedule. They would remember how he handled it. He chose to be flexible.

Another situation where these holidays can become complicated is in families with two mothers or two fathers. In these families, both parents share the same role, so the holiday can't be divided traditionally.

Here again, it may take some creativity and a willingness to think outside the box. There are many ways to approach holidays when they need to be shared. You might split the day or, my favorite, treat it as a weekend celebration. Think of it as Mother's Day Eve. The children spend the day before with one parent and the holiday itself with the other, then alternate the following year.

Observing Religious Milestones, Christenings, and Spiritual Traditions

Religious holidays hold a particular emotional weight because they shape identity, culture, and family meaning. After a breakup, parents sometimes discover they hadn't fully discussed their beliefs while they were together. What once felt like an unspoken agreement becomes a debate about whose tradition will guide the children.

When parents have differing beliefs, the healthiest approach isn't to persuade the child toward one tradition but to communicate openly and acknowledge that both perspectives matter. Courts typically avoid "choosing" a religion for a child and instead permit children to attend the services or observances each parent values. The way parents speak about each other's beliefs is crucial. Respect is the foundation.

Christenings, baptisms, and inclusion

Ceremonies marking the start of a child's spiritual life — christenings, dedications, and baptisms — often bring extended family together. After a breakup, parents sometimes struggle to determine who belongs at these events.

A divorced couple I worked with, Mark and Janine, were cordial co-parents for years. When Mark and his new partner had a baby, Janine expected she would be included in the christening simply because they'd always behaved warmly with one another. But the idea felt uncomfortable for Mark's partner, Sloane. For Sloane, like some others, the ceremony symbolizes their nuclear family, not their co-parenting relationship.

Co-parents walk a fine line in these situations. Being friendly doesn't automatically translate to being family. Boundaries help everyone feel safe.

First Communion, Confirmation, and other religious milestones

Catholic families often navigate First Communion and Confirmation with the same emotional complexity. These rites are steeped in tradition and often involve lengthy preparation, catechism classes, meetings, and rehearsals. If one home becomes disengaged or inconsistent, the child feels the disruption intensely.

When co-parents treat religious obligations as optional, the child experiences stress, embarrassment, and confusion. But when parents recognize that the milestone belongs to the child, they often find workable compromises. Co-parenting decisions become easier when the lens stays firmly on the child's experience rather than the parents' preferences.

Coming-of-age celebrations

Coming-of-age ceremonies are among the most memorable events of childhood, often carrying the emotional intensity of a wedding. They're expensive, heavily planned, and deeply symbolic. When parents are separated, the planning process can become strained.

> A family preparing for their daughter Isabella's Quinceañera ran into a wall when her parents disagreed over the role her father's new partner should play. Her father, Luis, felt strongly that his partner, Camila, should attend and even help with the preparations. Isabella's mother, Marisol, worried this would reduce her own role or confuse the extended family, who didn't know Camila well.
>
> What helped was reframing the event: it wasn't about repairing past hurts or establishing new boundaries. It was about Isabella. She wanted her father's partner present, nothing elaborate, quietly, respectfully, without stepping into the spotlight roles. Once everyone honored Isabella's wishes, the day unfolded beautifully.

Coming-of-age ceremonies work when parents ask what arrangement helps their child feel celebrated, not caught in the middle.

Bar and Bas Mitzvas

Milestone events like a Bar or Bat Mitzvah carry deep meaning for a Jewish boy or girl. This is the day a child is recognized as stepping into adulthood — age 13 for boys, and 12 or 13 for girls. The child is called to the Torah (the Jewish sacred text), may read from it, and often leads part of the service. They may also give a short speech reflecting on their portion and what the milestone means to them.

If that's the message, then it's also a signal for the parents to rise to the same level of maturity. This is not the time to argue over details, compete for recognition, or revisit old conflicts. It's a time to model what you hope your child has learned, how to handle important moments with respect, cooperation, and maturity.

Bar Mitzva preparations are often quite elaborate, so start early and divide responsibilities. Decide how expenses will be handled, seating, and how both parents will be included. This is your opportunity to stand up and be counted, to put your differences aside and show your child, and your community, what truly matters.

Birthday parties

Birthday parties are often the most challenging child-centered milestone for co-parents. Unlike holidays, birthdays belong to the child, and parents sometimes feel emotional ownership over the day.

When Sophie turned six, both of her parents planned separate birthday parties without telling the other. Her mother scheduled a cupcake-and-crafts party at home. Her father arranged a trampoline park celebration with the same group of classmates. By the time the invitations crossed paths in backpacks, Sophie was terrified someone would get angry if she expressed a preference.

Both parents believed they were trying to bring joy. Neither realized they were placing Sophie in a loyalty bind.

This would be a time when having alternating parties would be simpler: One parent hosts the party in odd years, the other in even years. The parent who isn't hosting attends if it feels comfortable, or they celebrate privately if not.

In families where tension is high, having two parties may be healthiest. In families with strong cooperation, a shared party can be wonderful. There's no universal rule, only what feels emotionally safe for the child.

School celebrations and extracurricular milestones

Recitals, science fairs, award ceremonies, debate tournaments, and sports banquets often bring both parents into the same space. For children, these events aren't holidays, but they carry enormous meaning. They're affirmations of effort and progress.

Children want to glance into the audience and see that both parents have shown up, if possible, and both parents are behaving well. Co-parenting doesn't require pretending to be close. It requires demonstrating that your child's moment is bigger than your past.

Graduations

Graduations often intensify co-parenting struggles because guest lists are limited, emotions run high, and the day marks a profound transition. Parents sometimes cling to feelings of ownership over the moment. But graduation isn't the end of a parent's journey; it's the celebration of a child's growth.

A father once told me his son quietly asked him, "Please don't make me choose who gets the extra ticket." Dad had not realized he was creating a no-win scenario. His son's mother wanted to bring her partner; Dad wanted his mother to attend. The school only allotted five seats.

Dad took a step back, reassessed, and made the simplest, most child-centered choice: he asked his mother to attend the reception instead. The ceremony became peaceful. His son later told him, "Thank you for not making it a fight."

Graduations, above all else, should reflect calm pride, not strategic planning.

Funerals

Funerals are difficult for any family, but for separated parents, the emotional stakes rise dramatically. When a child loses a grandparent or relative, the surviving parent's role isn't to revisit old arguments but to anchor the child through their grief.

Parents may struggle with whether to attend the funeral of, say, their former partner's mother. The divorce may have been ugly, and you might not have spoken since outside of exchange logistics, but the children are devastated. Under the circumstances, you might fear your presence will upset your ex, yet your children may need the extra shoulder because your co-parent and extended family are so distraught.

When my mother passed unexpectedly, we were all distraught and taken by surprise. My oldest daughter, her first grandchild, was particularly close to her and was struggling with the shock of her passing. My entire family — my husband, his children (my bonus children), aunts, uncles, and cousins — were crowded into a small room waiting for the service to start. Slowly, the door opened, and in walked my first husband, my oldest daughter's father. She was 13, and I remember the relief on her face as he walked in. His presence created unexpected healing. We were all mourning. Old grievances seemed small in that room.

In grief, the question is always about what the child(ren) needs right now. The answer is usually presence, not distance.

Anniversaries and personal milestones

Anniversaries aren't always about romance. A "sober date," the anniversary of completing cancer treatment, the day a parent adopted a child, or even the date the family moved into a new home: These are moments families mark for personal reasons.

In co-parenting, the question becomes whether both homes honor these dates and how to do so without pressure. Some milestones may be celebrated privately. Others may be acknowledged in both homes.

Children benefit from learning that life contains a variety of turning points. You can help them appreciate that not all celebrations require both parents to be present, only an atmosphere of respect.

Making Adjustments When Introducing New Partners

Introducing a new partner is one of the most delicate changes a co-parenting family experiences. Holidays and milestones often intensify the emotions around this shift. Parents may worry that a new partner will "replace" them or that celebrations will become awkward.

> A mother named Dana described her discomfort when her ex-husband introduced a new partner, Mae, at their daughter's spring recital. "I wasn't ready," she said. "It felt like I was being evaluated."
>
> Yet when she looked at her daughter, who was beaming because both her father and Mae were clapping for her, Dana realized the focus had quietly shifted. The audience wasn't a referendum on past relationships; it was a support system for a child on stage.
>
> It would have been preferable if Dana had met Mae prior to attending her daughter's special event. New partners must enter gently, observing before participating, and asking, not assuming, what feels appropriate. Co-parents

can help by setting expectations early. Just remember, the kids are watching. Appearing in public as a united front can go a long way to set a positive stage. Handled thoughtfully, new partners expand the support system, not complicate it.

Reminiscing and "Remember Whens"

Even strong co-parents stumble into nostalgia. Sometimes one parent wants to share a brief moment of reminiscing, believing it will be harmless. But timing matters, and intent matters even more.

One co-parent, Jess, texted her former partner a photo of their child carving a pumpkin, adding, "Remember when we used to get the big ones from the farm?" Her ex read the message while sitting next to his new partner, who felt uncomfortable and asked, "Is this about the pumpkin or something else?"

It wasn't about the pumpkin; it was about Jess feeling wistful. Nostalgia must be handled privately or expressed in neutral spaces. If you wouldn't say something in front of your co-parent, their partner, or your child, it probably belongs in a private journal, not a text thread.

IN THIS CHAPTER

» Announcing the commitment in the right order

» Preparing your co-parent and children

» Managing emotional undercurrents

» Considering vows, invitations, and the ceremony

Chapter 14
Making a New Commitment, and Planning the Festivities

When families live across two homes, occasions such as weddings or commitment ceremonies are no longer only about two people. They become meaningful turning points within a family system that has already been reshaped once before. Parents who remarry or recommit often carry a complex mix of emotions, a quiet fear of repeating past mistakes alongside genuine hope for a new beginning. Their children, meanwhile, navigate questions of loyalty, belonging, and an unspoken worry that sits just beneath the surface: *Where do I fit now?*

In this chapter, I explore how to introduce a new marriage or formal commitment into an established co-parenting system. I cover how to announce the decision thoughtfully, prepare children and communicate with your co-parent, design a ceremony that reflects the reality of two-home families, and craft vows and rituals that honor both partnership and parenthood. A new commitment isn't simply a celebration; it's a symbolic and practical shift in the family structure. The goal is to move forward with clarity, steadiness, and respect for every relationship involved.

This chapter focuses on co-parents who choose to remarry or make a new commitment while still actively raising children across two homes. These are families in motion, where a new partner enters a system already shaped by established routines. This chapter is also mindful of co-parents with adult children, whose experiences continue to shape the family landscape.

Here, communication isn't about announcements; it's about coordination, intention, and sharing information in ways that keep the family system steady and supported. Acceptance isn't about approval; it's about recognizing the impact of change. Respect isn't about etiquette; it's about preserving dignity. Finally, empathy isn't a feeling; it's a practiced pause to recognize another person's experience.

When parents decide to commit, they often believe the hardest part will be choosing the right partner. In two-home families, that's rarely true. The real work begins long before a ring is chosen or a date is set. It's in the quiet questions parents ask themselves when no one else is listening.

Before announcing a commitment, it's best to step away from the excitement and reflect on the decision. Your children have already seen how conflict affects a union. They've felt how uncertainty can affect every aspect of their lives. So have you and your partner. What are some of the things you'll do to ensure communication improves and the family continues to feel united?

Looking Inward First

Before you involve anyone else in your plans, you have a private responsibility to look inward with honesty. New commitments are often born out of relief: relief that loneliness has ended, that companionship has returned, that life feels hopeful again. Those feelings are real, and they're earned. But in co-parenting families, personal relief doesn't automatically translate into family readiness.

This is the step most parents skip, not because they don't care, but because they don't realize how much emotional preparation is required before an announcement is made.

The questions that follow aren't meant to delay your happiness. They're meant to offer self-examination and help you have a realistic attitude about your recoupling and how it can affect your children.

Ask yourself:

- What problem am I hoping this commitment will solve in my life?
- Is it companionship, financial security, healing, validation, belonging, or something else I haven't named yet?
- What parts of my child's daily life will change because of this decision, even if I intend everything to stay the same?
- Have I finished grieving the family my child once knew, or am I asking this new relationship to close that chapter for me?
- How will authority and influence shift once my partner is emotionally or legally recognized?
- What fears might this awaken in my co-parent, and can I acknowledge them without becoming defensive?
- Am I ready to protect my child from adult tension even when I feel vulnerable, misunderstood, or impatient?

Get clear on all these points. They're not romantic questions, but they're stabilizing ones. When parents contemplate the changes before announcing a new commitment, children experience the change as thoughtful rather than abrupt, as an evolution rather than a disruption.

Considering Alternatives to Marriage

More people are asking if there are better alternatives than marriage for co-parents who have found new relationships. For many families, the answer is yes. During my years as a child custody mediator working primarily with parents under 35, I saw far more unmarried parents than married ones. I did an unofficial poll of my clients over a three-month period. Sixty-eight percent of those who used the family court to solve their custody disagreements had never been married to their child's other parent. For some, this choice was deliberate. They had lived through their own parents' divorce and were determined not to repeat that story.

Yet, children don't experience less disruption when parents separate simply because their parents were never married. A breakup is a breakup. The emotional impact on children is the same whether there was a license or not.

For couples who want to formalize their commitment without entering a traditional marriage, a domestic partnership may be an option. Before same-sex marriage became legal nationwide in 2015, domestic partnerships were often the only path available to the LGBTQ+ community. Today, older adults especially might choose a domestic partnership if they want to commit without changing long-standing financial or legal arrangements.

A domestic partnership is a legally recognized union between two people who live together, but it's primarily governed by state law. A marriage, by contrast, is recognized at the federal level. Because of this, the rights connected to domestic partnerships can vary depending on where you live. A domestic partnership may provide some of the same rights and obligations as marriage, such as inheritance considerations, hospital visitation, or access to health insurance through a partner. However, domestic partners typically file taxes separately and can't receive Social Security benefits based on a partner's record. Further, the domestic partnership status isn't recognized in every state. Marriage carries additional federal protections and benefits that a domestic partnership doesn't.

While some couples feel no formal designation is necessary and choose to live together without paperwork, it's important to remember that avoiding marriage doesn't shield children from the emotional consequences of a breakup.

COMMITMENT CEREMONIES FOR DOMESTIC PARTNERSHIPS

Some couples choose to mark their decision with a commitment ceremony, a gathering that publicly acknowledges their intention to build a life together. Whether or not to have a ceremony is a personal choice that belongs to the couple.

A commitment ceremony is simply a gathering that marks a couple's intention to share their lives. It carries no legal weight. Unlike a wedding, a commitment ceremony has no prescribed format. Partners may exchange vows, present rings or symbolic gifts, and invite anyone they choose to witness their promise. An officiant is optional, and the ceremony may be shared with guests or kept private.

Children or grandchildren can be included in the celebration in whatever way feels meaningful. Because a commitment ceremony isn't a legal contract, it also doesn't require a legal divorce if the relationship ends. However, the emotional meaning of the ceremony is real. Regardless of whether the commitment is formalized with paperwork, reshaping the family system deserves the same care and preparation as any wedding.

Announcing Your Intent

Before you share your plans, consider who will be told and in what order. In most cases, your co-parent should be among the first to know. Of course, you may also share the news with family and extended relatives, but what you're guarding against is your child breaking the news to their other parent.

Announcements about engagement, cohabitation, or commitment should never travel through a child. Even in cooperative systems, major transitions require adult-to-adult communication first. Handling the news directly and respectfully preserves trust between homes and models the transparency children deserve to witness.

Telling your co-parent

When a co-parent hears about an engagement or even the decision to move in together from a child instead of from you, trust between the homes erodes quietly and immediately.

Announcing your engagement to your co-parent or notifying them of your decision to register as domestic partners isn't about asking permission, although it may feel that way. It's more about showing respect for the shared parenting relationship and protecting your child from emotional crossfire.

Keep the conversation focused on logistics, not emotions.

Start with a brief, direct message:

> "I wanted you to hear this from me. I've decided to get married (or formally register as a domestic partnership), and I care about how this affects our children."

Then, add the information your co-parent actually needs:

- Whether you're legally marrying or planning a commitment ceremony
- When you're thinking about sharing the news with the children
- How the children may be involved in the ceremony

Finally, invite cooperation, not approval:

> "I hope you'll support the kids as we all adjust to this. Let me know if there's anything I should be mindful of to help them adjust."

This approach doesn't erase discomfort, but it keeps the child out of the role of messenger and allows the adults to carry the weight of the change themselves.

Telling your young children

I look at an engagement as a time for preparation, a space for families to adjust to the reality that the family dynamic is changing once again, and to consider what that change means for everyone involved.

Many parents rush through this stage because they're eager to share their happiness. They change social media statuses, send group texts, and allow news to travel faster than their children can emotionally process it. What looks like a celebration from the outside often feels like insensitivity on the inside.

Not every co-parent meets a surprise announcement graciously. Some react in the moment, tightening their voice, asking sharp questions, or turning visibly cold. Children absorb those reactions instantly. It can determine whether they feel safe passing on information. If they become anxious about how you'll respond, they may simply stop sharing.

A better approach might be to incorporate C.A.R.E. into your approach.

Coping with C.A.R.E.: Telling your children

Sharing the news of your marriage with your children is an emotional transition, not just a conversation. The language you choose matters less than the steadiness you bring to the moment. Children rarely experience this news as pure excitement or disappointment; they experience it through the lens of safety.

> What does this change about my life? Where do I belong now? Will anything be taken from me?

Approaching this conversation through C.A.R.E. allows you to answer those questions without ever having to speak them out loud.

Communication: Make sure they feel heard

Choose a time when nothing else is competing for your child's emotional attention. Sit down. Put the phone away. Begin with stability, not the ring.

Instead of saying, "I have amazing news!" try this:

> "I want to talk with you about something important, and I want to hear what you think too."

Name what's staying the same before you name what's changing:

> "I'll still be your parent in the same way. Your routines will stay the same. We'll still live in this house (if you will, or explain if you'll be moving and when). Your dad/mom will still continue to love you and be your parent, too, and you'll see them just like you do now."

You may be asked a question comparing their parent and your new partner:

> "Will I have two dads/moms?"

This is how I answer that question:

> "You can't really compare them. You'll always have one dad/mom, but (name of person) will also be there for you and part of our family. Consider them an extra person in your corner, ready to help whenever they can."

If your child reacts with silence or distance, don't fill the space. Help them feel safe in their silence. Invite a conversation: "Are you surprised by the news?"

Acceptance: Make room for mixed feelings

Your child may be excited and smile or shrug, cry, change the subject, or leave the room. None of these responses is wrong. Children process change in layers. The first layer is rarely the whole story.

Avoid interpreting reactions. Don't say things like,

> "Don't worry; you'll come around."

That phrase or something like it minimizes your child's concerns and rushes them past their own emotional truth. Instead, say,

> "This may seem like a lot all at one time. We'll keep talking about it. I'm always here to listen."

Respect: Protect their loyalty

Children of divorce often feel that loving one person means betraying another. If they're enjoying their time with you, does that mean they're betraying their other parent? The same holds true with bonus parents. If I enjoy this new person in my life, am I betraying my dad or mom? Your job is to remove that burden immediately.

Say it clearly. Remember that comparing can get confusing, so something like this helps:

> "You don't have to choose sides. Your relationship with Mom/Dad doesn't change because of this."

If your child later asks, "Does this mean I have to call them Mom or Dad?" answer with clarity and choice:

> "You have a dad (or mom), but we can check with them about how they feel about that. For now, why don't you sit down with (name of person) and figure out a special name for them that only you use?"

Empathy: Stay present after the news is shared

The most important work happens after the conversation ends. Watch for changes in behavior: sleep, irritability, withdrawal, or defiance. These aren't discipline issues; they're information.

Create brief, predictable check-ins. No lectures. No fixing. Just presence.

Testing the waters

Don't correct your child if they say something that stings, like, "I wish it were just us again." Instead, try this:

> "I understand why you might miss what was familiar. But something new is just different, and we'll all work together to make sure you feel safe with the changes."

That sentence doesn't weaken your decision. It strengthens your bond.

Reaching out for support in unexpected places

Recently, a client shared that the only thing she would change about her wedding was not involving her bonus children's mother earlier in the process. She assumed that since the two of them rarely spoke, it was easier to stay quiet. Instead, her bonus daughter ended up carrying the news between homes, and the tension that followed colored every planning decision.

Telling your adult children

When a marriage ends after decades, or when a spouse has passed away, parents naturally hope their adult children will understand their desire for companionship. Many are surprised to discover that adult children can be even more resistant to change than younger ones.

Society often focuses on how hard it is for young children to accept a parent's new partner, but adult children face their own struggles. They have longer histories with the parent who's gone and often feel a powerful allegiance to that relationship. When widowed or divorced parents move forward quickly, adult children may experience it not as healing but as betrayal. That makes it difficult for the adult child to see their parent's new partner as a potential family member.

Some adult children understand their parents' desire to move forward. This is usually the result of the effort the two have made to understand each other after the parents' previous relationship ended. Make a special effort to connect with your adult child so that when you do find someone with whom you'd like to build a life, your child understands that you're not abandoning them or their other parent's memory, but wish to share the future with a partner.

Many parents who take care of terminally ill partners put their lives on hold and begin the mourning process when they first hear the news of their partner's condition. They devote years to supporting their loved one, so by the time they pass, they're ready to live life again. To family members, particularly the children and grandchildren of the deceased parent, it looks as if the parent is moving on without any thought. However, they've been quietly mourning for years. The children's mourning begins much later, when the parent passes.

Parents and grandparents who choose to commit again must be clear, compassionate, and patient. A new partner isn't a replacement for a deceased or divorced parent; they're a companion for this chapter of life. It can help to remind adult children that measuring one relationship against another removes the integrity of each one. (It's something you should remind yourself of as well.) These are two different people and two different stories, not in comparison to one another. Allowing each relationship to stand on its own gives everyone the best chance to move forward.

Setting Expectations for Family and Friends

Before announcing widely, set expectations. Ask relatives to avoid probing your children for reactions, making comparisons to the past, or commenting on "moving on." When families understand that this is a system transition, not a romance campaign, they become allies rather than amplifiers of stress.

Try this: If relatives overstep, use respect with clarity.

> "We're keeping the focus on helping the kids adjust. Please let us lead those conversations."

When announcements are guided by communication, held with acceptance, shaped by respect, and delivered with empathy, the family doesn't brace for impact; it steadies itself for change.

Announcements and Invitations

An engagement party is optional, and if you choose to have one, the key is to present the anticipated union from the point of view of those making the commitment and those who are hosting the party. If it's a formal engagement party, the invitation language will be formal, but most co-parents opt for casual language.

If a family member or friend is hosting, the wording could be this:

> Jim and Elena
>
> Are getting married!
>
> Please join their children and families
>
> In celebration of their engagement.
>
> Hosted by: The bride's parents, Fred and Ethyl Mertz.
>
> Date and time: [day of week], [date and time]
>
> Location: [name and address of venue]

Or, you could include something like:

> Sonja, Sean, and their children would like to make an announcement!
>
> They're getting married!

If you're announcing your own engagement, the wording would simply reflect that at the beginning of the announcement. Include something that acknowledges the combining of families, either the names of the combined children or,

> Please join our bonus family in celebration of our engagement.
>
> Or,
>
> Please join our family on our first step toward bonus status.

LANGUAGE MATTERS

The wording of your invitation tells the story of who's actually committing — and it's not only the couple. Their children are also part of the transition and investing in change.

When invitations acknowledge only the couple, children who are part of the transition feel overlooked, left out of this newly formed family. Even when this is unintentional, the message lands: This is about them, not us.

In two-home families, invitations should reflect that families, not just partners, are coming together. When co-parents remarry, traditional wording often misses the mark. "Together with their families" may feel inaccurate when the families exist in separate homes. Consider language that honors the family system being formed rather than pretending it already exists seamlessly.

For example:

> Together with their children, Sarah and Mark invite you to celebrate their marriage.

When children of co-parents are marrying, invitations may need to acknowledge multiple family lines. Adult children often struggle with how to name parents and bonus parents without creating tension, especially if they are helping to host the wedding. This isn't the moment for parents to insist on placement or order. The wording belongs to the couple.

But, to clarify, here are two somewhat informal approaches to spark some ideas:

If the parents hosting the wedding wish to be mentioned:

> Mr. Bill Smith and Mrs. Joyce Liberman and Drs. John Miller and Samantha Miller invite you to the wedding of their children, LeeAnne Smith and Michael Miller (place time and date).

(continued)

(continued)

Or, even more informal, and bonus parents are helping to host:

> The parents and bonus parents of LeAnne Smith and Michael Miller invite you to the wedding of their children (time, place and date).

When extended family members are remarrying, such as grandparents, invitations may feel complicated to the younger generation. Clear, inclusive language reassures their children and grandchildren that the family they know isn't being replaced but expanded.

The invitation isn't only a formality. It's the first public signal of how this commitment understands family.

To Shower or Not to Shower. . .

Originally, bridal showers were designed to help a couple begin their life together, with much of the focus placed on the bride creating a "home" for the marriage. Today, that sentiment has shifted toward a more equal distribution of responsibility. While gifts may still include household items, many co-parents already have established homes, complete with blenders, linens, and everything in between. The couple may even be living together before the wedding or commitment ceremony, meaning the household is already set.

A shower is ultimately a celebration of intention. It allows the people who care about you to gather, offer support, and share in your excitement as you step into a formal commitment. Couples in bonus families sometimes wonder whether they're entitled to the same traditions as everyone else. The answer is simple: Choose the customs that reflect your partnership today.

If a shower feels meaningful to you, plan one. Invite the people who have walked with you through change and growth. Let the day reflect the life you're building now: a family defined by commitment, care, and the courage to begin again.

Considering couples' showers

When both partners have been married before, some couples prefer a more relaxed or personalized theme. Lingerie showers, wine tastings, cooking showers, camping showers, honeymoon showers, and even family showers that include the children can feel more fitting. These gatherings focus less on setting up a first household and more on celebrating shared interests, acknowledging the couple's journey, and honoring the life they're creating together.

Including children in engagement or shower preparations

Bridal showers hold special meaning for those getting married, regardless of whether this is their first marriage. They also offer a natural opportunity to include your children or your fiancé's children in the preparations. When children participate, the "flavor" of a shower may shift, especially if you're planning something more adult-themed. The bottom line is this: When children are included, the celebration becomes less about the event itself and more about belonging.

If you prefer something more intimate or playful, you might consider two gatherings: one family-oriented shower that includes the children, and another for friends. Inclusion doesn't mean every event must look the same. It simply means children shouldn't feel overlooked in the larger transition taking place.

Invite the children to help create small favors or keepsakes for the shower or wedding. These projects give them a tangible way to contribute and feel invested. They can also assist with simple preparations and tidying afterward, learning that family celebrations are shared efforts.

On the day of the shower, children often enjoy welcoming guests, showing them where to sit, and making everyone feel at ease. This role can transition naturally into the wedding itself if a child serves as an usher, reinforcing their importance at both occasions.

When gifts are opened, older children can record what was given and by whom. This simple task places them in the heart of the celebration and sends a lasting message: This wedding is not only about two adults, but about the family being built together.

If your child feels excluded or displaced by the shower or any of the preparations, begin with empathy. Put yourself in their shoes. Although you may be celebrating, they may be struggling. In your elation, it's important not to minimize what your child has shared about their experience.

Then use communication that reflects the experience of change they're living through, rather than focusing only on the celebration:

> "This is a big shift for you, with a lot changing all at once. Let's slow down and make sure you feel comfortable and included. If it starts to feel like too much, I want you to tell me."

After you've shown empathy and opened with communication, follow with acceptance, which means not trying to fix, argue away, or rush past your child's disappointment or confusion. Instead, work together to understand what your child is experiencing and guide them through it.

If relatives treat the shower as the launch of a "new family" while ignoring the existing one, set boundaries early. Approaching the situation with respect can mean gentleness and firmness at the same time:

> "This celebration matters to us, but so does honoring the kids' place in our family."

A shower shouldn't establish a household before the children feel invited into it. It should be a soft opening, not a grand reveal.

Creating Guest Lists

Whether you're planning a bridal shower, a couples shower, or the wedding or commitment ceremony itself, the guest list reflects the relationships that support you as you step into this formal commitment. Showers tend to gather those who surround and encourage the couple in a more intimate setting. The wedding or commitment ceremony widens that circle to publicly acknowledge the life you're building.

For showers, the bride or couple typically creates the guest list and shares it with the host, keeping it aligned with the wedding or commitment ceremony invitation list so expectations remain clear and respectful. As a general rule, you don't invite someone to a shower who won't be invited to the ceremony.

Most bridal showers include women from both sides of the family and, if it's a couple's shower, members of the couple's shared community. The ceremony guest list may extend further, including extended family, longtime friends, and others who have shaped your journey. Both lists may move beyond traditional roles and include older children from previous relationships. It's not uncommon for people to remain close to bonus parents or former in-laws who continue to hold emotional significance. When a prior relationship ended through the death of a partner, these connections often carry deep meaning and deserve thoughtful consideration.

GUEST LISTS WHEN ONE OR BOTH HAVE CHILDREN

In a co-parenting family, the guest list is never just a list. It's a map of emotional history. Every name you add, and every name you omit, sends a message about belonging, loyalty, and who's being carried forward into the next chapter.

Parents often underestimate how closely children watch this process. They notice who's spoken of warmly, who's avoided, who's described as "too complicated," and who's treated as if they no longer exist. Even when children say nothing, they're building a story about what kinds of relationships survive change and which ones don't.

If you and your partner disagree about inviting someone from the past, pause the logistics and talk about the emotional meaning of the invitation instead. Is this about comfort, loyalty, history, or protecting the children's sense of continuity?

When co-parents remarry, the ceremony guest list is shaped by the current parenting system. Former spouses are rarely invited unless the co-parent relationship has evolved into a genuinely friendly one. However, former in-laws who remain actively involved in a child's daily life may still belong. Some relationships survive a breakup because they were built around the children, not the marriage.

The goal isn't perfection, but clarity. A shower may celebrate your partnership. A ceremony may publicly affirm it. In both cases, the guest list should reflect the family story you're choosing to honor as you move forward.

Seating for Inclusion

Seating for weddings is traditionally arranged with the bride's side and the groom's side. Family and guests invited by the bride sit on the left side of the room, the groom's family and guests sit on the right. However, when those who are marrying are parents, particularly if they've lived as a family prior to the ceremony, the separate bride's side/groom's side approach is often put aside.

When a couple has children from previous relationships, the wedding is an acknowledgment of unity and combining past and present to create a future together. They're looking for a feeling of inclusion, so no "side" is designated. The first few rows are set aside for "family," like grandparents, uncles, aunts, and cousins. The first row is set aside for the children and possibly grandparents to oversee if they're small because the children may be asked to join the parents at some point in the ceremony, and this would give them easy access to where the bride and groom are standing.

DEALING WITH UNEXPECTED EMOTIONS

What looks simple on the surface is often not. Weddings and commitment ceremonies do more than mark a new beginning. They gather history. Memories of the marriage that ended, the partner who's no longer present, or the family life that once seemed certain have a way of resurfacing. These emotions aren't signs of disloyalty or resistance. They're part of what shaped this family. Many parents describe a bittersweet quality when remembering these moments.

When parents don't expect this emotional layering, they're often caught off guard. They assume that their newfound happiness should dominate the day and are confused when tears arrive without invitation. The danger isn't in the feeling itself, but how you handle it.

Unacknowledged or unaddressed emotions can easily drive a wedge between family members. When feelings are ignored or pushed aside, they tend to surface elsewhere, often in ways that strain relationships. A comment that normally wouldn't bother you feels pointed. A simple request feels like pressure. You snap, not because of the present moment, but because of what it triggered. Making room for mixed emotions — happiness for the future alongside acceptance of what has changed — helps the family system remain steady.

If you anticipate that the wedding may stir unresolved pain, arrange support ahead of time. Reach out to a friend you can text, schedule a therapy appointment before or after the ceremony, or create a quiet plan for decompression once the celebration ends. Just remember one thing: Don't rely on your children to manage your emotions. Their story is different from yours. You're there to steady them, not to lean on them.

Tradition can remain intact, but it must be flexible enough to honor the realities of families that no longer fit neatly on one side of the aisle.

Including Children in the Ceremony

In a co-parenting system, a wedding or commitment ceremony does more than unite two adults; it reflects how existing relationships intertwine and how they'll be handled moving forward. Every choice, from who stands beside you to who sits in the front row, communicates something about belonging. The ceremony may last only a few hours, but the messages it sends can linger.

If you and/or your partner have children, they're not guests at your wedding or commitment ceremony. They're part of the family being formed.

Excluding children, whether intentionally or through well-meaning "adult-only" decisions, doesn't communicate unity. Although a marriage is a union of adults, those adults are parents. And when parents unite, the goal is not simply to commit to one another, but to unite a family. When children are left out, they don't hear "private." They hear "separate." They feel like an afterthought to a decision that will reshape their daily lives.

Including children doesn't mean scripting emotion or forcing them into roles they don't want. It means asking them how they'd like to be part of the moment and honoring their answer.

Some children want visible roles:

- » Walking a parent down the aisle
- » Holding rings or a written family vow
- » Lighting a candle with the couple
- » Reading a short poem or promise

Others prefer quieter participation:

- » Standing with the couple at the end of the ceremony
- » Choosing a song for the family dance
- » Helping design a family symbol or keepsake

The key is consultation. When children are invited into the planning, they don't feel that something is *happening* to them. They feel something is being *built* with them, and that distinction shapes how they remember the day long after the music fades.

The most respectful inclusion is flexible. Some children want a visible role: lighting a candle, reading a poem, or walking in at the beginning. Others want to sit with a trusted adult and simply observe. Both are valid. What matters is that children are given real choices without emotional consequences.

Navigating challenges

Even in families where everyone supports the marriage or commitment, emotional and logistical challenges can arise. These moments are opportunities to slow down, communicate with intention, and guide the family through change with steadiness.

» **Choosing your children to be your maid of honor or best man:** If you're having a ceremony without traditional pre-wedding events, such as bachelor or bachelorette parties or bridal showers, asking your child to stand beside you as your maid of honor or best man can be a lovely gesture. However, remember that the maid of honor and best man are typically responsible for coordinating many of the additional activities for the couple. If you choose to include these celebrations, someone other than your child will most likely need to be designated as the coordinator.

» **Loyalty conflicts between homes:** Children may worry that participating in one parent's wedding means choosing sides. A simple reminder can reduce that pressure: "You don't have to choose sides here." Supporting a parent's new commitment doesn't take anything away from their relationship with the other parent.

» **Introducing the new partner's extended family:** Blended gatherings often bring unfamiliar relatives into a child's world quickly. Allow relationships to develop naturally rather than assigning instant closeness. Familiarity grows through shared experiences, not labels.

» **The role of the other biological parent:** Questions about attendance, participation, or boundaries should be discussed privately between adults ahead of time. Clear expectations help prevent children from feeling responsible for managing social dynamics during the ceremony.

» **When your child says no to participating:** Respond with acceptance rather than persuasion. "Thank you for telling me. You don't have to do anything that doesn't feel right for you." Another way to include a child who prefers not to take an active role is to offer quiet inclusion, such as sitting in the front row or having their name acknowledged during the vows.

» **Uneven excitement among siblings:** One child may feel excited, while another feels cautious or unsure. Avoid comparison or pressure. Emotional timelines differ, and acceptance allows space for each child's process.

» **Timing of the announcement:** If a child feels blindsided by the news, repair begins with acknowledgment rather than explanation. "I wish I had told you sooner. I understand why this feels sudden." Repair builds trust more effectively than justification.

- **Language around titles and roles:** Questions about names or labels often arise during wedding planning. Allow children to choose what feels comfortable, whether first names, bonus titles, or no labels at all. Respect grows when language evolves naturally.
- **Revisiting old rituals:** Ceremonies can awaken memories of earlier family traditions. Rather than re-creating the past, focus on creating new meaning that reflects the family as it exists today.
- **Public vs. private celebration:** A child may support the marriage privately but feel uncomfortable with public attention. Offer flexible ways to participate, whether through smaller roles, fewer photos, or quiet involvement behind the scenes.

Finding their place in the ceremony

When children are included in a ceremony, their tasks should feel real, gentle, and free of emotional symbolism. They're not there to represent unity or heal history; they're there because they belong.

Here are roles that honor children without asking them to carry adult meaning:

- **Opening roles:** Some children like to begin the ceremony in quiet, non-performative ways. Lighting a candle at the start can feel grounding rather than spotlighted. Others may enjoy carrying in a framed photo of their family, placing it on a small table that remains visible throughout the ceremony, not as nostalgia, but as continuity.
- **Witnessing roles:** Older children may feel more comfortable reading a short, neutral passage about love, kindness, or family. This isn't about proclaiming loyalty; it's about witnessing the moment in their own voice. Younger children can ring a bell, release bubbles, or carry a simple object that signals the start or close of the ceremony without placing words in their mouths.
- **Support roles:** Some children prefer to stay near a trusted adult. Sitting in a front row with a designated support person, holding a flower, or helping guide guests to their seats allows them to participate quietly without being watched.
- **Closing roles:** At the end of the ceremony, children may join the couple in a low-pressure way, standing together for a moment of silence, holding hands briefly, or walking out together if it feels natural to them.

WHAT IF YOUR CHILD DOESN'T WANT TO PARTICIPATE?

This is a situation that needs to be handled carefully, because it's rarely about the wedding itself. It's about what the wedding represents to the child. A child who resists attending or participating in a parent's wedding is usually not being difficult. They're reacting to change, loyalty conflicts, or a sense of loss. For some children, a remarriage can feel like a final closing of the door on the original family. In their mind, if they don't attend, it's not happening.

Before making any decisions, it's important to understand what's underneath the resistance:

- Are you going too fast for them to adjust?
- Are they feeling replaced?
- Are they worried about hurting the other parent?
- Are they uncomfortable with the new partner?
- Or are they simply overwhelmed by the attention and expectations?

Parents should resist the urge to force participation and instead focus on understanding what's underneath the child's resistance. A child may not want a formal role but may still be able to attend as a guest, so it helps to separate participation from presence and offer options.

Acknowledge the child's feelings without correcting them, letting them know they don't have to feel excited or ready. Keep the door open by making it clear they are welcome, without making attendance a test of loyalty or respect. When possible, consider lower-pressure ways to include them or alternative ways to connect.

The goal is not to secure compliance, but to preserve the relationship and help the child feel safe during a significant change.

Writing Your Vows

Vows are intimate promises between adults, and when blending a family, often between all family members. Avoid language that publicly assigns parental roles, announces replacements, or elevates the new relationship above all others. Children don't need to hear who "finally shows up." They need to hear that love can expand without erasing.

A vow that centers on partnership rather than position protects the emotional neutrality children rely on. Communication here isn't about romance; it's about containment.

The following examples of co-parent vows aren't performative; they're stabilizing. These vows honor the adult relationship without rewriting the family system or placing emotional weight on the children.

Example 1: Grounded partnership

"I promise to love you with patience and honesty.

I'll build our life with care, remembering that the family around us already carries history, meaning, and love.

I commit to being a partner who listens before speaking, who protects before reacting, and who leads with respect, not only with you, but with everyone whose life is touched by ours."

Example 2: Choosing partnership over control

"I promise to walk beside you, not ahead of you, and not over anyone else in our family.

I'll honor the past that shaped us without letting it define us.

I choose you today, knowing that love grows strongest when it makes room rather than demanding space."

Example 3: Continuity for children

"I promise to love you without asking anyone else to carry the weight of our happiness.

I'll be thoughtful about the system we're joining, gentle with the people who already belong to it, and steady in my role as your partner."

Example 4: Respecting all bonds

"I vow to protect what we're building without diminishing what already exists.

I'll speak with respect about the people who matter to you, even when it's inconvenient.

I promise to choose empathy when things feel complicated and patient when you need me to listen."

Example 5: Quiet strength

> "I choose you not to change the story that came before us, but to add to it.
>
> I promise to be mindful of the lives our love touches and to treat those connections with care."

These vows unite the couple without making children responsible for validating the relationship, which is the heart of good co-parenting ceremony language.

Including Children in the Reception

Whether to include children at the reception is a question I'm often asked. Alcohol, late hours, and unpredictable adult behavior can feel overwhelming for younger children. For this reason, when children do attend, it's often earlier in the evening before celebrations become too lively. If your choice is to include them, consider a family table, a shared dance, or a brief moment that clearly welcomes them into the celebration.

The reception is also where weddings can drift from intention to impulse. Traditions that feel warm and predictable in first marriages can feel complicated in co-parenting families. Father-daughter dances, mother-son dances, toasts about "starting a family," or jokes about finally getting it right may land heavily on children who are still integrating what this new commitment means. Thoughtful planning, especially around toasts, keeps the focus on inclusion rather than comparison.

The question isn't whether children *can* be included. The question is whether inclusion supports their emotional safety. Children should never feel asked to choose sides or demonstrate loyalty publicly. A dance, a toast, or a shared moment that feels natural to adults may feel like a test to a child. If a child hesitates, respond with sensitivity. They're not being difficult; they're navigating change while protecting the bonds that still matter deeply to them.

A more stabilizing approach is to offer choice without expectation. If a child expresses interest in participating, explore that interest privately first. Let them know that saying "yes" isn't required and that saying "no" will never be interpreted as rejection. This is how acceptance is practiced: by allowing children to belong without performing.

For many families, it helps to reimagine traditional roles rather than replicate them. Instead of a formal father-daughter dance, a child may prefer a casual moment earlier in the evening or a shared song while remaining at the table. Some families choose a short, inclusive family dance where no one is singled out. The goal is not to re-create tradition exactly as it once was, but to support everyone's emotional stability as the family moves forward.

Planning Photos and Memorabilia

Photographs become the long-term record of a family's story. They'll be pulled out at graduations, shared with future partners, and eventually shown to grandchildren. In co-parenting families, how those images are arranged matters far more than how they look. Children don't remember whether the lighting was perfect. They remember whether their family history was honored or quietly edited.

The most helpful approach is to think in terms of layers rather than replacements. Create sets of photos that reflect the current partnership, but also preserve images that acknowledge continuity. Children benefit from seeing themselves with each parent separately, with both parents when appropriate, and within the new family structure, not because it creates symmetry, but because it creates wholeness. No single photograph needs to tell the entire story, but the collection should.

Plan the photo list in advance and share it with the photographer. This removes pressure from the moment and prevents the scramble that often leads to exclusions. Decide who will stand with the children, who will be present for blended shots, and which combinations might feel supportive rather than performative. If relationships are strained, neutral arrangements are often the safest: children photographed with each parent individually, then with the couple, without asking anyone to stand in emotional proximity that they're not ready for. Feel free to buffer the emotions of estranged co-parents or other former couples by placing other relatives between them.

Memorabilia deserves the same care. Albums, frames, keepsakes, and wall displays shouldn't announce that the past has been replaced. They should show that it has been integrated. Children who can see earlier chapters of their life honored alongside new ones grow up believing that change doesn't require erasure.

Balancing New Commitments with Your Co-Parenting Role

As the ceremony ends and everyday life resumes, new commitments naturally reshape the rhythm of both your family and your co-parenting. Schedules evolve, traditions expand, and more voices join the family conversation. What matters most now is staying intentional, keeping communication steady, and revisiting expectations when needed because children watch how adults adjust as much as they promise. Committing to a new partner doesn't end co-parenting; it often makes collaboration even more important.

Reaching out, looking for solutions, and staying inclusive in your approach to problem-solving reinforces the team philosophy your children depend on. In many ways, the relationship you now model becomes a counterweight, offering them another, ideally more positive, example of partnership. But it's up to you. Change isn't magic, and it doesn't happen simply because you signed a paper.

What you've learned in the previous chapters becomes the foundation you put into practice every day. The ceremony may be over, but the consistency you bring to everyday moments helps your children feel secure as your family continues to grow and change. Where things may once have felt uncertain, this commitment has the potential to bring greater steadiness, allowing your children to experience family life as something reliable and secure.

IN THIS CHAPTER

» Protecting the couple from being caught in the middle

» Clarifying the co-parent's role in your adult child's celebration

» Managing emotional undercurrents with maturity

» Presenting a united message across both homes

Chapter 15 Supporting Children of Co-Parents When They Commit or Marry

Marriage can look different for adult children who grew up across two homes. Their planning often reflects years of navigating more than one family system, learning to read emotional dynamics, adjusting to shifting roles, and at times managing adult discomfort before their own. Even in families that have done meaningful healing work, these patterns can resurface when the child of divorced or separated parents becomes the one planning a ceremony.

For these adult children, a wedding means romance, but beneath the surface, a thoughtful navigation of roles, placement, and long-standing family rhythms influences how the day comes together. Alongside choosing vows and flowers is an awareness of relationships, where people will sit, how moments may be interpreted, and how to include everyone without losing personal clarity.

Within this context, the parents' role changes. Rather than directing the day, they provide steadiness. Their presence communicates emotional maturity and support, allowing their adult child to move forward without carrying unresolved history. Parents shift from shaping the moment to stabilizing it, keeping the focus on the couple and the future they're creating together.

This chapter explores how parents can support their adult child's commitment with steadiness and clarity. It looks at how to protect the couple from being caught in the middle, clarify the co-parent's role in the celebration, and manage the emotional undercurrents that weddings can stir. It also addresses the practical decisions that often carry deeper meaning, from choosing vows, walking down the aisle, and hosting, toasting, and seating to navigating those choices across both homes with maturity and respect. When both parents approach these moments thoughtfully, the focus remains where it belongs: on the couple and the life they're beginning together.

Preparing Emotionally in Both Homes

When the child of active co-parents becomes engaged, emotional preparation reflects the entire family system that helped raise them. Wedding planning often draws on skills these adult children developed from both homes, weighing words carefully, anticipating reactions, and staying aware of how each decision may affect the people they love. These patterns aren't signs of drama or oversensitivity; they reflect lived experience. Growing up across two homes often teaches children to carefully read emotional climates. Those same instincts can shape how they approach one of the most meaningful transitions of their lives.

This is where coping with C.A.R.E. becomes an essential tool to manage and prevent conflict:

- **Communication** begins with greater awareness. Wedding planning can bring long-standing family patterns into clearer view, and many adult children of co-parents are accustomed to managing emotional balance between homes. When parents communicate directly with one another and with their child in a steady, thoughtful way, they ease that dynamic rather than reinforce it.
- **Acceptance** means recognizing that your child's wedding won't heal the divorce. That realization can bring up unexpected feelings for parents as well, including grief, nostalgia, or even a sense of displacement. Those emotions deserve care without being placed back onto the couple.
- **Respect** means allowing your child to design a ceremony that reflects who they are, not who you are.
- **Empathy** means remembering how heavy it felt to live between homes, even when you believed you protected them.

Consider this: If you notice yourself feeling territorial, nostalgic, or displaced, don't be surprised. These reactions are more common than many parents expect. A child's wedding often brings parents face-to-face with the history of their own relationship and the hopes they once held for their family. Those feelings deserve acknowledgment, but they are yours to manage, not your child's. Your first instinct may be to confide in them, but pause before you say anything.

Sometimes, the most stabilizing first step is reaching out to your co-parent. A simple conversation, such as "No matter what comes up, let's agree to make this easier for them," can set the tone long before the ceremony begins. Many parents tell me that forming a quiet pact to be especially supportive during wedding planning shifts the emotional atmosphere immediately.

Once that foundation is in place, communication with your child becomes steadier and more supportive. Preparation works best when communication is proactive rather than reactive. Instead of waiting to be invited into every decision, reach out with clarity and humility. A message such as, "I want to support your planning without adding pressure. What would feel most helpful from me right now?" lets your child know you're present without positioning yourself at the center of the process. When parents communicate with intention first, their child no longer has to manage the emotional balance between them.

Your child may not always say how much they're carrying, but you may notice it in delayed decisions, emotional fatigue, or hesitation to ask for help. When that happens, resist the urge to interpret or solve. A simple acknowledgment, such as "I can see this is a lot. You don't have to protect me," reassures them that their role isn't to manage adult emotions.

Handling Financial Contributions without Emotional Strings

Money has a way of reviving history if it's not handled with clarity. Weddings are expensive, and in co-parented families, the question of who contributes, how much, and under what expectations can quietly reopen old dynamics.

In some families, both parents contribute equally. In others, one parent has greater financial capacity. Bonus parents may want to contribute as well. Sometimes the couple pays for most of the celebration themselves. No single arrangement is the be-all and end-all. What matters most is that financial support doesn't become leverage. A contribution to a wedding is a gift, not a negotiation tool.

COPING WITH C.A.R.E. APPLIES HERE

Communication means discussing financial expectations directly and early. Clarify whether a contribution is a gift or whether it carries specific responsibilities, such as hosting a rehearsal dinner or shower. Ambiguity is where resentment grows.

Acceptance means recognizing that your financial support doesn't entitle you to design the day. Even generous contributions don't shift ownership of the ceremony away from the couple.

Respect means honoring the couple's priorities, even when they differ from your own.

Empathy means remembering how heavy wedding planning can feel when money carries emotional weight.

When emotions begin to rise, C.A.R.E. can serve as a simple internal reminder: Am I communicating clearly? Am I accepting what's not mine to control? Am I respecting the couple's vision? Am I responding with empathy rather than expectation?

When money begins to carry implied authority, decisions can shift from collaborative to conditional. "If I'm paying, I should decide." "If I contribute more, my side should have more seats." These statements are not always spoken aloud, but adult children feel them quickly. The wedding becomes less about partnership and more about balancing influence.

Some parents find it helpful to communicate their posture clearly from the start:

> "We would love to contribute, and we trust your decisions."

If financial contributions are unequal between homes, dignity still matters. Equal respect doesn't require equal funding.

The most stabilizing financial gift isn't the largest check. It's clarity without conditions.

Interferences from the Extended Family

Grandparents, siblings, and long-standing relatives sometimes carry their own unresolved feelings about the divorce. A wedding can feel like an opportunity to revisit history, protect "their side," or quietly influence decisions about seating, invitations, or participation.

It's important to remember that extended family members are guests, not decision-makers.

If a grandparent pressures the couple to exclude someone, change seating, or prioritize one household, the responsibility to address it belongs to the parent connected to that family member. Adult children shouldn't have to defend their guest list or justify their choices to aunts, uncles, or grandparents.

A simple statement often works best:

"This is their decision, and we're supporting it."

That posture stabilizes the entire system.

When the extended family sees parents aligned, interference usually subsides. When parents appear divided, interference multiplies. This is not the time to stage family alliances. It's time to celebrate the couple.

Addressing Parents Bringing New Partners

Few dynamics surface tension more quickly than deciding whether and how new spouses or long-term partners will attend. For many parents, this is the moment when old emotions unexpectedly resurface. Seeing a former partner arrive with someone new can stir memories, comparisons, or unresolved feelings, even years after the divorce.

Some adult children continue to run defense for their parents. Even when they know that one or both parents have recoupled, seeing everyone together in the same room can still feel unexpectedly disconcerting. And because it's their wedding day, even small tensions can feel magnified.

For parents, maturity in this moment often looks like restraint. You don't have to be warm, but you do need to be composed so the focus remains where it belongs: on the couple.

For the bride or groom, it can help to remember that your parents' relationships are their responsibility to manage. Your role isn't to mediate between them, but to celebrate the commitment you're making.

If a parent has remarried or is in a committed relationship, excluding that partner may feel dismissive. On the flip side, including them may feel uncomfortable for the other parent. The key question, however, isn't comfort; it's stability for the couple.

When a relationship is established and significant, excluding a long-term partner often creates more tension than including them. At the same time, a wedding isn't the place to introduce a brand-new relationship that hasn't yet settled into the family system.

Parents can ease pressure by addressing expectations early. A direct conversation between co-parents, rather than through the couple, prevents triangulation and sends a clear message that the adults are handling the situation responsibly. For example:

> "We both deserve to attend with our partners, and we both deserve a peaceful day. Let's agree to keep interactions respectful and minimal."

Mature co-parenting at a wedding often looks like simple civility. You don't have to be warm. You don't have to be friends. But you do need to be composed. Public displays of affection, territorial behavior, or visible tension shift attention away from the couple and back onto the past.

Your child should never have to monitor how you interact with someone you once loved.

Seating without Divided Loyalties

For children of divorce, the seating anywhere is rarely neutral. As they grew up, where their parents sat at little league games or school concerts often prompted concern. Who sits near whom, who's placed in front, and who's separated can communicate alliances that adult children have spent years trying to avoid. Even when the ceremony is calm, the room itself can reactivate old roles. Don't sit too close to Dad, or Mom will notice. Don't laugh too loudly on one side. Divorced parents don't always realize how often children have weighed these kinds of decisions.

The most helpful arrangements are those that replace ranking with balance, recognizing both parents as equally significant. This reduces loyalty binds and keeps the ceremony focused on the couple rather than lingering family divisions. If a parent was less than supportive in the past, "equal significance" is about the wedding day, not the past. It's not meant to slight an especially attentive parent. Equal footing in a ceremony doesn't mean equal history, equal behavior, or equal repair; it means equal dignity in the moment of the wedding.

There are many ways to acknowledge an attentive parent's contributions without slighting the other parent. A heartfelt toast at the reception, a special mention in the couple's remarks, a named role in the program, or a moment of acknowledgment during speeches can be deeply meaningful. Equal seating doesn't erase gratitude.

Before adapting seating for divided families, it helps to understand how conventional ceremony seating is typically arranged. Traditionally, the bride's family is seated on the left side of the ceremony space and the groom's family on the right, though many couples now choose arrangements that feel more balanced or inclusive. The first row is typically reserved for immediate family, parents, bonus parents, grandparents, and those playing significant roles in the ceremony. The second row often includes adult siblings and close relatives, while additional rows fill in according to relationship and availability.

Younger siblings are usually seated in the front rows because conventional seating reflects relationship rather than age. Very young siblings may sit with a parent or trusted adult who can help them feel comfortable. If a younger sibling has a role in the ceremony, their seat may be nearby rather than directly within the parents' row. The goal is thoughtful placement that reflects connection and support.

In co-parented and blended families, seating rarely follows a simple left-and-right structure. Rather than focusing on which side someone "belongs" to, many couples choose seating that emphasizes connection and comfort. The goal is to create an environment where the couple feels supported by everyone present, without asking guests to navigate old divisions.

If the couple chooses conventional seating, support it with clear expectations. Ask extended family not to move seats during the ceremony, not to make comments about who is where, and not to treat proximity as proof of relationship status. Small behaviors either stabilize or destabilize the entire room. Remind family members to follow the expectations of the bride and groom. It's their day.

Once everyone has found their place in the room, the focus shifts from where people sit to what the ceremony itself will communicate.

Planning the Ceremony

For children of co-parents, the ceremony often holds more emotional meaning than anyone expects. It's the moment when separate traditions, relationships, and histories come together in one room. Even adult children who appear confident may feel unexpectedly tender as familiar rituals bring past experiences close to the surface.

Couples benefit from making intentional decisions about how they enter the space, who stands beside them, and what the ceremony communicates about their partnership. Beginning with an entrance that clearly reflects the couple's autonomy and shared agency sets the tone. Whether the bride or groom enters alone, with one parent, with both, or with a bonus parent meeting partway, the movement should communicate choice, not possession.

When the couple arrives at the front, the officiant's opening words can hold the room steady. A brief acknowledgment of the many relationships that shaped them is often enough. Complexity doesn't need a spotlight; it needs respect.

Walking the bride down the aisle

Few wedding decisions bring co-parenting tensions to the surface faster than deciding who will walk the bride down the aisle.

Adult children can be placed in a difficult position. A parent who asks a child to choose between biological and bonus parents on a wedding day shifts the focus away from celebration and back onto old divisions. One of the central principles of good co-parenting is simple: Put your children first.

In many families, remarriage introduces additional parent figures who play meaningful roles. When those relationships are loving and supportive, their presence reflects lived experience rather than replacement.

Several approaches work well. A father and bonus father may walk on either side of the bride. One parent may begin the walk, and the second joins partway down the aisle. Some brides reverse the order depending on personal history. The decision belongs to the bride. The role of the adults is to support it graciously.

Not every bride chooses a father or bonus father. Some ask their mothers, grandfathers, uncles, siblings, or close friends. Others walk alone. Walking alone isn't rejection. It can be a declaration of autonomy. Parents who respond with maturity strengthen the relationship far beyond the ceremony itself.

Just as significant is the question of who responds when the officiant asks, "Who gives this bride in marriage?" Some couples keep the tradition; others modify or remove it. Responses can reflect those who raised and supported the bride. Increasingly, couples reframe the wording to emphasize support rather than ownership.

Supporting same-sex weddings

Just as children of co-parents reconsider traditional roles when deciding who walks with them, same-sex couples often reimagine many parts of the ceremony to reflect equality and shared agency. Traditional wedding customs developed around clearly defined roles for "the bride's family" and "the groom's family." When those roles don't apply, couples have an opportunity to design a ceremony that reflects their partnership rather than tradition alone.

For adult children of divorced parents, this can introduce an additional layer of sensitivity. Parents may wonder where they stand in the ceremony or how their roles will be recognized. Sometimes those questions are influenced by old family dynamics rather than the needs of the couple.

Same-sex ceremonies often invite families to move away from rigid expectations and toward more thoughtful choices. Some couples walk together, some invite both parents to accompany them, and others choose entirely different ways to begin the ceremony. The goal isn't to replace one tradition with another but to create a moment that reflects the couple's relationship.

For parents, the most supportive posture is flexibility. A wedding isn't the place to interpret symbolism or measure inclusion. When parents allow the couple to define their own rituals, the ceremony becomes a reflection of the partnership being celebrated rather than the history that came before it.

These decisions don't erase family history; they simply reduce comparison. They allow the focus to remain where it belongs: on the commitment the couple is making and the life they're building together.

Restoring calm when parents refuse to cooperate

Few moments test emotional maturity more than a wedding decision that doesn't go your way. The aisle, the seating, the guest list, the inclusion of a bonus parent — these choices can stir feelings that run deeper than many parents expect.

Occasionally, a parent responds with an ultimatum:

- "If they're included, I won't come."
- "If I'm not walking her down the aisle, I'm not attending."
- "If that's how it's going to be, count me out."

This isn't simply a disagreement. It's emotional leverage.

A wedding isn't the place to renegotiate your divorce, assert territory, or correct the past.

When a parent threatens absence to gain influence, the emotional cost is carried entirely by the adult child. Even if the statement is delivered calmly, the message underneath is unmistakable: Choose between us.

No child, regardless of age, should be placed in that position.

It's important to separate disappointment from participation. You may feel hurt, overlooked, or even replaced. Those feelings are real, but they are yours to work through on your own time. They don't justify withdrawing your support from your child.

As I've mentioned before, if you're struggling, speak to a therapist, a trusted friend, or even your co-parent directly. Don't process your frustration through your child. Don't ask them to solve what belongs to you.

Healthy co-parenting at a wedding requires this simple principle: Attendance is unconditional.

You may not love every decision. You may wish the ceremony looked different. But your presence shouldn't depend on preference.

The most stabilizing sentence a parent can offer is this:

> "I may not agree with every choice, but I'll be there."

That statement restores emotional safety immediately. It tells your child they don't have to manage you. It reminds them that your role is to support, not to negotiate.

A wedding marks the beginning of their partnership. Let it not become a measure of your past.

Considering the groom's side

Wedding traditions have historically placed more visible structure around the bride's family, but grooms often carry similar emotional considerations. Decisions about seating, acknowledgment, and participation affect them just as deeply.

Many grooms think intentionally about how to include the people who helped raise them. Some escort a mother or bonus mother to her seat before the ceremony begins. Others greet family members at the front. These gestures need not mirror the bride's processional; they reflect the groom's relationships and the tone he hopes to set.

Communication is especially important when assumptions arise about what the groom's family "should" do. A brief conversation with both parents about expectations can prevent misunderstandings and allow everyone to participate with clarity.

Finding a role for the bonus parent

Bonus parents often occupy the most delicate position in a child's wedding. They may have provided years of daily care and emotional support, yet feel uncertain about what space they're allowed to hold.

The most meaningful roles are often behind the scenes. A bonus parent can be the steady presence in the dressing room who notices rising nerves and offers water instead of advice. They can coordinate vendors, manage timelines, and ensure details unfold smoothly so the bride or groom can remain emotionally present.

Even though I was no longer married to her father when she married, my bonus daughter asked me to walk with her grandfather and sit beside him in the second row before her father escorted her down the aisle. She trusted that I would understand the history, support her choice, and help the moment unfold without drawing attention to myself.

Visibility is less important than stability.

Choosing readings, rituals, and vows

Readings and rituals work best when they focus on partnership, growth, and mutual care. Poems that frame love as rescue or redemption can unintentionally pull attention backward. Adult children of co-parents benefit from language that reflects intention and shared responsibility.

Within the ceremony, vows become the most personal expression of what the couple is choosing to create. For adult children raised across two homes, vows carry added weight. They're heard not only as promises between partners, but as statements about how this marriage will stand on its own foundation.

Words such as patience, partnership, responsibility, steadiness, dedication, belonging, trust, and care often communicate that posture more clearly than dramatic promises. Language that reflects how partners intend to listen, repair, and move forward together keeps the focus on the life they're building rather than the past they're leaving behind.

The most stabilizing vows focus on how each partner intends to show up in everyday life: how they'll listen, repair, and remain steady. Rather than telling a story about what they've survived, these vows describe what they're choosing to build.

As vows are spoken, the role of the family shifts. Parents and extended relatives move from guiding the couple to supporting them.

In the end, when children of co-parents marry, the most meaningful message families can offer is steady acceptance. The wedding becomes a moment in which the couple steps forward on their own terms, surrounded by support rather than management. The awareness that once helped them move between homes now helps them build a life of their own.

When parents stand behind them, even after years of separation or divorce, the message is clear: We trust you, we support you, and you're free to create your future.

That is the family's lasting gift, not perfection. It's the experience that commitment can feel safe, steady, and chosen.

5

The Part of Tens

IN THIS PART . . .

Learn good ex etiquette to make life better for both your children and you

Use a set of practical resets to adjust your approach and try again

IN THIS CHAPTER

» Deciding to cooperate

» Handling the most common disagreements

» Putting your children first after divorce or separation

» Respecting each other's turf

Chapter 16
Ten Rules of Good Ex Etiquette

More than a hundred years ago, Emily Post defined proper etiquette as "a code of behavior based on consideration, kindness, and unselfishness." When I first began working with co-parents, there was no code for handling life after a breakup. When an ex behaves badly, people often shrug and say, "Well, they're the ex." Poor behavior is expected, tolerated, and passed down from one generation to the next.

According to the National Institutes of Health, about 1 to 1.5 million children experience their parents' divorce each year. But that number reflects only divorces, not breakups between unmarried parents. Recent U.S. government data shows that about 40 percent of all live births are to unmarried mothers. That means the number of children affected by parental breakups is likely much higher. Whatever the exact percentage, millions of children are caught in the middle of their parents' battlefield.

That reality is why I developed ten straightforward rules for parents to follow when faced with disappointment or conflict. This chapter introduces ten rules of good ex etiquette and explains why good behavior matters so much. Relying on these rules helps parents make well-balanced decisions even in the most stressful situations.

The rules of good ex etiquette are similar to the unwritten rules of common decency and fair play. Many divorced parents have asked for a formal list — something they could turn to when emotions run high and decisions feel difficult.

I often suggest parents keep the Ten Rules where they can see them: as a screen saver on their phone or computer, or even on the Ten Rules refrigerator magnet available on the Bonus Families website. The idea is simple: When a problem arises, refer to the rules before reacting.

As always, examine your intent first. Do you want to make your life better? Do you want to change the negative status quo? Some are so stuck in the errors of the past that it never occurs to them that things can be different. When you intend to heal, move forward, set the stage for a new beginning, and raise your children with their best interest in mind, these ten rules will be an indispensable guide to getting along with your ex, your ex's new partner, their children, and even extended family.

Put the Children First

The cornerstone of this list is to put the children first. When you truly do that, decision-making becomes surprisingly clear. The work isn't complicated, but it's intentional: Set aside your own interests, hurt, resentment, or anger, and use your children's well-being as the lens for every choice.

When you make that shift, the ex who once felt unbearable often fades into the background. Compared to your child's welfare, the old conflict simply matters less. You may even hear yourself thinking, "Maybe it's okay if he takes Johnny to his football game on my week."

That's the moment you know you're leading with good ex etiquette and putting the children first.

Ask Each Other for Help If You Need It

I can't tell you how many times I've heard parents call themselves "single parents" when they're really co-parenting. They'll say, "Now that we've broken up, I'm raising the kids all by myself."

It's common to feel that way sometimes. But if your ex sees the kids regularly, contributes to expenses, and shows up for games and recitals, you're not doing this solo. You have help available that you can ask for. And yes, asking can be tough. That's exactly where these rules come in.

> "But I have asked, and they always say no. It's a waste of time."

Ask again. This is your new co-parenting relationship, not your old relationship where you argued to make a point and were so frustrated that both of you always said no. It's up to you to make the shift and put it into action by reaching out and asking for help.

No Badmouthing

Badmouthing isn't just obvious insults like, "Your mother/father is such a !#$@^&*." It also shows up as an impatient sigh or in smaller comments said in passing. Children take those remarks personally because criticizing a parent feels like criticizing a part of them. It also puts children in the middle, forcing them to weigh what's being said, decide whether it's true, and figure out which parent is right.

Badmouthing also tends to backfire. Children instinctively protect the parent they perceive as being attacked. "You're saying something bad about my Mommy" can quickly translate into, "I don't want to be here. He makes me feel bad." Instead of strengthening your bond, the commentary pushes the child away.

Biological Parents Make the Rules; Bonus Parents Uphold Them

This is the only rule on the list that requires a preface. Family systems are rarely simple, and in some homes, a bonus parent is also a parent with children of their own. In these blended households, rules often existed before the bonus family was formed. Routines are already established, and coordination matters. In those situations, the bonus parent should absolutely be consulted, particularly when expectations affect all children in the home.

That said, the core principle remains: Biological parents are responsible for setting the rules for their own children. Bonus parents play a vital, supportive role by reinforcing those rules, not redefining them. When expectations are aligned, children experience clarity rather than competition between adults.

Don't Be Spiteful or Hold Grudges

If you stay angry at your co-parent, you're making your decisions with that in mind, not the kids. You'll find yourself reacting rather than being proactive when problem-solving.

Here's what that looks like in real life: Your ex makes a suggestion, and your first thought is, "Five years ago she pulled that stunt at my sister's wedding, and I'm still not over it." So, you say no not because the suggestion is bad, but because you're still mad about something that happened half a decade ago.

The thing is, you never actually say that. You just dig in your heels and refuse. Your ex has no idea you're still upset about the wedding incident, or whatever it was, so from their perspective, you just look unreasonable and impossible to work with. You know exactly why you're being difficult, but they don't, and that makes you look even more unreasonable.

Don't Hold Grudges

Spite and revenge keep you stuck in the past. When you hold onto anger, you're "ex-ing" by refighting old battles in your head. The kids didn't break up. You did. Don't make them pay the price for it.

Use Empathy When Problem-Solving

I talk about empathy a lot. It's the *e* in the C.A.R.E. acronym I've mentioned throughout this book. Empathy is the great equalizer. If you can put yourself in your ex's shoes and feel how they might be feeling, you may not be so quick to lose your temper or judge their point of view.

This can be simplified by saying, "Don't ask your ex to do anything you wouldn't want to do." If you don't like your ex being late, don't be late. If you want to switch weekends because you have something special planned, don't say no when they ask you for the same thing. If you want your ex to respond to texts about the kids promptly, don't leave their messages unread for two days. The list goes on and on.

Basically, it's the Golden Rule. Treat your co-parent the way you'd like to be treated, and you'll be amazed at how much more inclined they are to cooperate.

Be Honest and Straightforward

Transparency while co-parenting is essential. When a child knows their parent has lied to their other parent, it puts the child in an impossible position. They become the secret-keeper, carrying information they know is false, and that's a huge burden for a kid.

Even more dangerous is when parents use phrases like "what happens here stays here" or "don't tell." That's classic grooming and abuse language. When you tell your child to keep secrets from their other parent, you're using the same manipulation tactic that abusers use.

Bottom line: Lying between co-parents and asking children to keep secrets undermines their sense of security. Kids need to trust that their parents are honest and reliable.

Respect Each Other's Turf

Once you and your co-parent break up, your children have two homes. And, as much as both parents want to dictate policy, they really can't. Divorced or separated parents must learn to respect each other enough to trust that the other will make the right decisions for the children.

This doesn't mean that you can't discuss things. In fact, you should coordinate as much as possible. Bedtimes? Homework rituals? Discipline?

But once the decision has been made, it's done. Harping on the other parent to do it your way will only get you into another argument, or they'll avoid you and stop returning texts and phone calls.

An easy way to cultivate the respect of an ex is to simply ask their opinion. Ironically, that's about the last thing an estranged co-parent wants to do. Some see it as a sign of weakness, a loss of power. But power comes from within, not from whether your co-parent says it's okay. Asking for an opinion isn't asking permission. It demonstrates respect. It's a gesture as much as a tool for problem-solving. You don't have to take the advice; however, when your co-parent feels heard, you're both well on the way to solving the problem.

Compromise Whenever Possible

I can't tell you how many times I've heard, "At least I don't have to listen to her (or him) now that we've broken up!"

Ironically, compromising may be even more important now than when you were together. Compromise is an excellent tool for problem-solving, and it begins with listening to your ex's concerns. The simple act of listening validates both parties. It's much easier to find common ground — the basis for compromise — when both sides feel heard.

If you listen, use empathy when problem-solving, are honest and straightforward, don't hold grudges, aren't spiteful, and put the children first, you're using good ex etiquette, and it will be easy to find a compromise in the best interest of your children.

IN THIS CHAPTER

» Simple tools to improve co-parenting interactions

» Strategies to keep communication child-focused and solution-oriented

» Using C.A.R.E. to reset your approach

Chapter 17 Ten Practical Resets

Even the most committed co-parents have moments when communication breaks down. Old frustrations resurface, messages are misunderstood, and conversations become tense.

A reset simply means pausing, adjusting your approach, and beginning again. Often, the smallest changes in wording or attitude can shift the tone of a conversation.

When things feel stuck, try one of these simple resets.

Pause Before You Respond

If a message makes you feel defensive or upset, give yourself a moment before replying. A thoughtful response protects your child far more than a quick reaction.

REMEMBER

If you're taking a break, let your co-parent know when you'll respond so the silence doesn't look like ghosting:

"Let me think about this one. I'll get back to you this evening before 6."

Assume Good Intent

Before reacting, consider that your co-parent may be trying to solve a problem rather than create one. This small shift in perspective can soften the conversation immediately.

Focus on the Child, Not the Conflict

When communication becomes tense, return to your shared purpose. Both of you want what's best for your child.

Change "You" to "We"

Sometimes, the quickest way to reset a tense conversation is to change one small word:

- "You" statements often sound like blame, even when that's not the intention. When a parent hears "you," the natural reaction is to defend.
- "We" statements sound more collaborative. They signal that both parents are working toward a solution together instead of pointing fingers.

For example, instead of saying, "You forgot to send his soccer gear again," try asking, "What changes can we make to be sure his soccer gear goes back and forth with him?"

When conversations shift from "you" to "we," the focus moves away from fault and toward solutions.

Ask Questions Instead of Making Accusations

Questions invite cooperation. Accusations invite defense. A simple question can open the door to a calmer conversation.

Beginning with "I'm curious . . ." can soften the tone and show that you're trying to understand rather than blame.

For example:

> "I'm curious why the pickup time changed today?"

Approaching the conversation with curiosity often leads to clearer communication and more cooperative solutions.

Keep Messages Brief and Clear

Long explanations can increase tension. When emotions are high, clear and simple communication works best.

Think BONUS: **B**rief **O**nly **N**ecessary **U**seful **S**tatements.

Keeping messages brief and focused can prevent misunderstandings and center conversations on solving the issue at hand.

Stay in the Present

A reset works best when the conversation stays focused on the current issue rather than revisiting old conflicts. When past frustrations are brought into the discussion, it becomes harder to move forward.

Staying in the present helps both parents focus on solving the problem at hand instead of reopening disagreements that have already passed.

Respect Differences between Homes

Your co-parent may handle some things differently from how you do. As long as your child is safe and supported, different approaches can still work.

Keep Your Child Out of Adult Conflict

Children should never be asked to carry messages between homes or manage disagreements between their parents.

Remember to C.A.R.E.

Not every conversation will go smoothly. When communication breaks down, take a breath, refocus on your child, and try again. This is a perfect time to remember to C.A.R.E.:

- **C**ommunicate clearly.
- **A**ccept differences between homes.
- **R**espect each other as parents.
- Lead with **E**mpathy.

Small resets guided by C.A.R.E. can turn difficult conversations into opportunities to work together again.

You don't have to be a couple to co-parent your children.

Index

Numerics

A

B

C

D

E

F

G

H

I

J

L

M

N

O

P

Q

R

S

T

U

V

W

About the Author

Dr. Jann Blackstone is a nationally recognized co-parenting expert, child custody mediator, and author dedicated to helping families move from conflict toward cooperation after divorce and separation. With more than three decades of experience studying and working with parents, bonus parents, and extended family systems, she has guided thousands of families toward creating stability across two homes.

Dr. Blackstone coined the term "bonus" after recognizing that traditional labels like "step" often carried negative cultural images rooted in Grimm's fairy tales and popular media portrayals of the "wicked stepmother." The word "step" also failed to reflect the reality of modern families, many of which grow and evolve without marriage. Because a significant percentage of children in the United States are born to unmarried parents, there is a strong likelihood that many will experience new partnerships and expanding family systems over time. "Bonus" offered language that felt more accurate, loving, and inclusive, translating naturally across roles — bonus mom, bonus dad, bonus child, bonus siblings, and of course, bonus family — and emphasizing addition rather than replacement.

She is also the creator of Good Ex-Etiquette: Good Behavior After Divorce or Separation, a philosophy centered on emotional leadership after divorce or separation. Her widely syndicated Ex-Etiquette advice column, distributed by Tribune Content Agency, appears in newspapers and digital platforms around the world. Each column ends with the tag line, "That's good ex-etiquette," reminding readers that the goal is always the same: good behavior after a breakup in the name of the children.

Through her writing, speaking, and mediation work, Dr. Blackstone emphasizes Communication, Acceptance, Respect, and Empathy (C.A.R.E.), helping families build healthier connections and stronger futures.

Learn more at `www.bonusfamilies.com` and feel free to contact her directly at `jann@bonusfamilies.com`.

Author Acknowledgments

No book about co-parenting is ever written alone. It grows from relationships, lived experience, and the many people who hold you steady while you do the work.

First, to my children, Melanie, Anee, Steven, and Harleigh, both biological and bonus, who have grown into remarkable adults and built families of your own. Some of you are now parents yourselves, and watching you create loving, thoughtful families has been one of the greatest privileges of my life. You have been my greatest teachers. Every lesson in these pages has been shaped by the reality of loving you, learning from you, and sometimes learning because of you. Thank you for accepting me into your life, both bio and bonus. You are and will always be my inspiration.

To Sharyl Jupe: Someone might rarely acknowledge her ex-husband's ex-wife, but Sharyl is a rarity. She is my bonus kid's mom, and I could not write a book on this subject without acknowledging that through my relationship with her, I learned the true nature of cooperative co-parenting. I met her over thirty years ago, and through our at times struggling interaction, we grew to become a team for the children we both loved. If we had not met, if we had not struggled and learned to put the children — *all the children* — first, the bonus philosophy would never have been realized.

To my partner, Peter Santin: Thank you for being endlessly understanding and supportive through long writing days, deadlines, edits, and rewrites. You understand the creative process firsthand, and your steady presence made it possible for me to keep moving forward even when the work felt overwhelming. This book carries your fingerprints more than you know.

A heartfelt thank you to Cynthia Guerrero, who somehow managed to type my craziness into a cohesive document. Your ability to organize chaos kept this project moving forward, and I am eternally grateful.

Thank you to my publisher, John Wiley & Sons (Wiley), and all the editors, beginning with Elizabeth Stillwell, Tim Gallan, Karen Gill, and Rick Kughen, for your professionalism, clarity, and genuine collaboration. The *For Dummies* process runs like a well-oiled machine, and your organization and guidance made the writing experience as stress-free as writing a book can possibly be, which is saying a lot, because writing a book is not a stress-free endeavor by any means. Your commitment to creating practical, accessible resources helped shape this work into something readers can truly use.

I am also deeply grateful to the many clients, readers, workshop participants, and families who have trusted me with their stories over the years. While your names are not written here, your experiences live within these pages. Your willingness to grow, to question old patterns, and to choose stability for your children continues to inspire everything I do.

Finally, this work is dedicated to the children whose parents will one day choose to raise them separately. Every parent who picks up this book has the power to change the emotional landscape in which those children will grow up. If these pages help even one family move from conflict toward cooperation, then every long night of writing has been worth it.

With gratitude,

Dr. Jann Blackstone

Publisher's Acknowledgments

Acquisitions Editor: Elizabeth Stillwell
Senior Managing Editor: Kristie Pyles
Development Editors: Tim Gallan and Rick Kughen
Copy Editor: Karen Gill
Production Editor: Umeshkumar Rajasekhar
Cover Image: © svetikd/Getty Images